P9-BZQ-670

Camping!
Washington

2nd Edition

Camping!
Washington

2nd Edition

The Complete Guide
to Public Campgrounds
for RVs and Tents

RON C. JUDD

SASQUATCH BOOKS
SEATTLE

Copyright ©2003 by Ron C. Judd
All rights reserved. No portion of this book may be reproduced or utilized in any form, or by any electronic, mechanical, or other means without the prior written permission of the publisher.

Printed in the United States of America
Published by Sasquatch Books
Distributed by Publishers Group West
09 08 07 06 05 04 03   7 6 5 4 3 2 1

Cover photo: Mike Brinson
Cover design: Karen Schober
Interior design: Kate Basart
Interior composition: Stewart A. Williams/Bill Quinby
Maps: GreenEye Design
Production Editor: Cassandra Mitchell
Copy editor: Julie Van Pelt
Proofreader: Joeth Whitley
Indexer: Bill Quinby
All interior photographs taken by the author unless noted here: Photographs on pages 27, 37, 71, 75, 161, 170, 172, 174, and 181 by Seabury Blair Jr.; pages 179, 185, 191 and 274 by Dan A. Nelson; pages 266 and 270 by Janice Ohlsen; page 235 courtesy Washington State Parks.

Library of Congress Cataloging-in-Publication Data
Judd, Ron C.
    Camping Washington / by Ron C. Judd—2nd ed.
        p. cm.
    Includes index.
    ISBN 1-57061-169-6
        1. Camping—Washington (State)—Guidebooks. 2. Camp sites, facilities, etc.—Washington (State)—Directories. 3. Washington (State)—Guidebooks. I. Title.
    GV191.42.W2J83 2003
    796.54'09797—dc21

                                                    2003050412

Sasquatch Books
119 South Main Street, Suite 400
Seattle, WA 98104
(206) 467-4300
www.sasquatchbooks.com
books@sasquatchbooks.com

Contents

Overview Map

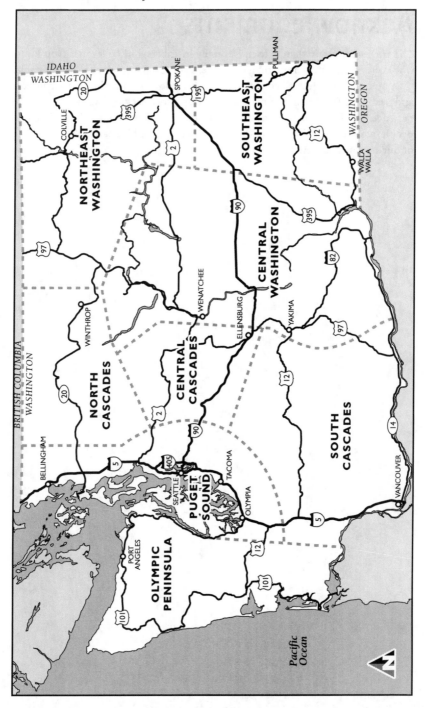

Acknowledgments

The author sincerely thanks friends, family members and colleagues (you know who you are, and, now more than ever, where not to camp!) who helped assemble, then update, this guide. Special thanks also to fellow fresh-air lovers Kate Rogers and Seabury Blair, Jr., and to my life tent/RV partner, Jackie, a woman of infinite patience. Lastly, but by no means leastly, continued thanks to those fabulous people, whomever and wherever they are, who make big blue tarps, the very fabric of our camping existence.

Introduction

Life tastes better outside.

This is a universal truth in the Evergreen State—assuming, of course, that said taste is not unduly influenced at a given moment by diesel fumes from a broken-down Metro bus on the parking lot formerly known as Interstate 5.

The idea here is to get away from all that, and it used to be quite simple. Back in the days before pantlegs flared out, then sucked back in, then inexplicably rewidened, you could arrive home from work on a Friday evening, pile the kids, dogs, blue tarps, broken-down canvas tent, cooler, matches, Oreos, six-packs of Tab, and piles of Tupperware with ill-fitting lids into the back of the Buick, and head to the hills—and a waiting campsite—before dark. Nowadays, you'd be lucky to get out of the Mount Baker tunnel by dark, and if you did, all the good campsites would have been long-ago occupied by retirees, encroaching Californians in Greyhound-size motorhomes, nosey guidebook authors, and other miscreants who, for some reason, don't live on normal schedules.

Like any other form of outdoor recreation, camping now requires a bit more strategizing. This is especially true in Washington, where, as we launch a second century of s'mores and smoke, interest in camping is at an all-time high—while available campsites are actually decreasing. When this book went to press, a budget crisis long in the making had put Washington State Parks—one of the primary providers of splendorous campsites found in this guide—essentially on financial life support. Four wonderful state parks in Southeast Washington had already closed to cut costs, their futures uncertain. And as many as a dozen others throughout the state were in danger of being turned over to private contractors, or lost forever. It's a disturbing trend—one, we hope, the growing camping constituency will reverse by screaming loudly that public parks and campgrounds should be a priority of the Evergreen State and its people.

Alas, we can't control that. But we can help you negotiate the curves in the road when it comes to securing one of those increasingly sought-after campsites.

Even more so today than when this guide first appeared in 1999, campground reservation systems are a fact of life for successful Washington campers. Ignore them at your own peril: They're the key to locking up that gorgeous site you used to claim first-come—before most of the rest of the planet started coming first.

Granted, this excises some of the spontaneity from getting out and away ("spontaneity" all too often translating to "sleeping in the car in the parking lot of the Forks Motel after finding every camping space on the Olympic Peninsula full"). But it also eliminates much of the guesswork. Somehow, heavy traffic on the way over Snoqualmie Pass seems a lot less stressful if you know an open site is waiting, with your name on it, at Steamboat Rock.

In that sense, camping in Washington is better than ever. You fellow natives might chortle over this. But think about it: As with other forms of outdoor recreation, numbers of campers have exploded in recent years. But unlike other activities, such as hiking, boating, skiing, et al., campgrounds still come with their own built-in restrictions. Witness: Kalaloch Campground has the same 177 sites it's had since the author was in diapers. True, some little things have changed—you can pay by credit card now, and reservations (!) were on their way at this writing. But otherwise, once you pitch the tent or drop the RV jacks, you're set. Time warped. Grandfathered. Why? A campground can only get so crowded. Latecomers don't muscle in; they go home. The same cannot be said of hiking a trail or fishing a stream or skiing a bump field at Mount Baker.

It's better in still other ways: Once at your coveted site, you'll probably be a lot more comfortable today than ever before. Technical innovations—camp stoves, heaters, lightweight, waterproof tents and clothing, synthetic insulations, completely worthless (other than for fireside joshing) electronic bug zappers, and inflatable sleeping mattress—have transformed Washington camping from a wet, cold Navy SEAL survivalist experience into something bordering on living-room cozy. And this applies equally to those in 3-by-6-foot tents and 48-foot motorhomes.

You know what all this means. It means you no longer have a good excuse to stay home and order pay-per-view this weekend. Can't ever get a site? Find an obscure one (plenty await herein). Or plan ahead six months and reserve one. Don't have the gear? Buy it. Borrow it. Rent it. You don't have to spend a fortune—or even a lot of money—to have fun camping in Washington.

Camping, quite simply, is the best adventure you can still undertake on a shoestring budget. It's a never-fail memory maker. It's as close as modern people come to pulling off a Columbus voyage of discovery—at least without enlisting the aid of a queen and fretting about dying of scurvy. It is the perfect personal "reboot" button for souls too cluttered by computers, deadlines, and team-building.

And it's difficult to imagine a better place to do it. From the sparkling beaches of Puget Sound to the pounding surf of the Olympic Peninsula, from the crisp, sweet alpine air of the Cascade highlands to the warm, sprawling lakefront lawns of the Columbia Basin, Washington is the Disneyland of American camping.

It's all here, campers. The trick is to put yourself in the midst of it and let fate have its way. We've spent a lifetime doing just that, learning lots along the way. Most of that accumulated campground knowledge is capsulized on the pages that follow. Use it in good health, and be prepared to get hooked.

For most of us, one taste is never enough.

—Ron C. Judd

Notes on the second edition

The camping world has been altered, mostly in small ways, since the first edition of this guide. And the guide's content, while retaining all its old useful features, has been substantially updated.

Three years of further intensive research travel around the state—split nearly evenly between tent camping and RV camping—gave us new insight into many campgrounds we hadn't visited in some time. As a result, we've added a substantial number of new campground writeups. We've also bolstered most of the existing written descriptions to include new levels of detail—and, notably, to update our evaluations as reflected in each campground's personalized quality rating. Unlike other, out-of-state guidebook publisher's glance-at-a-map-and-make-a-guess ratings, these are based on personal visits either by the author or an associate. Argue with them if you choose, but know that they're based on our personal opinions—not the park's owners or operators contacted by telephone!

Campground reservation systems, most notably for Washington State Parks, have changed—mostly for the better, we're happy to report. If you're a longtime user of this guide, be sure to re-read the specifics, below—or some newbie might beat you to your favorite site.

As noted above, a handful of Washington State Parks were in danger of closing at press time, due to state budget problems. Trying to be optimistic about their futures, we have left descriptions of all these parks in the guide, noting with each listing that campers should call and check their status before making travel plans. Please do so. And call or write your state legislator to insist that parks become a budget priority.

Finally, astute guide users will note that this edition contains wholesale improvements—both in number and quality—in photographs, which we've worked hard to collect on our travels in the past several years. We hope they'll give you an even better visual image of where you're headed before you even leave the front door.

How to use this book

The easy-to-read format of this guide should make using *Camping! Washington* fairly self-explanatory. But a few notes on its construction, as well as on our philosophies in describing and rating each campground, should make it even more helpful. Here's a look at how each campground listing is set up.

Sample Listing:

---

❶ Lincoln Rock State Park 🌲🌲🌲🌲

Lincoln Rock has long been one of our favorite state parks, mostly because of the amount of local character revealed by its namesake. History records that somewhere back around 1889, a local man, Billy Schaft, photographed a large rock outcrop across the river from this park and remarked how much it looked like a profile of Abraham Lincoln. Plenty of other local people who, let's face it, living in Wenatchee and all, had plenty of time to consider such things, agreed. Someone sent the picture to a photo contest in Ladies Home Journal, and it won first prize. Voila! Lincoln Rock went on the maps, and public gatherings soon followed. The park, on a broad, flat Columbia River

sites	94
🏕️🚐	32 full hookups, 35 water/electrical hookups, RVs to 65 feet
open	All year
reservations	Up to 11 months in advance; Reservations Northwest, (800) 452-5687
contact	Washington State Parks, (800) 233-0321; Lincoln Rock State Park, (509) 663-9603

shoulder across the river from the rock, now bears its name. If you look through the little fixed pipe near the Lincoln Rock upper restroom, you can see it. By George, it does look like Abe. Wake the kids. The campground here is worthy of a visit on its own, however. It's the prototype for a series of Washington State Parks on the middle Columbia, all of which follow a wildly successful formula: sprawling grassy playfields, boat launches, a swimming area, and flat, open trailer and tent sites separated by young shade trees. All these parks are popular with boaters, who flock here in summer months to water-ski and soak up the sun. Lincoln Rock, on the Columbia's Entiat Lake behind Rocky Reach Dam, has all of these pleasures and more, including two boat launches, multiple moorage docks, tennis and basketball courts, coin-op showers, horseshoe pits, and an amphitheater. It's a very pleasant spot—too hot for some tastes in the summer, but just right for the lizard people among us. Just across the river is the popular Rocky Reach Dam visitors center, which you can only get to by driving back south to Wenatchee, crossing the river, and driving up US 97A.

Getting there: The campground is 7 miles north of Wenatchee on US 2.

Ratings

Each campground is rated on a scale of one to five trees; one being lousy, five being tops. These ratings are based on personal visits and camping experiences of the wildly opinionated author and his mildly opinionated associates. In other words, like any ratings, they're highly subjective. Please understand that they have no underlying mathematical equation that takes into account distance from home, number of spaces, weather, or the likelihood that a garage band called "Used Food" will set up camp in the space next door. Rather, the ratings reflect each campground's overall feel, natural beauty, quality of facilities, ease of use, and other intangibles. It's important to understand that campgrounds, being out there in the wild and all, can change dramatically from one season to the next. That Forest Service campground we rated a solid "4.5 trees" might be a lot less attractive once you arrive and find that a November blast has leveled every tree in the place. Because of this, not to mention variations in taste, your camping experience may, and likely will, vary. If it does so markedly, please write and tell us about it. Thanks to all of you who did so after the first edition; we've considered your input and, in some cases, made adjustments.

The ratings system is somewhat stingy. You'll find, for example, only a handful of campgrounds rated "5 trees" in this book. That's an honor we take quite seriously. Campgrounds designated as such are those we consider essential to the serious Washington camper's résumé. (You also might be surprised at some of the lesser-known campgrounds we rate "4 trees" or better: Many of these are places outside the camping "mainstream" that we've come to love and appreciate during a lifetime of camping in the state.)

Conversely, you'll find few campgrounds herein rated lower than "2 trees." Most "1-tree" campgrounds were either purposefully left out of this guide, or listed under Other Campgrounds at the end of each section. Why list them at all? To help you know what you're getting into when you see the name on a map and it's your only option, or when you get steered toward it by someone who doesn't know better. We've attempted, in other words, to make a lot of your mistakes for you.

Camping! Washington ratings key:

🌲🌲🌲🌲🌲: The crème de la crème. A can't-miss Northwest classic. You haven't truly camped until you've camped here.

🌲🌲🌲🌲: A stunner. Among the best. Bring lots of digital film and site-finding patience.

🌲🌲🌲: Very nice. A pleasant, occasionally beautiful getaway—but don't set aside two weeks.

🌲🌲: Passable. It'll do for an overnight spot on the way to somewhere else.

🌲: A stinker. We spent the retirement money on a Winnebago—and guide-book—for this?

Sites

Total numbers of sites are listed for each campground. As frequent users of both a tent and an RV, we relate to frequent confusion about what kind of sites are suitable for whom. So unlike some other guidebook authors, we've chosen not to distinguish between "tent" sites and "RV" sites, for a simple reason: Experienced campers know that tents usually can be pitched comfortably in sites that are designated as "RV" sites simply because they have some sort of utility hookup. Designating these sites strictly as "RV" is misleading, because it suggests tents aren't welcome. Not so. Some of the nicest Washington State Parks tent sites, in fact, are listed as "RV" or "utility" sites in some guides. That doesn't mean you could not or should not pitch a tent there. Example: All except three of 63 campsites at Grayland Beach State Park, one of the most pleasant on the Washington coast, are designated "RV" sites because they have full hookups. But all 63 sites also are spacious, grassy, flat—and extremely popular with tenters. Tent campers who overlook this camp because of the RV designation would be making a mistake.

We've tried to work around this problem: Listings include the *total* number of campsites, "RV" and "tent" inclusive. To assist the RVer or trailer owner who's interested in utility hookups and campsite lengths, we separate out both the number of sites with utility hookups, and the overall length available to RVers. Thus, our sample park above, Lincoln Rock, contains this listing: "Sites: 94; 32 full hookups, 35 water/electrical hookups; RVs to 65 feet." Savvy tenters who read between the lines will note that all sites are available to them, but 25 of them don't have any sort of utility hookups, and thus are probably either designed for tents, or available to tenters at a lower price than the RV sites.

Tent and RV symbols 🏕️ 🚐

Each campground is marked by a tent and/or RV symbol. Those with both symbols have sites catering on some level to both tenters and RVers. Those with a tent only mean that literally: Tents only. Most of these are smaller, difficult-to-access campgrounds in the mountains, where RVs of any size cannot reach. The rules are slightly different for campgrounds marked only by an RV symbol. These typically are paved, cramped RV quarters where only the most desperate tenter would dare pitch his or her abode. You'd probably be allowed to pitch a tent here. You just wouldn't want to.

Open (the camping season)

Each listing indicates the campground's *scheduled* opening and closing dates. This is a matter of increasing importance to Washington campers, particularly RV owners, who are fighting the jam-packed madness of summer camping by extending their outdoor seasons all the way through the winter. Even tenters often can find "shoulder season" camping in the early spring or late fall a pleasant switch from the crowds of summer. Latch onto a down sleeping bag, and give it a shot. You just might get hooked. Or frostbite.

Opening and closing dates vary widely, and they're all subject to change. But some trends can be noted. Washington State Parks, the vast majority of which are in low-elevation locations less affected by snow or unseasonable weather, usually open and close precisely on the dates listed. U.S. Forest Service and national park campgrounds, which are often found in high-elevation areas, are less consistent. That's why most of those campground listings will be more vague: "mid-September" as opposed to "Sept. 15." National park and Forest Service operating dates can vary by as much as three weeks from year to year, because of unusually heavy or light winter snowfall. For these campgrounds, consider the listed dates a mid-range target. Then call the contact number listed to get exact dates as your trip approaches.

Persistent campers will find that camping is possible in some places even after the campground officially "closes." This is particularly true of some Forest Service campgrounds. Many ranger districts will close and gate most of their campgrounds, but leave one or two open for hardy late-season campers, hunters, and other warm-blooded outdoor lovers. Generally, if the campground gate is open in the fall, you can camp there, *usually* free of charge (see "fees," below), until snows close the campground for good. Note that water and garbage services probably won't be available after seasonal "closings." You'll need to pack everything in and out. Again, check with the contact agency about off-season camping. Opening and closing dates also can change from one year to the next because of budget shortfalls and other unnatural factors.

Reservations

You already know "why." This guide should help you with the "where" and the "when." Unfortunately, campers in people-clogged Washington keep getting tripped up by the "how."

Just knowing where you want to go and during what season no longer cuts it in the Evergreen State, where landing a non-reservation campsite on any given summer Friday night ceased being simple about the time the Mariners came to town (for you newcomers: 1977). It's increasingly a good idea to take advantage of campgrounds that accept reservations. Doing so removes much of the uncertainty (also known in some old-fashioned circles as "fun") from camping: You'll know before you ever leave home whether your favorite campground is booked. If it is, reservation operators usually can help you choose an alternate site—a guaranteed alternate site—in the same area.

The bulk of Washington's reservation campgrounds use one of three systems:

Washington State Parks use a private vendor to handle telephone and Internet campground reservations for more than 50 state parks. Note that the new vendor, unlike the old one, does not handle reservations for both Oregon and Washington state parks—it's Washington only. To reserve a spot at one of 60 state parks, call 888-CAMPOUT (888-226-7688), or go online to www.parks.wa.gov, and click on "reservations."

We like the new system for several reasons, chief among them the online access, which allows you to pull up campground maps, click on a site, and see a reasonable description of each one. The site also tells you which specific sites are available on specific dates. A nice feature, and a valuable trip-planning tool.

Under the new system, you can reserve campsites (also cabins and yurts at several parks) up to nine months advance, and can pay by check or credit card. A reservation fee is added; at this writing it is $7 per reservation. Summer holiday weekends require a two-night minimum stay. A cancellation fee is charged if you change your mind later. Remember three important things about this service:

• The 9-month advance window is crucial. If you're looking to get a site in, say, Steamboat Rock on the Fourth of July, you'd better be punching up "redial" at 7 a.m. (when reservations are first accepted every day, by phone or online) on the preceding fourth of October.

• While a handful of state parks (notably: Deception Pass and Fort Canby) now operate under the reservation system all year, most use it only between May 15 and Sept. 15. These parks revert to first-come, first-served during the winter. If you're frustrated at trying to get into your favorite park during the reservation season, try it in the early spring or late fall. Some very pleasant camping conditions often can be found in October, in particular.

• Don't overlook the fact that the majority of Washington State Parks are not on the reservation system. Sites there can still be nabbed the old-fashioned way: showing up early. Call the Washington State Parks information line, (360) 902-8844, for information on campgrounds that are not part of the reservation system.

The **National Recreation Reservation System**, another private vendor, has been taking reservations for National Forest Service and other federal-agency (such as the Bureau of Land Management) campsites since 1999. Many of Washington's approximately 500 Forest Service campgrounds now use the system, reached by calling toll-free, (877) 444-6777, or pointing your Web browser to www.reserveusa.com. Individual campsites booked through NRRS can be reserved 240 days in advance. Group sites can be reserved 360 days in advance. Note that, unlike Washington State Parks, most Forest Service campgrounds offering reservations still set aside about half their sites for first-come, first-served campers. Call the contact number listed with each campground for advice on site availability.

The **National Park Reservation Service,** (800) 365-CAMP or online, http://reservations.nps.gov/, accepts reservations at the two most popular campgrounds at Mount Rainier National Park, Cougar Rock and Ohanapecosh. Reservations also are accepted at computer kiosks at Cougar Rock Campground and the Ohanapecosh Ranger Station. These reservations are *required* during the peak summer season—the last Tuesday in June through Labor Day. See the listings for those campgrounds for more information about the ins and outs of this system.

As this guide was being printed, Olympic National Park had its popular Kalaloch Campground on this reservation service beginning in Summer 2003. No other national park campgrounds in Olympic or North Cascades National Parks offered campsite reservations.

Contact
Numbers listed reflect the closest and best information source for each campground. We strongly recommend phoning before you go, no matter where you're going or when.

Campground descriptions
We've attempted to describe the campground, its surrounding area, and its attractions and drawbacks in the main text of each listing. Generally, the more noteworthy the campground, the more long-winded we become—a handful of top-rated campgrounds are described in far more detail than standard listings. At the end of each chapter, under Other Campgrounds, unrated campgrounds are noted with just the bare-bones facts.

The main text is also the place to pass on vital information about the campground's facilities. For brevity's sake, we've made the assumption that a basic Washington campground is minimally equipped with a picnic table, fire pit, piped water, and flush toilets. If facilities aren't discussed in the text, assume the camp will offer those services. Any variances—the lack of piped water or flush toilets, the presence of hot showers, and so on—are typically noted in the description.

Facilities vary widely from campground to campground, but these trends generally hold true: **Washington State Parks** are the most creature-comfortable public campgrounds. All are equipped with fire pits, picnic tables, piped water, and flush toilets; most also offer a true nicety for tent campers: coin-op showers (although sadly, some of these are in a sorry state of repair). Many state parks offer full hookups (water, sewer, and electricity) for RV campers. The vast majority also have RV dump stations, while many feature picnic facilities, boat launches, and other amenities. Most **U.S. Forest Service** campgrounds in Washington have picnic tables, fire pits, piped or hand-pumped water, and pit toilets (note for true loo aficianados: Yes, some modern Forest Service toilets are technically "vault" toilets; we've used the term "pit toilet" to describe all non-flushable commodes). None offer utility hookups, and only a small number have flush toilets, RV dump stations, picnic areas, boat launches, or other services. As a general rule, Forest Service camps do not have showers. Campsites in Mount Rainier, Olympic, and North Cascades **National Parks** are equipped with picnic tables, fire pits, and, with only a couple exceptions, piped water and flush toilets. Some have RV dump stations, picnic areas, and other facilities. None of them offer showers, and one in particular—not to mention any names, but it's Mount Rainier—has gone so far as to tell us that even portable solar showers are forbidden. Please join us in writing your Congressperson.

Getting there

Each campground listed includes detailed road directions, most of which begin at the nearest sizable town or landmark. To make your travel and camping plans easier, campgrounds in this guide generally are arranged according to common highway travel from the Puget Sound area. For example, listings in the Stevens Pass and Lake Wenatchee section begin at Gold Bar and proceed a west-to-east order along US 2. If you're traveling in the opposite direction, start at the end of the section and work your way forward. (The alternative is turning the book upside down, which is not recommended, particularly if you are piloting a large motor home.)

Other Details:

Fees

Because campground prices often change, individual campsite prices are not listed with campground descriptions in this guide. Generally, however, the following rules apply:

In **Washington State Parks,** primitive campsites (no tables, sometimes no fire pits) cost $8 per night; standard sites (tables and fire pits, but no hookups) are $15 per night; and utility sites (tables, fire pits, and sewer and water hookups) are $21 per night. A $1 summer surcharge is added at some popular parks between Apr. 1 and Sept. 30. Other fees: $2 for each additional person beyond the allowable four adults per campsite; $6 for a second vehicle, unless it's towed by an RV; $5 for trailer dumping (included in site fee if you're camping there). Also expect to pay a fee to use a boat launch if you're not staying at the park. Day-use fees for state parks—$5 per carload per day—have been proposed for the 2003 season.

Most **national, city, and county park** campgrounds range from $10 to $17 per night for standard sites. Add $5-$7 more per night for hookup sites.

U.S. Forest Service campsites charge $8 to $14 per night, but some, especially those without piped water, are free. Note that a federal lands pass, such as the ubiquitous Northwest Forest Pass for trailhead parking, is now required at many of these "free" campgrounds. State Department of Natural Resources campgrounds also tend to be free and usually offer very primitive facilities; some are hike-in or boat-in campgrounds.

Private campgrounds

The observant camper, particularly those in RVs, will notice that with a few exceptions, we haven't listed great numbers of private campgrounds in this guide. The reasoning is simple: There are far too many of them to make listings practical, and private campgrounds can change ownership so often it's difficult to vouch for their quality or level of service. We've also omitted them for philosophical reasons: While we on occasion enjoy a hot, clean KOA shower as much as the next person, we sought to create a guide that fully explores the "wild" camping experience more commonly found at public parks. A number of exceptions crop up. In areas that receive heavy summer traffic, but offer few public campgrounds, we've listed phone numbers and locations for the most popular private parks. Examples include the San Juan Islands and the area around the Gorge Amphitheater summer concert venue near George in Central Washington. Comprehensive "Yellow Page" listing books are available to RVers. We have one in our own rig—it makes a nice companion to this volume!

Pets

Pets are allowed—on leashes—in nearly all Washington public campgrounds. Any exceptions are noted in the text. Even in national parks, where pets are strictly prohibited on trails and other wild lands, pets are permitted within campgrounds, provided they're kept leashed or caged, quiet, and under control. Check with administering agencies for local regulations regarding pets on beaches, in playfields, and in other areas adjacent to the campground. As a general rule, however, no public campground is a suitable place to let your dog roam. Earn the right to bring along your pooch by picking up after it and being courteous of non-pet-loving neighbors. It's common sense, and common courtesy.

More information

The contact numbers listed with each campground are, for the most part, year-round numbers. They're usually your best source for specific information. More general questions about campground choices, or recreation on surrounding public lands, can be addressed to the **Outdoor Recreation Information Center**, located in REI's Seattle flagship store, 222 Yale Avenue North. Call the center at (206) 470-4060. For further information about the Cascadia Marine Trail, a string of marine campsites from Olympia to the Canadian border, contact Washington Water Trails Association at (206) 545-9161 or e-mail, wwta@wwta.org. The Marine Trail Web site is found at www.wta.org/trails/cmt.html. For full details on all recreation opportunities at or around campgrounds listed in this guide, consult this author's previous guide, *Inside Out Washington* (Sasquatch Books). It's arranged under the same geographical headings as this camping guide, making it an excellent companion volume with details on hiking, fishing, wildlife watching, kayaking, boating, picnicking, winter sports, and other activities. For current road construction and winter weather information, call the **Washington Department of Transportation** hotline, 800-695-7623 or go to http://traffic.wsdot.wa.gov/sno-info/. For general **Washington State Parks** questions, call (360) 902-8844. For **U.S. Forest Service** information, contact the ranger district listed as a "contact" with each campground.

Puget Sound

They turned us into campers. No, not our parents. Not Boy Scout or Brownie leaders. Not even friends and relatives, although the co-conspirators who taught generations of Puget Sound natives to be nature fans almost qualify as such. We're speaking of the magically comforting old-growth trees of Whidbey Island; the taffy-sweet saltwater breezes rising from warm, rocky San Juan Island beaches; those unforgettable sunsets over Samish Bay.

Each and all of them came—and still come—to us at campgrounds around Puget Sound, an inland sea blessed by hundreds of miles of calm saltwater beaches, patches of old-growth forest, and grand places to pitch a tent and breathe it all in.

Not surprisingly, the best campsites around Puget Sound, from the rocky beaches and stiff breezes of Birch Bay to the maritime splendor of Penrose Point, are on the Sound itself. A series of majestic Washington State Parks, nearly all of them abandoned World War II military sites on prime, waterfront property, stand guard over this natural heritage, allowing the region's ever-inflating population to stealthily bow out of the urban rat race for overnight splurges in fresh air.

These parks are the highlights of Puget Sound camping, and they contribute much to the area's vaunted reputation for a high "quality of life." While campsites within a short drive of downtown Seattle are relatively scarce, an abundance lies on the Sound within a two-hour drive of the metro area. They're ample in quantity and perhaps unparalleled in scenic quality, thanks mostly to a fortuitous topography that provides a wealth of heavily forested areas intersecting fine saltwater beaches and million-dollar views.

A lot of us natives have come to take them for granted (witness: Washington State Parks' ongoing battle to simply remain budgetarily afloat). We're jolted from this complacency only during those odd years when out-of-town visitors make the trip to Moran, Larrabee, or Scenic Beach State Park, and return literally agog. Why, they always want to know, aren't you out there all the time?

It's hard to explain to them but, in our own way, we are. The body of a Puget Sound resident might be chained to a keyboard. But the spirit can always smell the saltwater.

1. Camano Island State Park
2. South Whidbey State Park
3. Fort Casey State Park
4. Fort Ebey State Park
5. Oak Harbor City Beach Park
6. Deception Pass State Park
7. Washington Park
8. Spencer Spit State Park
9. Odlin County Park
10. San Juan County Park
11. Moran State Park
12. South Beach County Park
13. Bay View State Park
14. Larrabee State Park
15. Birch Bay State Park
16. Wenberg State Park
17. Kayak Point County Park
18. Flowing Lake County Park
19. Saltwater State Park
20. Dash Point State Park
21. Kopachuck State Park
22. Penrose Point State Park
23. Joemma Beach State Park
24. Jarrell Cove State Park
25. Millersylvania Memorial State Park
26. Kanaskat-Palmer State Park
27. Fay Bainbridge State Park
28. Kitsap Memorial State Park
29. Scenic Beach State Park
30. Illahee State Park
31. Manchester State Park
32. Blake Island State Park
33. Belfair State Park
34. Twanoh State Park

Puget Sound Map

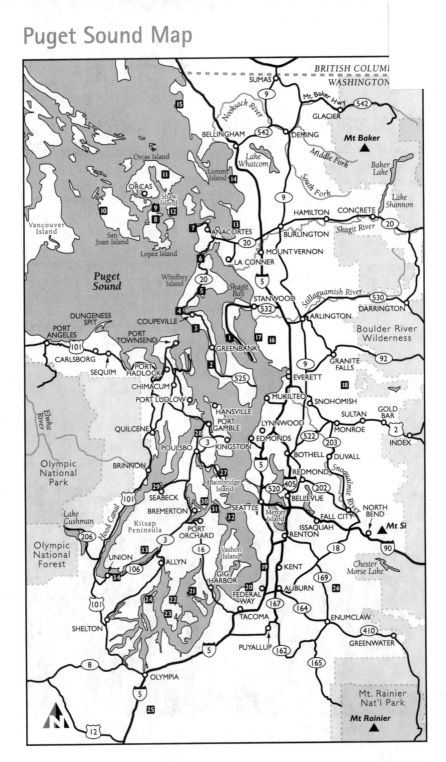

North Sound and Islands

① Camano Island State Park 🌲🌲🌲⛺

The squiggling toes of many a Puget Sound tyke got their first dip into the world of camping at Camano, a sprawling park with 6,700 feet of waterfront on sparkling Saratoga Passage. The 134-acre park's unusually good weather (it's at the far end of the same Olympic Mountains "rain shadow" that keeps Sequim and the Dungeness Valley dry), exceptional beaches, and plentiful wildlife make it a grand family spot. Campsites are snuggled nicely among the madronas on a high bluff. Trails lead a couple hundred vertical feet (and a mile or less) down to the gravely beach, which is the real highlight here, with majestic views of sunsets behind the Olympic Mountains. A two-lane boat launch makes the beach area a high-traffic boating venue, particularly during summer salmon-fishing season. Surf fishing for bottomfish (perch, flounder) can be decent here, crabbing is conducted offshore (in season), and

sites	88
🏕️ 🚐	No hookups, RVs to 40 feet
open	All year
reservations	None
contact	Washington State Parks, 360/902-8844; Camano Island State Park, 360/387-3031

More than a mile of saltwater shoreline greets Camano Island State Park visitors.

clams are found at very low tides. About 3 miles of hiking trails run through the park's upper, woodsy area, connecting the three main campground loops, the beach area, and the picnic area. The park has a trailer dump station, coin-op showers, and a group camp for 160 people. The state plans to add several rental cabins to the group camp. Some sites in this older, somewhat timeworn campground are small; RVers are advised to stick to the roomier upper loop.

Getting there: From Everett, take Interstate 5 north 18 miles to exit 212. Turn west on Highway 532 and follow signs about 14 miles to the park.

❷ South Whidbey State Park 🌲🌲🌲🌲

A quiet park tucked onto the southwest shore of the island, South Whidbey is a pleasant, close-to-home getaway for anyone and everyone sick of all the Seattle metro-area bustle. The park's campsites are found in mature second-growth forest (no water views), with trails leading down to 4,500 feet of gravel beach and saltwater shoreline on Admiralty Inlet. For another major attraction, look upland to find a 300-acre-plus stand of old-growth forest, mostly Douglas fir, that's unique in this area. The trees, which include some grand western red cedars, are best seen by following the Wilbert Trail (easy, 1.5-mile loop) on the east side of Smuggler's Cove Road, opposite the developed park area.

sites	54
🏕️ 🚐	9 water/electrical hookups, RVs to 50 feet
open	February through November
reservations	Up to 9 months in advance; 888/226-7688 or www.parks.wa.gov
contact	Washington State Parks, 360/902-8844; South Whidbey State Park, 360/321-4559

Cyclists should take note of an additional six walk-in campsites on the south side of the park. The park has an RV dump station and coin-op showers. Off-season day-users will find the forested picnic area a relaxing, though shady, retreat with a shelter to flee to in bad weather.

Getting there: From the ferry terminal at Clinton, follow Highway 525 9 miles north, turn left (west) onto Bush Point Road, and follow signs to the park, on Smuggler's Cove Road.

❸ Fort Casey State Park 🌲🌲🌲🌲

Here's a Puget Sound classic. Old Fort Casey, on Whidbey's west shore across Admiralty Inlet from Port Townsend, truly is one of the most picturesque spots in the Northwest. The lineup is formidable: 467 sunny acres, much of which are wide open, grassy uplands with stunning views of the north Sound and Mount Baker; more than 10,000 feet of saltwater shoreline for uninterrupted beach strolling, surf fishing, or lounging; gun emplacements with restored cannons—always a hit with the kids; and a beachfront campground that's highly sought after year-round, particularly by RV owners.

Most day visitors and campers flock to the day-use area, high on a bluff near the old gun mounts. Frisbees, softballs, stunt kites, and enthusiastic dogs share the airspace over the lush, spacious grass here. Trails lead along the bluff to several grassy viewpoints (unfenced; be careful with kids), all grand sunset-watching perches. Back by the gun mounts, interpretive signs describe the fort's history as a World War I–era gun emplacement and World War II–era training facility. A large picnic area is nearby. Don't miss the grand old lady back in the woods. The Admiralty Head Lighthouse, built in the 1860s and literally hidden at the north end of what's now the day-use area, is a graceful beauty, one of the stateliest light stations in the West. The light was intentionally obscured from water view after the military moved in. The building now contains an interpretive center filled with park history. The park also has coin-op showers, a boat launch, a couple miles of hiking trails, and an underwater park for scuba divers. The beach is a popular spot for surf fishing for bottomfish, salmon, and steelhead in season.

sites	35
	No hookups, RVs to 40 feet
open	All year
reservations	None
contact	Washington State Parks, 360/902-8844; Fort Casey State Park, 360/678-4519

Ferries and RVs rub shoulders at Fort Casey.

Unfortunately, Fort Casey's campsites don't keep up with the park's crowds, at least in terms of numbers. The 35 sites are almost literally on the water, on a sand spit below the bluff-top gun emplacements, adjacent to the Keystone ferry terminal. The waters of Admiralty Inlet lap just outside your tent flap or doorstep. Needless to say, it's a popular spot—particularly among RVers, who are less troubled by the persistent winds on the mostly exposed beach.

Getting there: Following signs for the Keystone ferry terminal, turn west off Highway 20 near Coupeville and proceed about 3 miles southwest to the park, near the ferry terminal.

❹ Fort Ebey State Park 🌲🌲🌲🌲

Another of Whidbey's abandoned military sites, Fort Ebey is much smaller, more secluded, and a lot less famous than its north Whidbey cousin, Deception Pass State Park, just a ways up Highway 20 (see below). But it offers a similar saltwater-beach experience, and its camping area is actually brighter, tidier, more private, less congested, and more relaxed. Sites in this treed, bluff-top campground are nicely spaced in two loops. Many are flat, very spacious

sites	50
🏕 🚐	4 electrical hookups, RVs to 70 feet
open	All year
reservations	Up to 9 months in advance; 888/226-7688 or www.parks.wa.gov
contact	Washington State Parks, 360/902-8844; Fort Ebey State Park, 360/678-4636

pull-throughs. Trails lead to old gun mounts, a quasi-lighthouse (more "light" than "house"), fine Admiralty Inlet views from the nearby bluffs, and to the lovely, 3-mile-long, sandy beach below Point Partridge. None of the campsites have actual views of the inlet, but some are separated from it by only a thin wall of low trees. The park has coin-op showers, but mysteriously lacks an RV dump station. Plans call for four rental cabins to be built in the near future. This is a particularly nice place to visit in the spring, when wild rhododendrons are out in pale pink splendor. And if you can muster 59 friends who want to qualify as a "group," don't hesitate to check out Ebey's group camp. It's one of the nicest we've seen, with a green lawn for tents right at the bluff top, plus a covered cooking and eating area. Also note that this park is home to the "Kettles" trail system, a series of 25 miles of mostly single-track mountain bike paths through the region's hilly geologic formations.

Historical note: Unlike nearby Forts Casey, Worden, and Flagler—all built early in the 20th century—Fort Ebey was a "second-generation" Puget Sound fortress, part of a triad of 16-inch cannon emplacements built during World War II. Ebey's sister installations were built at Cape Flattery and at Striped Peak west of Port Angeles. (See Fort Casey State Park above; and Fort Worden State Park, Fort

Flagler State Park, and Salt Creek Recreation Area in Olympic Peninsula and the Pacific Coast.)

Getting there: From Highway 20, about 8 miles south of Oak Harbor and 2 miles north of Coupeville, turn west onto Libbey Road, proceed 1.5 miles to Hill Valley Drive, turn left and follow signs to the park.

❺ Oak Harbor City Beach Park 🌲🌲🌲

This mid-Whidbey spot in downtown Oak Harbor is basically an RV stopover, although we've seen tents pitched on the grass behind the flat, gravel spaces for big rigs. It's not exactly a back-to-nature experience, but it is close to the water, the city marina, downtown shopping, and parks. And it's a short drive from both Deception Pass and Fort Ebey State Parks, making it attractive to campers who can't get into one or the other. The park has an RV dump station and coin-op showers.

sites	56
🏕️🚐	All have water/electrical hookups, RVs to any length
open	All year
reservations	None
contact	Oak Harbor City Beach Park, 360/679-5551

Getting there: The park is on 80th Street SW in downtown Oak Harbor, a short distance from the intersection of Pioneer Way and Highway 20.

❻ Deception Pass State Park 🌲🌲🌲🌲🌲

It's all here. And then some. Washington's flat-out most spectacular state park (if not single chunk of real estate), Deception Pass is a showcase for all the elements that make the Northwest magic: sprawling saltwater beaches, jutting cliffs, deep forest, freshwater lakes, and great views. As a bonus, they threw in a magnificent bridge that might be the most artful assemblage of steel in the country. All told, it's a magnificent package—one that every Washington nature lover must unwrap at least once in his or her outdoor career.

sites	261
🏕️🚐	83 full hookups, RVs to 30 feet
open	All year
reservations	Up to 9 months in advance; 888/226-7688 or www.parks.wa.gov
contact	Washington State Parks, 360/902-8844; Deception Pass State Park, 360/675-2417

Plan to stay awhile. This is a park that can't be fully explored in a single day. Deception has an impressive 4,134 acres of wooded uplands, a remarkable 77,000 feet of saltwater shoreline, two campgrounds, multiple day-use areas, and 34,000 feet of shoreline on four freshwater lakes. If you only have time for the highlights,

Deception Pass bridge, an artful assemblage of steel.

park in one of the Highway 20 pullouts and walk out on Deception Pass Bridge, which spans one of the most treacherous, tumultuous saltwater channels in the Northwest. After you catch your breath, get back in the car and follow the winding road from the park's main entrance (a short distance south of the bridge) downhill to the beach day-use area. From here, trails lead along North Beach to viewpoints of the impressive bridge—actually two steel spans linking Whidbey and Fidalgo Islands. The southern end of the main day-use area fronts on both Rosario Strait and Cranberry Lake, offering fine salt- and freshwater swimming in the summer. A separate, splendid picnic area on the opposite shore of Cranberry Lake has a boat launch and a dock, where trout fishing is often good. The park also has an RV dump station and coin-op showers.

Even more of the park is found on the opposite (north) side of the bridge. Pass Lake, a productive fly-fishing venue, is right off Highway 20. Nearby, a road leads steeply downhill to Bowman Bay, where a saltwater fishing pier, small (16-site) campground, and boat launch are found. It's all tied together by an astonishing 30 miles of well-worn hiking trails.

The vast majority of campsites are found in three loops in the southern, Cranberry Lake sector, which has been substantially upgraded with utilities, regrading, and other major work in the past half decade (most utility sites are in the Forest Loop). Compared to the park's overall grandeur, this main campground is still somewhat wanting: The spaces are close together, with little privacy. But if you scout around, you can find a good one. If you have a choice (which you probably won't), go low and get one of the open-air sites closest to the water, and thus farthest away from busy Highway 20. Finally, note that this is one of only a few state parks where reservations are accepted—and probably necessary—year-round. And beware those loud, loud jets from nearby Whidbey Naval Air Station.

Getting there: From Interstate 5 at Mount Vernon, follow Highway 20 east to Whidbey Island and Deception Pass Bridge, 9 miles northeast of Oak Harbor.

⑦ Washington Park 🌲🌲🌲

Washington Park is a great little secret, well-kept by the city of Anacortes, which is lucky enough to own it and does a nice job running things. Visiting Washington Park is a lot like going to the San Juans without ever leaving the mainland. This beautiful, 220-acre park on Fidalgo Head, just beyond the Anacortes ferry terminal, is one of the loveliest waterfront getaways in the Northwest. Alas, the forested campground is comparatively cramped and pedestrian, lacking privacy in most sites. The last time we visited—in the interest of full disclosure, on a sunny August weekend—sites seemed to be occupied by an average of about 3.5 cars each. Rangers would be well served to crack down on the demolition derbyness of the place. But some decent sites are available, and if you're here in the off-season, any or all of them can be

sites	75
🏕️ 🚐	46 full or water/electrical hookups, RVs to 40 feet
open	All year
reservations	City of Anacortes residents only
contact	City of Anacortes, 360/293-1918

Snoozing away an afternoon at Fidalgo Island's Washington Park.

quite pleasant. Besides: You don't have to sit in the Winnie all day, and the rest of the park is a gem. The day-use area near the campground has a pleasant saltwater beach, picnic area, and boat launch, but the highlight is a 2.3-mile loop road that skirts the shoreline all the way around the park. The narrow road can be driven one way, or better yet walked or cycled, to waterfront picnic spots with views of Rosario Strait, the San Juans, and all the pleasure craft headed toward them. The park also has a laundry room, RV dump station, and hot showers. The park is about a 20-minute walk or 5-minute bike ride from state ferries to the San Juans.

Getting there: From Commercial Avenue (Highway 20) in downtown Anacortes, turn left (west) on 12th Street and proceed about 2 miles, staying left where the road to the Washington State Ferry terminal veers right.

⑧ Spencer Spit State Park 🌲🌲🌲🌲

If exploring all or part of Lopez Island is high on your to-do list, Spencer Spit should be your base camp. Spencer, one of the very best campgrounds in the San Juans, doesn't have the drive-through, full-hookup amenities many modern campers are looking for, but its seven walk-in, beachfront spots make it a true gem for cyclists, tent campers, and sea kayakers. The 138-acre park is a designated Cascadia Marine Trail campground, and its 16 moorage buoys make it a popular boat-in stopover for mariners of all sorts. The rest of the campsites are in a pleasant, wooded upland area; about half accommodate RVs. Kids will have a blast on the park's trails and on its narrow, sandy spit, with salt water on each side and a sizable lagoon in the center. The park also has a group camp that accommodates 60. A wealth of great Lopez Island day trips beckon. Watch for whales and sea lions across the island at Shark Reef Sanctuary, Otis Perkins Day Park, or Agate Beach Day Park, or hop the ferry to Friday Harbor. Special close-quarters alert: The park has an RV dump station, but unlike most state parks, this one has no hot showers.

sites	37
🏕️ 🚐	No hookups, RVs to 20 feet
open	March through October
reservations	Up to 9 months in advance; 888/226-7688 or www.parks.wa.gov
contact	Washington State Parks, 360/902-8844; Spencer Spit State Park, 360/378-2044

Getting there: From the Lopez Island ferry terminal, follow signs 5 miles southeast. Go left at Center Road, left at Cross Road, right at Port Stanley Road, and left at Bakerview Road, which leads into the park.

⑨ Odlin County Park ▲▲▲▲

This is a perfect first-night stopover for cyclists bound for a tour of Lopez, the favorite San Juan island of most two-wheeled tourists, thanks to its many miles of relatively flat roads. The camp is a short roll (just over a mile) from the ferry dock on Lopez, so getting there even late in the evening doesn't pose too much of a challenge. For boaters, the 80-acre campground has a boat launch and low-bank waterfront access, with nine sites right on the rare sandy beach (5 for hikers/bikers/kayakers only). The campground has pit toilets. Reservations are recommended; be patient with the limited hours of the reservation number. Spencer Spit State Park (see above), a Lopez highlight, is a short ride or drive away.

sites	30
🏕️🚐	No hookups, RVs to 30 feet
open	All year
reservations	Up to 90 days in advance; 360/378-1842
contact	San Juan County Parks, 360/378-8420

Getting there: From the Lopez Island ferry terminal, follow Ferry Road 1.3 miles south to the park, on the right.

⑩ San Juan County Park ▲▲▲▲

One of the rare public campgrounds in the San Juan Islands, this 12-acre camp near Smallpox Bay on San Juan itself has a boat ramp and good beach access, plus a boat launch and lush green lawn. It's a favorite of scuba divers, who find some of the richest (natural) underwater treasures in the continental United States just offshore; orcas and other sea creatures are also common to these waters. Most of the campsites are in an upland area; site 18, a waterfront special, is likely to be the one you want, but can't get. Reservations are strongly recommended, even though the campground has no piped water.

sites	20
🏕️🚐	No hookups, RVs to 25 feet
open	Summers only
reservations	Up to 90 days in advance; 360/378-1842
contact	San Juan County Parks, 360/378-8420

Getting there: The campground is about 10 miles west of Friday Harbor on San Juan Island, via Beaverton Valley, Mitchell Bay, and West Side Roads.

⑪ Moran State Park 🌲🌲🌲🌲🌲

Umm, where's the water? That's the first question asked by many a first-time Moran visitor. Give 'em a half hour to look around, however, and few ever regret the irony that the San Juan Islands' largest park lacks easily accessible saltwater shoreline. There's so much more to Moran, the beach seems almost irrelevant. This sprawling 5,200-acre park is one of the jewels of the state park system, with a rich mix of old-growth forests, picturesque freshwater lakes (there are four), pleasant campsites (in five separate areas, with sites at two of the lakes), and a 2,400-foot mountaintop where the view is as gorgeous as any in the Northwest. Named for shipbuilder and former resident Robert Moran (who donated the park land and whose mansion now is the focus of nearby Rosario Resort), most of the park is wooded, mountainous terrain.

sites	*166*
🏕️🚐	*No hookups, RVs to 45 feet*
open	*All year*
reservations	*Up to 9 months in advance; 888/226-7688 or www.parks.wa.gov*
contact	*Washington State Parks, 360/902-8844; Moran State Park, 360/376-2326*

Of the three primary camping areas, the Southend camp, with nearly all sites on the lakeshore, is the most popular; Midway is another favorite with boaters who favor the nearby launch; Mountain Lake sites offer more privacy. Fifteen sites in the park are walk-ins; great for cyclists. Your best bet is to book well in advance.

This is a huge, diverse park, with pleasant picnic grounds, two boat launches, bathhouses, swimming beaches, and moorage docks with rental boats. The park has an RV dump station and coin-op showers. Also on site is a large Extended

An American dipper or water ouzel—a frequent Northwest streamside companion.

Learning Center, which rents cabins to large groups. Activities include fishing, kayaking, canoeing, or boating in Mountain or Cascade Lake, and hiking on the park's 30-mile trail system. One of those trails leads from the park's lowland camping areas to Moran's highlight—2,400-foot Mount Constitution, the highest spot in the San Juans. At the summit (which you can also drive to during daylight hours), the view in all directions is spectacular. Climb up the stairway in the 12th-century replica stone observation tower (built by the Civilian Conservation Corps in 1936) and you can see as far south as Mount Rainier and the Olympics, west to Vancouver Island, British Columbia, north to Vancouver, British Columbia, and east to the North Cascades.

Getting there: From the Orcas Island ferry landing, turn left follow signs about 14 miles northeast to the park.

⑫ South Beach County Park 🌲🌲🌲

The beach is the main draw at this small (30 acres) public park on Shaw, the quietest of all the "developed" San Juan Islands. The 3,200 feet of splendid sand make this one of the finer picnic spots in the San Juans, and campers lucky enough to snare one of the pleasant, upland campsites here are in for plenty of rest and relaxation. This task got easier in the spring of 1999, when the campground began accepting reservations. South Beach also serves as a popular boat-launch site for canoeists and kayakers, who can paddle the short distance across Indian Cove to Canoe Island, home of a summer camp for teens. On shore, a short walk on a local road leads to another quiet beach on Squaw Bay, just to the west. The park is a popular boat-in destination for powerboaters and paddlers based in Friday Harbor, which is less than 4 nautical miles away. The campground has pit toilets.

sites	12
open	All year
reservations	Up to 90 days in advance; 360/378-1842
contact	San Juan County Parks, 360/378-8420

Getting there: From the Shaw Island ferry terminal, follow Blind Bay Road southwest to Squaw Bay Road, turn left, and follow signs a short distance to the park.

⑬ Bay View State Park 🌲🌲🌲

Bay View, a sleepy campground off Highway 20 in the Skagit Valley, is notable not so much for what's in it, but what's near it. Namely, the Padilla Bay National Estuarine Research Reserve—a long name for a fine bird-watching venue that's a relatively short drive from most Puget Sound-area homes. Many RV-equipped birders flock here in the winter (best birding season), parking in Bay View's grassy, some-

The calm waters of Padilla Bay are a Bay View State Park highlight.

what closely packed sites, all across the road from the saltwater day-use area, which has 1,285 feet of shoreline. Padilla Bay in winter months is home to one of the state's largest populations of migratory raptors and waterfowl. They are sometimes visible from viewing blinds or the boardwalk at the Padilla Bay interpretive center (a short walk from the campground; 360/428-1558; open 10am–5pm, Wednesday through Sunday); or from a nicely maintained, 2.25-mile barrier-free trail along a dike at the south end of the bay, about a half-mile south. The campground has an RV dump and coin-op showers. Sites are split into three areas: 1–9, in the front section, are the only true "bay view" sites, and they're often booked well in advance in summer; sites 10–30 are utility spaces in a partially forested loop surrounding a large, open playfield. The remainder of sites have no hookups and largely consist of small back-in sites in a wooded area, with average to below-average privacy. Plans call for three cabins to be built in the campground.

sites	76
🏕️	
🚐	30 full hookups, RVs to 40 feet
open	All year
reservations	Up to 9 months in advance; 888/226-7688 or www.parks.wa.gov
contact	Washington State Parks, 360/902-8844; Bay View State Park, 360/757-0227

Getting there: From Interstate 5 in Mount Vernon, take the Highway 20 exit, turn west under the freeway, and proceed about 7 miles to Bay View–Edison Road. Turn right (north) and drive about 4 miles to the park, where the campground is on the right (east) side of the road.

⑭ Larrabee State Park 🌲🌲🌲

Put this one on the must-visit list. Washington's oldest state park (established 1915) is also one of its finest, offering in one 2,700-acre nutshell a tasty sampling of what makes north Puget Sound so soothing—and the Northwest itself so famous. Perched on a bluff between the smooth, stony cliffs of Chuckanut Mountain and the gently lapping shores of Samish Bay, Larrabee is so well-known as a primo day-use area for Bellinghamsters that it's often overlooked as a quality overnight getaway by everyone else. Campsites are adequate, but don't quite match the big-splash status of the rest of the park. Renovated in 1997, they're situated in tall (some old-growth) fir, madrona, and maple trees (no water views). Unlike many of the RV sites, the tent sites offer decent privacy, and eight walk-in sites are favored by cyclists. All sites are pleasantly cool in the summer, but can be dark and dreary in bad weather. And if you're a light (or even medium) sleeper, late-night Burlington Northern trains might be a problem.

sites	85
🏕️ 🚐	26 full hookups, RVs to 60 feet
open	All year
reservations	Up to 9 months in advance; 888/226-7688 or www.parks.wa.gov
contact	Washington State Parks, 360/902-8844; Larrabee State Park, 360/676-2093

That said, hikers and beachcombers will love the park's nine miles of trails, including two that climb to Fragrance Lake, high onto Chuckanut Mountain,

Lummi Island is a backdrop to the beach at Larrabee State Park.

offering sweeping views of the San Juan Islands. (Look for the trailhead opposite the main entryway on the east side of Chuckanut Drive.) The park also has an RV dump station, coin-op showers, and a boat launch popular with sea kayakers, swimmers, divers, and Frisbee-chasin' dogs. Less than a half mile south on Chuckanut Drive is Clayton Beach, a fine Department of Natural Resources day-use area with ample parking, restrooms, and a gentle (mountain-bike accessible) trail that leads about a half mile downhill to the sandy, Puget Sound waterfront.

Getting there: Larrabee is 7 miles south of Bellingham on Chuckanut Drive (Highway 11). From the south, take Interstate 5 exit 231, north of Mount Vernon; follow signs along Chuckanut Drive 14 miles to the park. Note: The south portions of narrow, winding Chuckanut Drive are not suitable for trailers or RVs, which should proceed to exit 250 in Bellingham and follow signs to Highway 11 from the Fairhaven neighborhood.

⓯ Birch Bay State Park 🌲🌲🌲🌲

If you can find an empty spot of sand amidst all the migratory Canadians, Birch Bay is a great place to while away summer afternoons, with gentle—OK, occasionally gusty—Strait of Georgia breezes keeping you company by day and a wealth of decent campsites greeting you at night. This camping area was used for centuries by local Semiahmoo, Lummi, and Nooksack tribal members, who came here for the same reasons you might: miles of open saltwater shoreline. Clamming, sunbathing, general beachcombing, and kite flying are the chief activities here, thanks to 8,255 feet of beachfront. The park has also an RV dump station and coin-op showers. But

sites	167
🏕️ 🚐	20 water/electrical hookups, RVs to any length
open	All year
reservations	Up to 9 months in advance; 888/226-7688 or www.parks.wa.gov
contact	Washington State Parks, 360/902-8844; Birch Bay State Park, 360/664-8112

there's much more to Birch Bay than just sand and gravel. The upland portion contains Terrell Creek Marsh, one of the last undisturbed salt/freshwater estuaries on north Puget Sound. A short nature trail loops through this rich wildlife habitat, where harlequin ducks and other rare waterfowl often are spotted through the reeds. Campsites in this 194-acre park are standard state park fare, spread in separate loops north and south of the park access road. Tip: The quieter northern loop, which contains all the utility sites, fills up first; it's tough to get into without a reservation during summer months. Local trivia: The bay was named by a botanist on the 1792 Capt. George Vancouver expedition, who noted the many black birch trees in the area.

Getting there: Follow signs west from Interstate 5 exit 270 (Grandview) about 8 miles to the park on Helwig Road. It's about 10 miles south of downtown Blaine.

A waterfront seat at Birch Bay State Park.

Other North Sound Campgrounds

Department of Natural Resources camps at **Lily** and **Lizard Lakes** (9 sites total, no piped water) are hike-in campgrounds reached by a 3.5-mile trail from the Blanchard Hill Trailhead on Samish Lake Road south of Bellingham.

In rural Whatcom County, **Berthusen Park** (8837 Berthusen Road; 360/354-2424), managed by the city of Lynden, is a clean, pleasant, wooded campground with 53 sites, 24 with hookups. Follow signs from Hwy 539 near Lynden.

In the Skagit Valley, **River Bend Park** (305 Stewart, Mount Vernon; 360/428-4044), a private campground along the Skagit River in Mount Vernon, is an alternative to Bay View, but it's primarily an Interstate 5 motorhome stopover, with 25 tent sites and 95 RV pull-throughs with hookups. Another private campground, **Burlington KOA** (646 N Green Road, Burlington; 360/724-5511), has 45 tent and 45 RV sites, many with hookups, along with the standard KOA amenities.

Other San Juan Islands Campgrounds

In the San Juans, a small number of private campgrounds compensate for the lack of available public campsites. On San Juan Island, the best campground is at **Lakedale Resort** (reservations, 800/617-CAMP), on Roche Harbor Road 4.5 miles from the ferry terminal. The park is open March 15 to October 15 and has 117 lakefront campsites (19 with full hookups) and three small lakes for fishing and swimming. Rental cycles, boats, and camping gear are also available. As the primary campground on the island, it's often overcrowded, so make a reservation. Other campgrounds include the **Pedal Inn** (reservations, 360/378-3049), 5 miles from the ferry terminal on False Bay Drive, with 25 biker/hiker sites; and **Snug Harbor Marina Resort** (reservations, 360/378-4762), on Mitchell Bay Road 8.5 miles from the ferry, with 16 campsites (4 with hookups), a boat launch, and other services. In Friday Harbor proper is **Town and Country Trailer Park** (360/378-4717), which has 40 sites (some with hookups), showers, and laundry facilities.

On Orcas, try **Doe Bay Village Resort** (360/376-2291), which offers 50 campsites (8 have hookups); primitive **Obstruction Pass** (see Boat-in San Juan/North Sound Campgrounds, below); or **West Beach Resort** (360/376-2240) at Eastsound, a private facility with 72 campsites (36 with hookups).

Boat-in North Sound/Islands Campgrounds

Private boaters will find an almost overwhelming array of quality public moorages with access to primitive beachfront or upland campsites, managed by Washington State Parks or the Department of Natural Resources. (Many of the campsites also serve as Cascadia Marine Trail camps; call Washington Water Trails Association, 206/545-9161 or visit www.wwta.org for details on the trail.) Most have moorage floats or docks. Fees are charged during the summer, and fresh water is limited. Avid boaters say these parks offer some of the best boat camping (or boat-in camping) in the country. Boaters should note that most state marine parks have picnic tables, pit or composting toilets, and moorage floats for pleasure boaters, while most DNR-maintained sites are more primitive.

The sites are too numerous to list here, but an excellent guidebook to the marine parks, written with the mariner in mind, is *The San Juan Islands: Afoot & Afloat*, by Marge and Ted Mueller (The Mountaineers Books). You can also consult the State Parks website, www.parks.wa.gov, or contact the DNR's Sedro-Woolley office, 360/856-3500.

Greater Seattle and Cascade Foothills

16 Wenberg State Park 🌲🌲⛺

Lake Goodwin and a healthy crop of evergreen trees are the star attractions at Wenberg, a park that's most popular in the summer, when swimming in the lake and fishing for smallmouth bass and planted rainbow trout reach their peaks (the park also has a boat ramp and ample day-use parking). Given the abundance of powerboats and Jet-skis on the lake in the summer, it's neither the quietest nor most scenic state park you'll ever find. But Wenberg, one of the few public camping venues within a day's drive of Seattle, is conveniently located, and just far enough from town to make you feel as if you're actually camping. The park has an RV dump station and coin-op showers. Hookup sites are in the lower (southern) portion of the campground.

sites	75
⛺ 🚐	30 full hookups, RVs to 50 feet
open	All year
reservations	Up to 9 months in advance; 888/226-7688 or www.parks.wa.gov
contact	Washington State Parks, 360/902-8844; Wenberg State Park, 360/652-7417

Getting there: From Interstate 5 about 12 miles north of Everett, take exit 206 (Smokey Point) and follow signs 6.7 miles west on Highway 531.

17 Kayak Point County Park 🌲🌲🌲⛺

ARCO's loss was our gain. The oil giant purchased this plum slice of Puget Sound waterfront—the site of an early-century would-be, never-was town called Birmingham—in 1967, planning to plunk yet another refinery here. Didn't work out, thank heavens, and Snohomish County was wise enough to snatch up 670 acres of the land five years later. The point, one of the finer stretches of public saltwater beach north of Seattle, is a favorite summertime getaway for Everett-area families drawn to the beach area's fine picnic sites. The park also has become a popular windsurfing and, appropriately, sea kayaking venue. A 300-foot public pier juts into Port Susan, offering decent bottom-fishing and crabbing in season.

sites	34
⛺ 🚐	34 water/electrical hookups, RVs to 25 feet
open	April to early October for all campers; RVs only in winter
reservations	For yurts only; 360/652-7992
contact	Snohomish County Parks, 360/652-7992

Often overlooked is the small but very nice campground tucked into the trees and shrubs. The sites all are nicely manicured. If you want to camp and don't want to mess with the gear, Kayak Point is one of only a handful of campgrounds in Washington State with rental yurts (round, frame-tent structures with skylights, wood floors, and heat). Ten yurts are grouped in a "yurt village" here, and can be reserved for $35 a night at this writing. Local trivia: The park gets its name from a pair of Eskimo kayaks displayed at the former private resort on the site.

Getting there: From Interstate 5 at Marysville, take exit 199 (Tulalip), cross under the freeway on Tulalip Way, and follow signs 13 miles west to the park on Marine Drive.

⑱ Flowing Lake County Park ▲▲▲

Flowing Lake, a great retreat from the sweltering summer heat that seems to hang in the Snohomish River valley, is way out there in the bowels of the Puget Sound's rural thickage; in fact, it's tough to find without precise directions. Tucked onto the shoulder of this small lake, in a space you'd expect two large Microsoft-executive homes to fill, is a tidy, picturesque county park, with a decent campground in a wooded area near the lakeshore. It's not exactly Wild Kingdom: Homes surround the lake on all other sides. And the campground has the kind of semi-crowded, busy feel of a private resort, which is what this space used to be. But if you close your eyes and stick your feet in the lake, it almost feels like wilderness. Highlights are swimming (in the fenced-off area, away from the water-ski boats), fishing, and just lounging in the shade.

sites	42
🏕 🚐	32 water/electrical hookups, RVs to 25 feet
open	Mid-May to September for all campers; RVs only in winter
reservations	None
contact	Flowing Lake County Park, 360/568-2274

Getting there: From Interstate 5 at Everett, follow US 2 east to milepost 10. Turn left onto 100th Street SE (Westwick Road). Just past the French Creek Grange, the road bears sharply to the left (north) and becomes 171st Avenue SE. Continue on 171st to 48th Street SE and turn right. Proceed to the entrance at the end of the road.

⑲ Saltwater State Park ▲▲▲

Considering its location, in a suburban area bordering on urban (Des Moines), Saltwater is a surprisingly diverse campground getaway. The 88-acre park is most often used by picnickers, sunset watchers, and scuba divers, who visit the underwater park just off the 1,445 feet of public shoreline. But the campground is adequate, and 2 miles of seldom-maintained, but well-trod, hiking trails lead into the

sites	50
	No hookups, RVs to 50 feet
open	Late April to mid-September
reservations	None
contact	Washington State Parks, 360/902-8844; Saltwater State Park, 253/661-4956

wooded uplands, offering nice views of Maury and Vashon Islands and the leeward Olympics. McSorely Creek, a salmon-spawning stream, runs through the camping and picnic areas. Unlike some Puget Sound parks, this one has long been public property. Original development here was conducted by the Civilian Conservation Corps in the mid-1930s. The park has an RV dump station and coin-op showers. The biggest drawback: plane noise. The park lies in the flight path for nearby SeaTac Airport.

Getting there: From Des Moines, follow the signs on Highway 509 (Marine View Drive) about 2 miles south to the park.

⑳ Dash Point State Park 🌲🌲🌲

This Federal Way–area park's campsites are pleasant enough, nestled in an alder/broadleaf maple forest. But it's Dash Point's scenic waterfront day-use area, not to mention its being one of the few public-camping venues close to Seattle, that makes it worthwhile for out-of-town visitors or locals looking to get the early-season kinks out of the RV or tent. The day-use area, reached via an underpass below Highway 509, has three well-developed picnic areas, with shelters and a slew of tables. It also has a Puget Sound rarity—a sandy beach. The campsites are scattered in two wooded loops across Highway 509, which bisects the park. Some

A pooch samples the wares at Saltwater State Park.

Summertime Seattle visitors take to Washington State Ferries.

of the sites are broad and level, making particularly nice tent spots. Utility sites are in Loop B, to your right as you enter. A group camp for up to 100 people can be reserved in advance. The park has an RV dump station and coin-op showers.

sites	*141*
	27 water/electrical hookups, RVs to 35 feet
open	*All year; upper loop closed in winter*
reservations	*Up to 9 months in advance; 888/226-7688 or www.parks.wa.gov*
contact	*Washington State Parks, 360/902-8844; Dash Point State Park, 253/593-2206*

Getting there: From Interstate 5 exit 143, near Federal Way, follow 320th Street West for about 4 miles to its end at a T intersection. Turn right on 47th Street and proceed to another T intersection. Turn left on Highway 509/ Dash Point Road and drive about 2 miles to the park. The camping entrance is on the west side of the street.

Other Greater Seattle–Area Campgrounds

In the south end of the metro area, **Orchard Trailer Park** (4011 S 146th Street, Burien, I-5 exit 154; 206/243-1210) has limited overnight facilities for RVs. **Seattle/Tacoma KOA** (5801 S 212th Street, Kent I-5 exit 152; 253/872-8652) has more than 140 sites for tents and RVs. **Aqua Barn Ranch** (15227 SE Renton–Maple Valley Highway, Renton; 206/255-4618) is one of the best local tent areas, with 240 sites, many of them grassy. To the north, **Holiday Park Resort** (19250 Aurora Avenue N; 206/542-2760) has 22 RV sites. **Lake Pleasant RV Park** (24025 Bothell–Everett

Highway SE, Bothell, take I-405 north to exit 26; 206/487-1785 or 800/742-0386) is the biggest campground (and one of the nicest) in the greater Seattle area, with more than 200 campsites, including a dozen tent spots.

To the east, not far from Lake Sammamish is popular **Trailer Inn RV Park** (15531 SE 37th Street, Issaquah, off I-90 exit 11a; 425/747-9181), with 115 pull-through RV sites. **Blue Sky RV Park** (9002 302nd Street SE, Issaquah; 425/222-7910) has 51 RV sites. **Issaquah Village RV Park** (650 1st Avenue NE, Issaquah; 425/392-9233 or 800/258-9233) has 112 RV sites, no tents allowed. On the west side of Lake Sammamish is **Vasa Park Resort** (3560 W Lake Sammamish Parkway, Bellevue, I-90 exit 13; 206/746-3260), a small park with decent tent sites. A bit farther out, but worth the drive, is the more natural-feeling **Snoqualmie River Campground** (on the banks of the river at Fall City; 425/222-5545), which has 50 tent sites and 30 RV sites, with utilities for RVs to 60 feet.

South Sound and Key Peninsula

㉑ Kopachuck State Park 🌲🌲🌲🌲

A fine forested/saltwater park on Key Peninsula that's a quick trip (well, assuming you're not tied up in Narrows Bridge traffic for 19 hours) from Tacoma and Gig Harbor, Kopachuck's campsites are nicely spaced in a Douglas fir–forested upland area. Down at the Henderson Bay beach (a short walk away), scuba divers, sea kayakers, cold-water-swimming fools, and other water fans will have a heyday. The waterfront picnic area offers grand views of the Olympics. The park has an RV dump station and coin-op showers. Also available are two group-camping facilities for a total of up to 55 campers.

sites	41
🏕️ 🚐	No hookups, RVs to 35 feet
open	April to early October
reservations	None
contact	Washington State Parks, 360/902-8844; Kopachuck State Park, 253/265-3606

Getting there: From Tacoma, drive 7 miles north on Highway 16 to the second Gig Harbor exit; follow signs 5 miles west to the park.

The vine maple, a common companion in Puget Sound campsites.

㉒ Penrose Point State Park ♠♠♠

Campers looking to sample the saltwater wonders of the south Puget Sound/Key Peninsula area won't go wrong at Penrose Point, one of the most enjoyable saltwater parks in the state. The campground, tucked on a wooded bluff inside Carr Inlet's Mayo Cove, is idyllic, quiet, and fairly secluded. All sites are at least partially shaded, and all are within a short walk of the beach. The day-use area at the beach is well equipped and wonderful, with a group camp, picnic facilities, boat moorage, and a shallow swimming beach on more than 2 miles of shoreline.

sites	83
🏕️ 🚐	No hookups, RVs to 35 feet
open	April through September
reservations	Up to 9 months in advance; 888/226-7688 or www.parks.wa.gov
contact	Washington State Parks, 360/902-8844; Penrose Point State Park, 253/884-2514

At low tide the beach becomes truly massive, and a long sand spit offers exploring opportunities for the kids. Several miles of hiking trails wind through the trees in the park's upland area, including Penrose Point itself, a thumb of land pointing northeast into Puget Sound. The park has an RV dump station and coin-op showers.

Getting there: From Tacoma, drive north on Highway 16 to Highway 302 (Key Peninsula Highway) near Purdy. Proceed south on Key Peninsula Highway for about 9 miles. Turn left at Cornwall Road and follow signs to the park, on 158th Avenue KPS.

㉓ Joemma Beach State Park ♠♠♠♠

You have Joe and Emma to thank. And after a day spent on the beach here, you probably will. Joemma Beach, one of Washington's newer state parks, is the former R. F. Kennedy Multiple Use Area. It was transferred from Department of Natural Resources management to State Parks in 1995, and renamed to honor Joe and Emma Smith, early settlers who lived here from 1917 to 1932. The 122-acre park on Key Peninsula's west shore now has campsites with a still-newish feel to them, in two small loops. Also on the premises are wheelchair-accessible vault toilets, two walk-in, hiker/biker

sites	21
🏕️ 🚐	No hookups, RVs to 35 feet
open	All year
reservations	None
contact	Washington State Parks, 360/902-8844; Joemma Beach State Park, 253/884-1944

sites, a couple of short hiking trails, 1,000 feet of gravelly beach, a pair of Cascadia Marine Trail waterfront campsites, a boat launch, and a very nice moorage dock for overnighting boaters. It's a good fishing and crabbing spot.

Getting there: From Tacoma, follow Highway 16 to Highway 302 (Key Peninsula Highway). Turn left (south) and drive about 15 miles to Whiteman Road. Turn right and drive 4 miles to Bay Road. Turn right and drive about a mile to the park entrance, staying on the asphalt road into the park.

㉔ Jarrell Cove State Park 🌲🌲🌲

This one's out there a ways; so far, in fact, that you really have to want to visit the north end of Harstine Island to get here. For that reason alone, Jarrell Cove is a quiet, occasionally lonely place, one that's visited by boat almost as often as by auto. The wooded campground is small, sufficient, but not spectacular. The cove itself is the attraction here, with two docks and moorage piers, 14 mooring buoys, a pumpout station, and other facilities. It's a great place to spend a week exploring the south Sound by boat. The park has one coin-op shower and a group camp for up to 64 people. One site is wheelchair accessible.

sites	22
	No hookups, RVs to 35 feet
open	All year
reservations	Up to 9 months in advance; 888/226-7688 or www.parks.wa.gov
contact	Washington State Parks, 360/902-8844; Jarrell Cove State Park, 253/265-3606

Getting there: From Shelton, follow Highway 3 about 8 miles north to Pickering Road. Turn right and proceed 4 miles to Harstine Island bridge. On the island, turn left at the stop sign at North Island Drive and follow signs 4 miles to the park.

The cove itself is the attraction at Jarrell Cove State Park.

㉕ Millersylvania Memorial State Park 🌲🌲🌲

Millersylvania, the best public-camping venue within a short shot of Olympia, got its start as the 850-acre estate of Johann Mueller, an Austrian general (and bodyguard of Emperor Francis Joseph I) exiled to these parts in the late 19th century.

sites	168
🏕️ 🚐	48 full hookups, RVs to 45 feet
open	All year
reservations	Up to 9 months in advance; 888/226-7688 or www.parks.wa.gov
contact	Washington State Parks, 360/902-8844; Millersylvania State Park, 360/753-1519

Now it's a very big, very pretty, very diverse state park with a nice camping area, hiking trails, coin-op showers, and swimming (and good trout fishing) in Deep Lake. The park even has its own 1.5-mile fitness trail. The campsites, set in a stand of stately old-growth firs, are popular with both tenters and RVers. The completing touch is a series of historic Civilian Conservation Corps–era buildings, which the Corps built while headquartered here as it worked on other local public parks in the 1930s. This is a good family park, with convenient Interstate 5 access. Note that the park's RV dump station at this writing had closed; ask park rangers for other nearby facilities.

Getting there: From Interstate 5 south of Olympia, take exit 95 and follow signs, driving east on Maytown Road, then north on Tilley Road.

㉖ Kanaskat-Palmer State Park 🌲🌲🌲

It may have a funny name, but it's hard to find, too. Kanaskat-Palmer, tucked into the Green River Gorge Recreation Area between Black Diamond and Enumclaw, is better known as a winter steelheader's parking spot than a campground. But it

sites	50
🏕️ 🚐	9 electrical hookups, RVs to 35 feet
open	All year
reservations	Up to 9 months in advance; 888/226-7688 or www.parks.wa.gov
contact	Washington State Parks, 360/902-8844; Kanaskat-Palmer State Park, 360/886-0148

switches gears just fine for summer, offering pleasant campsites that increasingly are glommed onto by kayakers, rafters (this stretch of Green River white water is not for rookies), and nature lovers who come for the park's unparalleled access to the river—13,000 feet of river frontage in all. The park also has 3 miles of hiking trails, coin-op showers, an RV dump station, and an 80-soul group camp equipped with a couple nifty Adirondack shelters. A nearby attraction is Flaming Geyser State Park, a day-use-only area just downstream.

Showing the kids how not to toast a marshmallow.

Getting there: From Interstate 5 at Tacoma, follow Highway 410 east to Enum-claw. Turn left (northeast) on Farman Road and proceed 9 miles to the park.

Other South Sound Campgrounds

The Capitol State Forest has a series of small, primitive campgrounds, all managed by the Department of Natural Resources. They are **North Creek** (5 sites), **Sherman Valley** (7 sites), **Porter Creek** (16 sites), **Middle Waddell** (24 sites), **Fall Creek** (8 sites), and **Margaret McKenny** (25 sites). Only the latter two are off-limits to the noisy dirt bikes and ORVs that frequent this area, and even they are too close for comfort for many campers. Also, most of these campgrounds are used by hunters in the fall. Another DNR-managed campground is **Mima Falls Trailhead** (5 sites), off Highway 121 near Little Rock. All these campgrounds are free, and are accessed either from US 12 or Highway 121, both west of Interstate 5. Call DNR's Chehalis office (360/748-2383).

For boaters and kayakers, boat-in-only state marine parks in the south Sound are on **Squaxin Island, Cutts Island, McMicken Island, Hope Island, Eagle Island,** and **Stretch Point.** Call Washington State Parks (360/902-8844) for details.

West Sound and Kitsap Peninsula

㉗ Fay Bainbridge State Park ▲▲▲

Bring your camera. Fay Bainbridge, one of the very best things about Puget Sound's most yuppified island, is the only place we know of where one can pitch camp and get a direct, cross-Sound gander at downtown Seattle. In fact, it's one of

sites	36
🏕️🚐	26 water hookups, RVs to 30 feet
open	Mid-April through September
reservations	None
contact	Washington State Parks, 360/902-8844; Fay Bainbridge State Park, 206/842-3931

the few saltwater-front campgrounds in the entire Seattle area. But there's a tradeoff: This park is in more of a neighborhood setting than a wild place. Beachfront homes are visible on either end of the small, 17-acre park, and there's little privacy. The somewhat cramped sites also are fairly exposed to the very active day-use area near the smooth, sandy beach, cluttered by picnickers and driftwood.

Still, spaces can be tough to land in the summer. The park also has coin-op showers, an RV dump station, a group camp, and good picnic facilities with cov-

Mount Rainier looms on a red letter—and blue balloon—day at Fay Bainbridge.

ered kitchen shelters, a boat ramp, and mooring buoys. Local trivia: There is not, and never was, a "Fay Bainbridge." The park's name combines that of the island and the original property owners, Mr. and Mrs. Temple S. Fay, who graciously sold the land to the state for $5,000 in 1944.

Getting there: From the Bainbridge Island ferry terminal, drive about 5 miles west on Highway 305 to the Day Road turnoff. Turn right (north) and proceed about 2 miles to a T intersection. Turn left on Sunrise Drive NE and continue about 2 miles to the park entrance, on the right.

28 Kitsap Memorial State Park 🌲🌲🌲

A Hood Canal alternative to the aptly named Scenic Beach State Park (below) is Kitsap Memorial, halfway between Poulsbo and the Hood Canal Floating Bridge. The park has 1,800 feet of rocky shoreline and a good day-use site, with acres of open, grassy fields that attract softball players, kite fliers, and dog runners. A set of large, reservable kitchen shelters also makes this a high-traffic day-use area, especially on weekends. The campsites are clustered in a somewhat dreary area of dense forest but recently were upgraded with water and electrical hookups. The park has an RV dump station and coin-op showers. A 30-person group camp also is available, as is a restored, historic cabin, the Hospitality House, which can be reserved by calling the contact number above.

sites	46
🏕️🚐	18 water/electrical hookups, RVs to 40 feet
open	All year
reservations	None
contact	Washington State Parks, 360/902-8844; Kitsap Memorial State Park, 360/779-3205

Getting there: From Poulsbo, follow Highway 3 north for about 4 miles to Park Street, near milepost 57 on the west side of the highway. Turn left and proceed a short distance to the park.

29 Scenic Beach State Park 🌲🌲🌲🌲🌲

Scenic Beach very well could be the nicest state park you've never heard of. We'll admit it's located in an odd, out-of-the-way place and doesn't offer the most modern amenities. Some RVers might well balk at this park's rare five-tree rating, given its lack of utility hookups. But Scenic Beach is one of the flat-out most beautiful tent campgrounds we've ever had the privilege to visit—and revisit, and revisit—over the years. The setting is sublime. Located on a thumb of land—a former homestead—jutting into Hood Canal near the quaint town of Seabeck, the campsites (18 are pull-throughs) are nicely spread through large firs in a hilly,

Eating at a picnic table at Scenic Beach.

upland area. And the waterfront picnic area, set on a majestically wooded bluff overlooking the gravelly saltwater beach, is magnificent. Wild rhododendrons burst into bloom in May, and the view across Hood Canal into the Olympics is stunning; from this angle, you're looking right up east-slope Olympic valleys (namely the Duckabush and Dosewallips), and the mountains appear many times larger than when they're viewed from Seattle. Late- or early-season visitors are likely to encounter as many harbor seals as human souls on the beach, which also is a notable oyster-picking spot.

sites	52
	No hookups, RVs to 60 feet
open	April through September
reservations	Up to 9 months in advance; 888/226-7688 or www.parks.wa.gov
contact	Washington State Parks, 360/902-8844; Scenic Beach State Park, 360/830-5079

Nearby, on elegantly landscaped grounds, is Emel House, the stately old homestead for this former resort property. The house can be reserved for weddings and other functions. Also reservable is the park's group camp, which accommodates 50 campers. The park has an RV dump station and coin-op showers. If it all gets to be old hat after a few days, troop down the road to the Seabeck Store and chew the fat around the potbellied stove with the local boys.

Getting there: From Highway 3 near Silverdale, take the Newberry Hill Road exit and drive 3 miles west to Seabeck Highway. Turn right and drive 6 miles, proceeding through Seabeck. Turn right on Scenic Beach Road (just after Seabeck

Elementary School), and continue about a mile to the park entrance at the end of the road.

30 Illahee State Park 🌲🌲🌲

An interesting park in an odd location, Illahee is a waterfront site tucked below one of Bremerton's suburban neighborhoods. The park is split in two, with a boat launch and small saltwater mooring dock in the lower, waterfront portion, and a picnic area and campground in the wooded upper sector—part of the "last stand of old-growth forest in Kitsap County," according to State Parks. The waterfront is the primary draw. It's a popular shore-fishing, picnicking, and sun-worshiping spot. The 56 mooring buoys and 365 feet of moorage docks are protected by a breakwater and often draw anglers and scuba divers.

sites	25
🏕️	
🚐	1 full hookup, RVs to 30 feet
open	All year
reservations	None
contact	Washington State Parks, 360/902-8844; Illahee State Park, 360/478-6460

The small camping area is unspectacular but sufficient, set in a forest very high above the waterfront (quite a hike). A group camp houses up to 40 people. Coin-op showers and an RV dump station are available. As a campground, it's nice enough. But something about traipsing through Bremerton's commercial and suburban sprawl to get wild doesn't exactly appeal to the natural camper in most of us.

Getting there: From Highway 303 in East Bremerton, follow Sylvan Way west to the park.

31 Manchester State Park 🌲🌲🌲

This 111-acre waterfront park in south Kitsap County—a short drive from Seattle via the Fauntleroy ferry—is a pleasant place with an intriguing history. It was built in the early 1900s as a U.S. Coast Artillery base to mine the waters of Rich Passage to protect Puget Sound Naval Shipyard in the event of war. The base was converted to a navy fuel supply depot during World War II. Remnants of those operations remain, including a giant concrete shell of a 1901 torpedo warehouse that's now used as a picnic shelter. (This for those of you who thought none of that military spending ever comes home to roost!) A trail leads from the day-use area to the rocky beach and some lin-

sites	53
🏕️	
🚐	15 water/electrical hookups, RVs to 60 feet
open	All year
reservations	Up to 9 months in advance; 888/226-7688 or www.parks.wa.gov
contact	Washington State Parks, 360/902-8844; Manchester State Park, 360/871-4065

A Vashon Island boater forgot to consult the tide chart.

gering gun emplacements. You're liable to see scuba divers here in the summer months. The camping area isn't quite as unique, unfortunately, with 50 sites split into two unremarkable wooded (fir and large maple) loops. Three hiker/biker sites also are available. The park has an RV dump station and coin-op showers. Two horseshoe pits are on the premises.

Getting there: From Port Orchard, follow signs from Beach Drive. From the Southworth ferry terminal, follow Highway 160 and Colchester Drive to Manchester, proceed north on Beach Drive, and follow signs. From Highway 16, take the Sedgwick Road exit and follow signs to the park.

③② Blake Island State Park 🌲🌲🌲

Seattleites who want to treat visiting relatives to the shiny side of the Northwest's cultural past can take a boat trip to Tillicum Village on the east side of Blake Island, where an authentic Northwest native salmon dinner is served up nightly in the summer. But those who want them to see the nitty-gritty of Seattle's cultural present take them by boat or kayak to the island's backside, where a boat-in-only state park offers a wide choice of boat- and hike-in campsites, many very private and secluded. Some areas even have piped water, and most have picnic tables and fire rings. Pit toilets are distributed throughout. The four main camping areas are separated by 15 miles of hiking trails. Boaters usually come from Port Orchard or

sites	54 primitive boat-in
open	All year
reservations	None
contact	Washington State Parks, 360/902-8844

Bremerton; sea kayakers can make it here on a short paddle from Manchester State Park, 1.5 miles to the west. Once they get here, they can stroll the 5 miles of saltwater beach and argue for several hours about how those 30 black-tailed deer got over here. Historical note: The

island was once used as a campsite for the Suquamish tribe. It's believed that Chief Sealth, in fact, may have been born here. Later, the island was acquired by William Pitt Trimble, who named it after himself and built a spectacular estate, which he abruptly abandoned after his wife drowned in Elliott Bay in 1929. The estate burned long ago after years of plundering and vandalism.

Getting there: Blake Island, 3 miles west of Seattle and 1.5 miles east of Manchester, is accessible only by boat.

③③ Belfair State Park 🌲🌲🌲🌲

Belfair is a longtime western Washington favorite. Campsites in the park, located near the town of Belfair at the southern crook of Hood Canal, are found in two main areas: a set of camping loops in broad, open, flat lawn just off the beach,

sites	184
🏕️🚐	47 full hookups, RVs to 75 feet
open	All year; beach loop closed in winter
reservations	Up to 9 months in advance; 888/226-7688 or www.parks.wa.gov
contact	Washington State Parks, 360/902-8844; Belfair State Park, 360/275-0668

with imported shrubs and trees; and a third, more natural (though darker) wooded loop just to the north. The latter loop, open summers only, has no utility sites, and has an RV size restriction of 25 feet. The beach has 3,700 feet of salt-water shoreline on shallow, tepid Hood Canal, much of it at the site of a long-since-abandoned commercial oyster bed. Shellfish commerce has fled, but many oysters still remain, making this a favorite spot for oyster pickers. In recent years, however, pollutants have closed the beach here to oyster gatherers and clam diggers. Big Mission and Little Mission Creeks flow through the park; they contain chum salmon runs in the fall. Just inland from the beach, Belfair has another unique feature: a tidal "swimming pool" that fills with warm salt water when the tide comes in. This is the best—and cleanest—place for a dip in the 65-acre park. The park has coin-op showers, and usually remains full for much of the summer. Reservations are recommended. Note that the RV dump station here has closed and the next closest aren't very close: They're at Kopachuck and Manchester State Parks (see above). Historical note: Thousands of ancient arrow points have been found in this area. The site of the current park likely was a village or meeting site for the Twana (a.k.a. Skokomish) people, who lived throughout what is now the south Hood Canal region.

Getting there: From Highway 3 at the town of Belfair, follow signs 3 miles west on Highway 300.

㉞ Twanoh State Park 🌲🌲🌲

Twanoh State Park, best known for its day-use beach area (great swimming in summer) on the north side of Highway 106, has a secluded camping area on the south side. The nicely manicured campsites are found among big trees, with

sites	47
🏕️🚐	22 full hookups, RVs to 35 feet
open	April to mid-October
reservations	None
contact	Washington State Parks, 360/902-8844; Twanoh State Park, 360/275-2222

smaller tent sites in one loop, RVs in the other. The scenery is pleasant, with cool shade along Twanoh Creek, which—like most Hood Canal streams—comes alive with chum salmon in the fall. The campground also has coin-op showers but no RV dump station. A group camp accommodates up to 50 campers. Several miles of trails follow the creek through the greenery on the hillside above (bring your bug dope). Note the old stone build-

The beach at Twanoh is noted for summertime swimming.

ings; most were built by Civilian Conservation Corps crews in the 1930s. Some facilities are barrier free. Local trivia: The trees in the campground are large, but by no means old-growth. This former private resort site was logged in the 1890s; note the very large cedar stumps.

Getting there: From Belfair, follow Highway 3 to Highway 106 and proceed 8 miles west to the park, which straddles the highway.

Other West Sound/Kitsap Peninsula Campgrounds

Winghaven Park on Vashon Island is a pleasant, 12-acre, undeveloped beachfront campsite, part of the **Cascadia Marine Trail** system. It's three-quarters of a mile from the ferry terminal, below Vashon Highway SW. Other designated Cascadia campsites in the immediate area are found in **Fay Bainbridge** and **Fort Ward State Parks,** on Bainbridge Island, and in **Lisabeula Park,** on the southwestern shore of Vashon Island on Colvos Passage. Kayakers also should note several other Vashon public beaches accessible only from the water: Department of Natural Resources **Beach 85** near Point Beals; DNR **Beach 83** on Maury Island near Portage; DNR **Beach 79,** northeast of Tahlequah; and DNR **Beaches 77 and 78,** two small beach patches on Colvos Passage on Vashon's west shore. Call the DNR's Enumclaw office (360/825-1631).

Two state forests in this area offer free DNR campsites. The most easily accessible is **Green Mountain Horse Camp** (9 sites, pumped water; 5 miles west of Bremerton, in Green Mountain State Forest). To the southwest are seven Tahuya State Forest campgrounds: **Toonerville** (4 sites, no piped water); **Aldrich Lake** (4 sites); **Tahuya River Horse Camp** (9 sites); **Kammenga Canyon** (2 sites); **Camp Spillman** (6 sites); **Twin Lakes** (6 sites); and **Howell Lake** (5 sites). All are popular with riders of beasts, both gas- and hay-powered. Call the DNR's Enumclaw office (360/825-1631) for directions and information.

Olympic Peninsula and the Pacific Coast

The rains shall fall, the winds shall blow, and the campers? Well, they shall get really, really wet—and put on a damp-but-happy face. Laughing at the rain—or possessing the ability to pretend to—is part of the recipe for camping success on the Olympic Peninsula, which didn't exactly become one of the world's greatest tree-growing factories by virtue of its arid weather.

Over the years, in fact, we've come to suspect there should be two certified "Guaranteed to Keep You Dry" ratings for Gore-Tex and other waterproof fabrics: one for those that'll keep you dry in October up in the Queets Basin, and another for those that'll keep you dry everywhere else on the planet, where it only rains downhill.

Not that it rains here all the time. Just most of it. Up to 140 inches a year, in fact, on the west side of the peninsula, where legendary forests on the Hoh, Bogachiel, and Queets Rivers suck it all up and turn it into grow juice, producing trees so big that Dr. Seuss himself could never have imagined them.

In spite of this—or perhaps because of it—it's a magical place, the peninsula. The jagged-edged Olympics rise from the center of it like 6,000-foot castle walls, protecting for centuries the splendid alpine interior from loggers, hunters, miners, and other riffraff. Oceans of forest surround—well, surrounded—these walls, stretching 50 miles or more in some places to the Pacific, which lands on some of the most unspoiled ocean beaches left in America, period.

Sound like a good place to camp? It really isn't. Trust us (and Yogi Berra): Nobody goes to the Olympics anymore. Too crowded. Please stay away.

By now, you've already figured out the obvious: The place is gorgeous, too gorgeous. And it's so close to the bulk of people living within the shadow of the Columbia Seafirst Center that it should be illegal.

Your camping choices on the peninsula are as diverse as the land itself, which seemed so frighteningly rugged for so long that no white settlers ventured into it until about 100 years ago. The northern area sets a saltwater table of campsites on Puget Sound and Strait of Juan de Fuca beaches that you'll want to keep coming back to. The east side combines the alpine wilderness highlands of Olympic National Park with the quiet saltwater shores of Hood Canal. The west side is a delicious concoction of massive trees and crashing waves. The southwest coast carries its own magic, from the "longest beach in the world" (yeah, we doubt it, too) at Long Beach to the stately grandeur of the North Head Lighthouse, one good rifle shot from the spot where Lewis and Clark finally stumbled into the Pacific.

Trudging in their long-vanished footsteps has become a life's pursuit for many of us, which explains why peninsula sand and mud is a leading cause of trunk rot in Washington. And it's not limited just to the trees.

1. Fort Flagler State Park
2. Old Fort Townsend State Park
3. Fort Worden State Park
4. Sequim Bay State Park
5. Dungeness Recreation Area
6. Deer Park
7. Heart o' the Hills
8. Elwha
9. Altaire
10. Salt Creek Recreation Area
11. Ozette
12. Fairholm
13. Sol Duc
14. Klahowya
15. Klahanie
16. Mora
17. Bogachiel State Park
18. Hoh
19. Kalaloch
20. Queets
21. Willaby
22. Falls Creek
23. Graves Creek
24. Pacific Beach State Park
25. Ocean City State Park
26. Twin Harbors State Park
27. Grayland Beach State Park
28. Fort Canby State Park
29. Falls View
30. Seal Rock
31. Dosewallips State Park
32. Elkhorn
33. Dosewallips
34. Collins
35. Hamma Hamma
36. Lena Creek
37. Lake Cushman State Park
38. Big Creek
39. Staircase
40. Potlatch State Park

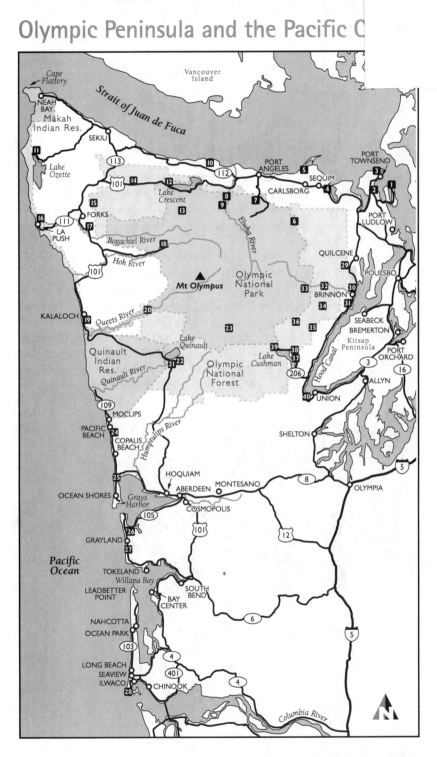

Strait of Juan de Fuca and Northside Olympics

❶ Fort Flagler State Park 🌲🌲🌲🌲🌲

If we had to pick one Washington campground to spend the entire rest of our camping days, it might well be Fort Flagler, one of the most scenic, diverse parks in the state, and arguably one of the finest in all the West. Flagler, another Puget Sound converted military post, is special not for any one thing, but for the so very many things it does so well.

Flagler is one of three 1890s forts surrounding Port Townsend, all of which can be seen from the shore of the park. The earliest fort, Old Fort Townsend, burned in 1895 and never was effectively rebuilt, although a state park still marks the site. But the other two, mighty Forts Worden and Flagler, lived long lives as keepers of the gates to Puget Sound. Big artillery guns at the two forts, coupled with similar firepower at Whidbey Island's Fort Casey, combined to form a "triangle of fire," guarding the door to the inner waters' thriving population centers. Today, replica guns shipped in from the Philippines (the original guns were scrapped after World War II) symbolically stand guard over one of the state's greater recreation treasures.

Wind powers much of the fun at Fort Flagler State Park.

sites	*115*
🏕️ 🚐	*14 water/electrical hookups, RVs to 50 feet*
open	*March through October; all year for day use*
reservations	*Up to 9 months in advance; 888/226-7688 or www.parks.wa.gov*
contact	*Washington State Parks, 360/902-8844; Fort Flagler State Park, 360/385-1259*

The campground itself isn't all that remarkable. Sites are clustered on a flat, tidal upland with very little privacy between sites. But the surrounding setting is spectacular, and the campground is the best base from which to explore this unique 784-acre park. Fort Flagler occupies the entire north end of Marrowstone Island and has a stunning stretch of beach, its own lighthouse, fascinating abandoned gun emplacements and other military artifacts, two boat launches, moorage floats, a fishing pier, an underwater park, a youth hostel, hiking trails, extensive group camps, and a host of other wonders. Campground amenities include an RV dump station and coin-op showers. Four rental cabins are scheduled to be built here. Because the park is so big and spread out, this is a good place to bring your bicycle.

The park has more than 19,000 feet of saltwater shoreline on Admiralty Inlet, Port Townsend Bay, and Kilisut Harbor, but the far northern beach is a standout day-use area. It's accessible either from the campground area or a narrow road that drops from the bluff-top Environmental Learning Center to the picturesque Marrowstone Point Lighthouse. The entire stretch of fine-graveled beach in between—more than a mile—is open for strolling, and the views across the water to Port Townsend, east to Whidbey Island, and northeast to Mount Baker are sublime. Seals often are seen playing offshore here, and it's a favorite destination of sea kayakers, scuba divers, beachcombers, and salmon anglers.

Getting there: Follow signs from Highway 20 and proceed to the park at the north end of Marrowstone Island, 8 miles northeast of Hadlock, on Fort Flagler Road.

❷ Old Fort Townsend State Park 🌲🌲🌲🌲

There's not much "fort" left in the Port Townsend area's oldest fort, but Old Fort Townsend State Park, 4 miles south of town, remains a decent camping area and saltwater playground. The campsites aren't as close to the beach as they are at the other two nearby forts (Flagler and Worden), and they're 150 feet above the water. But this campground received major upgrades in summer 2002, beach-bluff access is easy, and the place doesn't fill up quite as fast. The park also has a group camp for up to 80 souls, a nice picnic area, and 6.5 miles of good hiking trails through its wooded uplands, most of which offer grand views of Admiralty Inlet and, in clear weather, Cascade Mountains peaks. It also has an RV dump station and coin-op showers. Historical note: Unlike its sister forts, this one was built to protect residents from a potential foe that pre-dated world wars: area natives. The

sites	*40*
🏕️ 🚐	*No hookups, RVs to 40 feet*
open	*Mid-April to late September*
reservations	*None*
contact	*Washington State Parks, 360/902-8844; Old Fort Townsend State Park, 360/385-3595*

first fort on the site was built in 1856–57 by the U.S. Army, using logs plastered together with an inventive paste—made from ground clam shells. The fort never saw much action, although its troops were bolstered during the July 1859 "Pig War" dispute with England over San Juan Island. The fort later served as an enemy-munitions defusing station during World War II. We trust they didn't leave any shells lying around. . . .

Getting there: Follow signs 4 miles south of Port Townsend on Highway 20.

❸ Fort Worden State Park 🌲🌲🌲

You don't need a tent, RV, or even sleeping bag to "camp" at Fort Worden, a 433-acre, well-preserved military fort whose old wood buildings—built around the turn of the century as noncommissioned officers' housing—today offer a variety of overnight accommodations. The

sites	*80*
🏕️ 🚐	*50 full hookups, 30 water/electrical hookups; RVs to 50 feet*
open	*All year; upper campground closed early December through mid-February*
reservations	*Up to 5 months in advance; by mail, e-mail, or fax only at Fort Worden office, 360/344-4400 or www.olympus.net/ftworden*
contact	*Washington State Parks, 360/902-8844; Fort Worden State Park, 360/344-4400*

park's grounds always seem active with a festival, retreat, or convention of some kind, and the entire property takes days to explore. But the campground is nothing to sneeze at, either. While it's not as scenic as the one at Fort Flagler (above), the RV-equipped campground is one of the region's most extensive. It's actually two camps in one: The lower loop boasts 50 spacious, level (not terribly private) full hookup sites on the bluffs of Point Wilson, with great views of the point's namesake lighthouse; the upper loop, closed in midwinter, offers 30 mostly level, very long campsites with water and electricity, with a dump station nearby. The park also has coin-op showers. Both areas have sweeping views across Admiralty Inlet to Whidbey Island on clear days. Camp spaces are booked solid during the summer; you'll need a reservation. It's not unusual for the lower camping loop to be full on weekends in the middle of winter. Note that Fort Worden, unlike other Washington State Parks, maintains its own reservation system; see reservations information above.

The park's wealth of other attractions—abandoned gun emplacements, a Coast Artillery Museum, 11,000 feet of gravelly saltwater beaches, marked hiking and cycling trails, museum exhibits, and more—make this a great place to camp with children. Fishermen also tend to congregate here. Point Wilson, one of the best places on Puget Sound to fish from shore for migratory salmon, gave birth to the "Point Wilson Dart," a slim, heavy fishing lure that local salmon anglers developed to cast far offshore from the beach near the Point Wilson Lighthouse.

Getting there: From Highway 20 at Port Townsend, follow signs to the park, about 1 mile north of downtown.

④ Sequim Bay State Park 🌲🌲🌲

Sequim Bay, tucked into thick trees just off US 101, is easily missed by traveling campers bound for grander Olympic Peninsula stops. But it rarely avoids the attention of RVers, who know it's the only state park in this area. They often make it a single-night stopover on a US 101 loop around the peninsula. Alas, the 90-acre park has only so-so campsites, with the exception of a small handful of tent sites near Sequim Bay. The park did make some recent improvements, removing some

sites	76
	16 full hookups, RVs to 45 feet
open	All year
reservations	Up to 9 months in advance; 888/226-7688 or www.parks.wa.gov
contact	Washington State Parks, 360/902-8844; Sequim Bay State Park, 360/683-4235

sites in the hookup loop to make the others more roomy. It made a difference, and we've upgraded the park's rating a half-tree in consideration. Also, the day-use area on the waterfront is very nice, offering boater services, moorage, and launching. Note: The park's only dump station was closed because of "technical problems" during our last visit.

Getting there: The park is 4 miles southeast of Sequim on US 101.

⑤ Dungeness Recreation Area 🌲🌲🌲🌲

Not far from the mouth of the Dungeness River—and adjacent to the scenic Dungeness National Wildlife Refuge—this bluff-top campground is one of two underrated sites operated by Clallam County. Campsites, some of which offer good back-window views of the Strait of Juan de Fuca, are separated either by head-high shrubbery or short, thick trees, offering good privacy but ample sunlight. A short walk away is the main trailhead to the wildlife refuge; you can

sites	67
	No hookups, RVs to any length
open	February through September
reservations	None
contact	Dungeness Recreation Area, 360/683-5847

Day hikers take a break on Dungeness Spit.

walk the sand spit formed by the Dungeness River about 4.5 miles to its end, where the historic New Dungeness Lighthouse is sometimes open for tours. The park has an RV dump station and coin-op showers.

Getting there: From US 101 at Sequim, proceed about 4.5 miles west to Kitchen-Dick Road. Turn right (north) and follow signs about 3 miles to the park.

❻ Deer Park 🌲🌲🌲

The view is to die for, but everything else about Deer Park will make you pine for that nice tent space in your backyard. This national park campground, open summers only, is primitive, very remote and, well, miserably dusty in the dry season.

sites	18
open	Approximately June to early October
reservations	None
contact	Olympic National Park, 360/565-3130

But the view is worth the trip up Blue Mountain. At 5,400 feet, this is one of the more lofty campgrounds in the state, and aerial views of the Strait of Juan de Fuca, Dungeness Valley, and most of northern Puget Sound are unique. The 18 tent sites are almost an afterthought. Deer Park, the former site of one of Washington's earliest ski lodges, is no place for RVs. Sites are too small, and the 17-mile, mostly gravel road is too rough (it's the kind of mountain road that makes nervous passengers wish they were driving). Call the park to make sure the road is open before embarking. This camp also serves as a trailhead for the Grand Ridge Trail, a 7.5-mile, one-way hike to

Obstruction Point. It's the highest trail in Olympic National Park, reaching 6,500 feet at its summit.

Getting there: From US 101 about 6 miles east of Port Angeles, follow Deer Park Road 18 miles to the campground at the road's end.

⑦ Heart o' the Hills 🌲🌲🌲🌲

Heart o' the Hills is one of the nicest campgrounds in Olympic National Park and one of the better camps in all of the north Olympics. The Port Angeles–area camp, perched at Olympic's northern gateway, is set in tall, thin trees. Suitable for tents

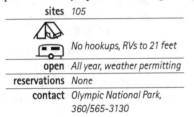

sites	105
🏕️ 🚐	No hookups, RVs to 21 feet
open	All year, weather permitting
reservations	None
contact	Olympic National Park, 360/565-3130

and/or smaller RVs, it's quiet, clean—and generally packed with RVs from Oklahoma all summer. But you can usually stumble across a site midweek without too much trouble. Beware the predatory night-stalking raccoons, particularly Old Three Legs, one of our longtime friends. Just across the road is a major trailhead, with paths leading to Lake Angeles, Heather Park, and on to Klahhane Ridge near the Hurricane Ridge day-use area, which is 17 miles above the campground via a steep, winding, but well-maintained road. The campground has an RV dump station.

Getting there: From US 101 at Port Angeles, follow signs 5 miles south on Hurricane Ridge Road.

The view from Hurricane Ridge never disappoints—when it's clear.

❽ Elwha 🌲🌲🌲

West of Port Angeles, nestled between the two controversial dams on the lower Elwha River, is the often-overlooked Elwha area of Olympic National Park. The road following the river here is home to two fine campgrounds. The first, Elwha, is about a half mile away from the river, with 41 campsites set in fairly thick forest. A kitchen shelter covers you in extremely bad weather, of which there is much in the winter. Not far up the road is the Whiskey Bend Trailhead, which provides access to Olympic National Park's famed Elwha River Trail. The lower Elwha offers fair trout fishing in the summer. Local trivia: A proposal to remove both dams and return the river to its former status as a major salmon producer has been approved; it's now just a matter of time and money until the Elwha becomes a majestic, free-flowing stream once more.

sites	41
	No hookups, RVs to 21 feet
open	All year
reservations	None
contact	Olympic National Park, 360/565-3130; Elwha Ranger Station, 360/452-9191

Getting there: From Port Angeles, follow US 101 9 miles west, turn left (south) on Elwha River Road, and proceed 3 miles to the campground, on the left.

❾ Altaire 🌲🌲🌲

The second Olympic National Park campground on the Elwha River, Altaire, is the most popular, thanks to its location right on the banks of the cool, clear Elwha. Some sites actually put the river at your feet—assuming you can snare one in the summer at this popular park. A major trailhead just up the road (it leads to Olympic Hot Springs, Boulder Lake, Appleton Pass, and on to the Sol Duc drainage) makes this a much sought-after overnight spot for hikers, either coming or going. The Glines Canyon Dam, the upper of two controversial dams on the lower Elwha River, is just up the road, and worth a look. This shady, damp campground is somewhat primitive, and can be very chilly in less than hot weather. But it's a lovely setting.

sites	30
	No hookups, RVs to 21 feet
open	June through September
reservations	None
contact	Olympic National Park, 360/565-3130; Elwha Ranger Station, 360/452-9191

Getting there: From Port Angeles, follow US 101 9 miles west, turn left (south) on Elwha River Road, and proceed about 4 miles to the campground, on the right, just after a bridge over the river.

⑩ Salt Creek Recreation Area 🌲🌲🌲🌲🌲

Every so often, we stumble upon one of those special outdoor places we love so much that we hesitate to ever write about it. This is one of them. Salt Creek, one of the state's best (and most overlooked) campgrounds, sits perched on a bluff above the Strait of Juan de Fuca. Like so many other prime waterfront campgrounds in Washington, this one takes advantage of the very qualities that made it public property in the first place—the kinds of sight lines needed for heavy artillery. Salt Creek, the jewel of Clallam County's park system, is the former home of Camp Hayden, a World War II–era 16-inch-gun emplacement. Not much of the military base remains, but a diverse, relaxing getaway has risen from its remains.

A misty morning greets hikers at Tongue Point.

sites	90
⛺ 🚐	No hookups, RVs to any length
open	All year
reservations	None
contact	Salt Creek Recreation Area, 360/928-3441

Salt Creek's campsites, all situated either on a steep bluff above Tongue Point or in a terraced, grassy field in the center of the park, are a wonderful escape any time of the year. The grassy sites afford no privacy, but each offers a gorgeous view of the strait, where you can watch the parade of cargo and military ships, peer across to Victoria, or scan for orca whales, otters, and sea lions. There's plenty to do here for active campers as well. Striped Peak, which looms above the campground to the east, is ringed by hiking trails and old logging roads that make for fine day-long exploration. Keep your eyes peeled for buried ruins of the park's military past.

There's not much sandy beach here, largely because of the strait's rocky, often treacherous shoreline (the inviting, sandy beach at Crescent Bay to the west is part of a private RV resort). But Tongue Point Marine Reserve, on the west side of the park, is one of Washington's best tidal-pool viewing spots, a true delight at low tide, when a jagged rock formation rises from the deep to offer acres of exploring. Salt Creek has an RV dump station and coin-op showers.

Getting there: From Port Angeles, follow US 101 and Highway 112 about 13 miles west to Camp Hayden Road. Turn right (north) and drive about 4 miles to the campground, on the right.

⑪ Ozette 🌲🌲🌲

Lake Ozette, Washington's largest natural lake, is one of the most popular destinations in Olympic National Park, largely because of the wildly popular Cape Alava/Sand Point Trail that begins near the north shore. A small national park campground—far too small to handle the crowds, unfortunately—awaits here. The

sites	14
⛺ 🚐	No hookups, RVs to 21 feet
open	All year
reservations	None
contact	Olympic National Park, 360/565-3130; Ozette Ranger Station, 360/963-2725

campground, free until recent years, is popular not only with hikers but canoeists and anglers who like to ply the waters and fish for trout, perch, kokanee, and other fish. No license is required here. The campground is fairly rustic, with pit toilets. Campers would be remiss not to follow the crowds out to Cape Alava and Sand Point, a classic Northwest beach hike that can be walked in an easy, 9.3-mile loop (actually, it's more of a triangle). Note: Between Memorial Day and Labor Day, you need an advance permit to camp overnight on the ocean beaches. Call 360/565-3100 for information.

Vacationers relax on the shores of Lake Crescent.

Getting there: From Port Angeles, follow US 101 west to Highway 112. Proceed west to Hoko-Ozette Road. Turn left (south) and drive about 22 miles to the campground, near the Ozette Ranger Station.

⑫ Fairholm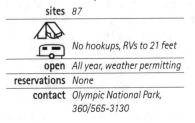

Fairholm, on the far western shore of deep, majestic Lake Crescent, is the most easily accessible public campground in this area. Nestled in the firs just off the lake, the park's shady sites are fairly private, and all are within a short stroll of the shoreline. The only caveat: You can hear traffic on US 101 from those on the east side of the camp. The campground has a boat launch, an RV dump station, a nice play area and swimming beach (brrrrr!), and good campfire programs in the summer. It's also a popular spot for hikers. Olympic's Spruce Railroad Trail, a nice, 4-mile, one-way Lake Crescent shoreline walk and one of the few trails in the Olympics open to mountain bikes, is a short distance up North Shore Road from here; it makes a good day-long cycle trip from the campground. Great trails in the Sol Duc River drainage are a 30-minute drive to the east. And the popular Marymere Falls/Mount Storm King Trail is a short distance back toward Port Angeles, as is Lake Crescent Lodge.

sites	87
	No hookups, RVs to 21 feet
open	All year, weather permitting
reservations	None
contact	Olympic National Park, 360/565-3130

Getting there: From Port Angeles, follow US 101 southwest about 25 miles, skirting the east shore of Lake Crescent, to North Shore Road. Turn right and proceed about a half mile to the campground, on the right.

⑬ Sol Duc 🌲🌲🌲🌲

This is the place to stay for people day hiking in the Sol Duc Valley, one of the primo summertime destinations in Olympic National Park. The nearby Sol Duc Trailhead is the take-off point to beautiful Sol Duc Falls and beyond to Deer Lake, Seven Lakes Basin, High Divide, and a connecting trail to the Hoh River drainage to the south. The shady campground has an RV dump station, and is suitable for RVs and tents, with spaces in a nicely wooded area just up the road from Sol Duc Hot Springs. A trail leads from the camping area to the privately operated hot springs resort, where you

sites	82
🏕️🚐	No hookups, RVs to 21 feet
open	May to late October
reservations	None
contact	Olympic National Park, 360/565-3130; Eagle Ranger Station, 360/327-3534

can soak in the warm waters of the springs, or in cool water piped from the crisp, clear Sol Duc River for $10 a day at this writing.

Getting there: From Port Angeles, drive west on US 101 to Lake Crescent. A short distance beyond the lake, turn left (south) on Sol Duc River Road. Proceed 13 miles south to the campground.

⑭ Klahowya 🌲🌲🌲

sites	55
🏕️🚐	Some electrical hookups, RVs to 30 feet
open	May through September; winters with no services
reservations	None
contact	Olympic National Forest, Pacific Ranger District, Forks office, 360/374-6522

Spectacular, no. Convenient, yes. This Olympic National Forest camp is one of only a few situated right along US 101. That makes it a busy place in the summer. The Sol Duc River is nearby, as is the highway. (Be thankful there aren't as many Jake-braked logging trucks over here as there once were.) The camp—like most in this area, set in the mossy temperate Olympics rain forest—has pit toilets and piped water. A boat ramp makes it a fisherman's favorite. The Pioneer's Path interpretive trail begins in the camp, and you can take in an interpretive program at the campground amphitheater in the summer. RVers' note: Electrical hookups are available for a fee when the camp host or a Forest Service employee is present.

Getting there: From Port Angeles, follow US 101 about 35 miles southwest (about 10 miles west of Lake Crescent) to the campground, on the right, near milepost 212.

Other Northside Olympic Campgrounds

Along the strait, a halfmile north of Highway 112 (about 20 miles west of Port Angeles), is **Lyre River** (near milepost 46; DNR's Forks office, 360/374-6131), a free, semiprimitive Department of Natural Resources campground. In the beautiful Dungeness River drainage of the Olympic Mountains southwest of Sequim are two Olympic National Forest campgrounds with 10 (tent-only) sites each: **Dungeness Forks**, on Forest Road 2880 at the confluence of the Dungeness and Gray Wolf Rivers; and **East Crossing**, on Forest Road 2860. Contact the Hood Canal Ranger District, Quilcene office (360/765-2200). In the Elwha River valley, one of Olympic National Park's better-kept secrets is **Olympic Hot Springs**, a natural spring at an old hotel site reached by driving to the end of Elwha Road and then hiking 2.5 miles. A walk-in campground, **Boulder Creek** (360/565-3130), is located nearby. At Lake Ozette, **Erickson's Bay** (on the northwest shore of lake; 360/565-3130; no fee, no reservations), a small, primitive campground, is accessible by foot or boat only. A swampy trail leads about 2.2 miles west to the ocean.

No public campgrounds are found at Sekiu or on the Makah Indian Reservation at Neah Bay, but private spots are available. Mostly gravel lots for anglers' RVs, they're not really suitable for tents, but RVers might favor amenities such as full hookups. Some have good views of the strait or the harbor at Neah Bay. The list includes Neah Bay's **Tyee RV Park** (360/645-2223); and Sekiu's **Van Riper's Resort** (360/963-2334), **Olson's Resort** (360/963-2311), **Surfside Resort** (360/963-2723), and **Coho Resort** (360/963-2333). In the Clallam Bay area, try **Sam's Trailer and RV Park** (360/963-2402). A somewhat pricey private camping option on Lake Crescent is **Log Cabin Resort** (3 miles north of US 101 on East Beach Road; 360/928-3325), which has 40 sites (full hookups, unlimited RV length) within a short distance of the lake's shore.

Westside Olympics and the Coast

⑮ Klahanie

sites	15
🏕️🚐	No hookups, RVs to 30 feet
open	May through September
reservations	None
contact	Olympic National Forest, Pacific Ranger District, Forks office, 360/374-6522

Klahanie, a small camp on the South Fork Calawah River, is a shady spot in a forest of hemlock, broadleaf maple, and big, old spruce. It's pretty basic, with pit toilets and piped water, but no garbage service. Sites are better geared to tents than RVs, but it makes a worthy overnight stop in a pinch on US 101 trips. A short day-hiking trail along the river begins in the campground. This camp has been closed on and off in recent years; call first to make sure it's open.

Getting there: From US 101 about 1 mile north of Forks, turn east on Forest Road 29 and proceed about 5 miles to the campground.

⑯ Mora 🌲🌲🌲

Two of the Olympic Peninsula's most gorgeous clear-water streams, the Sol Duc and Bogachiel, merge near the town of Forks, masquerading as the Quillayute River for the final miles to the ocean. Just downstream from the confluence is

sites	94
🏕️🚐	No hookups, RVs to 21 feet
open	All year
reservations	None
contact	Olympic National Park, 360/565-3130; Mora Ranger Station, 360/374-5460

Mora, an Olympic National Park campground that's a longtime favorite. The camping area itself is not remarkable. Spaces are in a heavily wooded, almost dark forest. But the campground's proximity to Rialto Beach makes it truly special. On a peninsula well stocked with fabulous sandy beaches, Rialto is a standout—one of those very few picture-perfect Washington scenes you can almost drive right up to. A series of sea stacks lurks in the mist to the north, and the unusually steep-sloped beach makes for frothing, always picturesque surf. The beach is almost always windy but great for strolling, with miles of unobstructed sand beckoning to the north. Rialto also is a major beach-hiking trailhead for coastal backpackers. Most day-use visitors walk 1.5 miles up the beach to Hole-in-the-Wall, a nifty surf-carved tunnel beneath the jutting headlands. It's all a short walk from the campground on an old access road. Mora has an RV dump station and a group camp for 15 to 40 campers. The group camp can be reserved after March 1.

Getting there: From US 101 2 miles north of Forks, turn west on La Push Highway and follow signs for 12 miles, keeping right at the Y where La Push Road departs to the left.

⑰ Bogachiel State Park 🌲🌲🌲

Bogachiel State Park is more popular for its location—halfway up the Olympic Peninsula on US 101—than for what it contains. But what it contains is plenty good enough for most, particularly for all you multiple-days-without-showers US 101 vagabonds. It's a simple place with 42 sites, most of which are a bit too close to the highway for our taste. But unlike most peninsula parks managed by the National Park Service or Forest Service, Bogachiel does have hot showers (the only ones on this whole stretch of US 101!)—the best investment of a couple quarters you'll make out here all summer. The park also has an RV dump station, a picnic area, and a boat launch on the lovely Bogachiel River, a noted steelhead fishery.

sites	42
🏕️ 🚐	6 full hookups, RVs to 40 feet
open	All year; limited winter facilities
reservations	None
contact	Washington State Parks, 360/902-8844; Bogachiel State Park, 360/374-6356

Getting there: The park is on US 101, 6 miles south of Forks.

The cold waters of the Bogachiel, viewed through an old-growth stump.

⑱ Hoh 🌲🌲🌲🌲

The majestic old-growth forest of the Hoh River valley is a national—indeed, worldwide—treasure, and the Hoh campground is where the great bulk of all those folks with sore necks (from craning) spend the night. As a result, it's one of Olympic National Park's most popular camps, and landing a site here in midsummer can be quite the feat. Campsites are spread through wooded loops near the Hoh River and a short walk from the valley's famous rain forest trails, such as the Hoh River Trail—it winds 17 miles up the river to Glacier Meadows on the slopes of Mount Olympus, the park's tallest peak at 7,965 feet. Any portion of the trail's first 13 miles, mostly flat, is great for day hiking. Shorter walks through the massive trees, fed by up to 140 inches of rain every year, also start nearby. The Hall of Mosses Trail (easy, three-quarter-mile loop), which begins and ends near the visitors center, is a good nature-trail primer. Nearby are two barrier-free trails, the Spruce Nature Trail (easy, 1.25-mile loop) and a separate paved, quarter-mile nature loop. The campground has an RV dump station. Wildlife note: Black bears are not uncommon here, so don't leave food out. And Roosevelt elk are frequent campground visitors.

sites	89
🏕	
🚐	No hookups, RVs to 21 feet
open	All year
reservations	None
contact	Olympic National Park, 360/565-3130; Hoh Ranger Station, 360/374-6925

Getting there: From US 101 14 miles south of Forks or 21 miles north of Kalaloch, turn east on Hoh Rain Forest Road and proceed 18 miles to the campground.

Hoh campers get up close and personal with the local elk.

⑲ Kalaloch 🌲🌲🌲🌲🌲

No two ways about it: This is one of the premier Therm-a-Rest plunking spots on the continent. Situated on a breezy bluff above one of the state's most gorgeous sandy Pacific Ocean beaches, Kalaloch (you know you're officially local when you pronounce it correctly, CLAY-lock) might be the best campground in the state. It's certainly one of the more difficult to get into during summer months. And it's one of very few where you can actually see the ocean—feel it, even—from some campsites.

On those rare days (even in the summer) when the fog lifts, sunsets from the beach at Kalaloch will carve their own spot in your soul. Not surprisingly, even though it's spacious, Kalaloch stays full for much of the summer. In the past, that forced prospective campers to play a prolonged game of campsite roulette—arriving early in the day, parking in the day-use lot or a road-side campsite, and then patrolling like greedy vultures for anyone who even looks like they're about to abandon a choice, waterfront spot. But things are changing, dear camper. Starting in the spring of 2003, Kalaloch finally entered the 20th century and began accepting campsite reservations up to five months in advance. This will be a major bonus for you organized types; a major bummer for spur-of-the-moment road-trippers. No more lurking and bribing departing waterfront-site dwellers with fresh fruit, meats, stove fuel, cash, or other bartering goods! Oh well. We'll leave it at this: The foolish man builds his Kalaloch hopes upon getting lucky. The wise man picks up the phone. Unfortunately, the fledgling Kalaloch reservation system doesn't allow campers to specify sites. This is a major bummer—especially at this park, where there's a wide disparity between roadside sites in the back and primo waterfront real estate. Still, the risk is probably worth it: There's really no campground like it on the planet.

Facilities are comparatively so-so. Kalaloch has an RV dump station, but the closest public showers are in Bogachiel State Park. Although most of the sites here were designed for 1950s-sized cars, tents, and small trailers(hence the official 21-foot RV "limit"), some have been redesigned to accommodate larger rigs, and we're constantly amazed by the size of some of the diesel push-and-shovers that shoehorn in here. But the park, to its credit, has now reserved a handful of the prime, beachfront sites for tenters only. Another great recent improvement is a machine in the day-use parking lot allowing you to pay camp fees with credit or debit cards.

The fun doesn't end in the campground proper. About 3 miles to the south is the South Beach overflow area, open summers only. This somewhat primitive, flat

sites	177
	No hookups, RVs to 21 feet
open	All year
reservations	Up to 5 months in advance; National Park Reservation Service 800/365-CAMP
contact	Olympic National Park, 360/565-3130; Kalaloch Ranger Station, 360/962-2283

Kalaloch: Washington's premiere oceanfront campground.

gravel lot began as a sloppy-seconds campground with no running water, tables, fire pits, or facilities of any kind. But now that a restroom has been built, it's become the campground of choice for many, particularly RV owners who can set up just about anywhere. Reason: It's almost right on the beach, with only an 8-foot bank and a pile of driftwood separating the dinner table from the pounding Pacific surf.

Getting there: The campground is on US 101, 35 miles south of Forks.

⑳ Queets 🌲🌲🌲

This quiet, remote campground on the surging banks of the Queets, one of the Olympic Peninsula's most powerful rivers, isn't easy to get to. Most times of the year, the Queets River Road, which winds 14 miles east from US 101 along the river's south shore, is a bumpa-torium, with some potholes large enough to swallow a Volkswagen. But it's worth the trip for those able to make it around or through them. The primitive campground, in a deep forest of moss-draped Douglas fir, western red cedar, and broadleaf maple, is at the end of the road, where you'll also

sites	20
open	All year
reservations	None
contact	Olympic National Park, 360/565-3130; Queets Ranger Station, 360/962-2283

An angler casts a line on the mighty Queets River in Olympic National Park.

find the trailhead for the Queets River Trail. Subtract points for the fact the forest is so thick that it always seems dark and damp in here. Deer and elk are plentiful. There's no running water, flush toilets, or showers. The summers-only Queets Ranger Station is nearby.

Getting there: From US 101, about 13 miles south of Kalaloch or 20 miles north of Lake Quinault, turn east on (gravel, often rough) Queets River Road and proceed 14 miles to the campground, to the left at the end of the road.

21 Willaby 🌲🌲🌲

Willaby, tucked into the trees on the south shore of Lake Quinault, a short walk from the venerable Lake Quinault Lodge, is one of our favorite Forest Service campgrounds. Sites in the 14-acre park are small but private, in thick, mossy, second-growth forest, with some along the lakeshore and many of the upper sites offering peekaboo lake views. The real beauty lies upland: Winding through the campground is the 3-mile Lake Quinault Loop Trail, which connects your campsite to the lodge, about half a mile of shoreline, and some

sites	22
🏕️ 🚐	No hookups, RVs to 16 feet
open	Memorial Day through September
reservations	None
contact	Olympic National Forest, Pacific Ranger District, Quinault office, 360/288-2525

magnificent surviving old-growth forest just up the hill. One segment of this trail, Big Tree Grove (also reached from a separate South Shore Road Trailhead), is a definite don't miss. The campground, now concessioner operated, has a boat launch and some moorage space, making it popular with boaters. Willaby does not have showers.

Getting there: From US 101 at Lake Quinault, turn east on South Shore Road and proceed about 1.5 miles to the campground, on the left.

22 Falls Creek 🌲🌲🌲

Falls Creek is like a twin-brother camp to Willaby (see above), located on the far side of Lake Quinault Lodge. It offers similar good access to local rain forest trails and, like its companion, often serves as a launching pad for backpacking and day-hiking expeditions up the East Fork Quinault Trail. The campground doesn't have quite the same pleasing aesthetic as Willaby, but it's a nice place, with some large firs and bigleaf maples looming over waterfront sites on Falls Creek

sites	31
🏕️ 🚐	No hookups, RVs to 16 feet
open	Memorial Day to Labor Day
reservations	None
contact	Olympic National Forest, Pacific Ranger District, Quinault office, 360/288-2525

and Lake Quinault. Local trivia: A short distance east is the world's largest spruce tree—58 feet in circumference and up to 1,000 years old—near the lakeshore at Rain Forest Village Resort.

Getting there: From US 101 at Lake Quinault, turn east on South Shore Road and proceed about 2.5 miles to the campground, on the left.

23 Graves Creek 🌲🌲🌲

If the road is open (it washes out frequently; be sure to call first), it's well worth the trek all the way to the end of South Shore Road to Graves Creek, near the trailhead of the East Fork Quinault and Graves Creek Trails. Well, for tent campers, anyway. This formerly free campground in a mossy, mixed-forest area, often serves as a base camp for backpackers exploring farther up the valley. The primary destination is Enchanted Valley (26 miles round-trip), one of

sites	30
🏕️ 🚐	No hookups, RVs to 21 feet
open	All year; limited winter facilities
reservations	None
contact	Olympic National Park, 360/565-3130; Quinault Ranger Station, 360/288-2444

Olympic National Park's more notable backcountry destinations. But day hikers can trek the same trail to a grand river view from Pony Bridge (5 miles round-trip). It's a basic camp, set in the forest, but offers plenty of peace and quiet, especially in the shoulder seasons of spring and fall.

Getting there: From US 101 at Lake Quinault, turn east on South Shore Road and proceed 15 miles to the campground, at the end of the road.

Other Westside Olympic Campgrounds

Don't overlook the string of very nice—and very free—year-round state Department of Natural Resources campsites along the Hoh River. **Hoh Oxbow,** just south of the Hoh Rain Forest Road near US 101 milepost 176, has seven sites for tents and small trailers, but no running water. A small boat launch makes it a favorite angler's hangout, especially during winter steelhead season. **Cottonwood,** just off Oil City Road (turn west off US 101 near milepost 177, about 15 miles south of Forks) is similar, with nine sites. On Hoh Rain Forest Road itself are **Willoughby Creek** (3.5 miles east of US 101), with three small campsites and limited facilities; and **Minnie Peterson** (4.5 miles east of US 101), which has eight small riverside spots. Another primitive, but private, option is **South Fork Hoh,** reached by turning east off US 101 on Hoh Mainline Road (about 15.5 miles south of Forks) and proceeding 14 miles east. The other free (and even more remote) DNR campgrounds in the area are **Coppermine Bottom** (9 sites), **Upper Clearwater** (9 sites), and **Yahoo Lake** (4 sites). Contact the DNR office in Forks (360/374-6131).

A private campground in the Forks/La Push area is **Hoh River Resort** (near the river on US 101; 360/374-5566), with 23 sites with hookups and other facilities. A small camp serving as overflow for Forest Service Willaby and Falls Creek Campgrounds at Lake Quinault is **Gatton Creek** (3.5 miles east of US 101 on South Shore Road; 360/288-2525), with five tent and eight parking-lot RV sites. Those who venture all the way to the end of North Shore Road (assuming it's not washed out) will come upon **North Fork** (360/288-2444), a quiet but nondescript Olympic National Park campground with seven tent sites set near the North Fork Quinault Trailhead. It's free but primitive, with no running water. An hour south of Lake Quinault is **Campbell Tree Grove** (on the upper Humptulips River, on Forest Road 2204; 360/288-2525), a free 14-acre Olympic National Forest campground near the southern border of the Colonel Bob Wilderness, with eight tent and three small RV sites.

Grays Harbor and Long Beach Peninsula

㉔ Pacific Beach State Park 🌲🌲🌲

Here's proof that once in a while, things do improve in the financially strapped Washington State Parks system. Pacific Beach, formerly a cramped parking lot of a private resort campground, was renovated in 1995 by Washington State Parks. Campsites were reduced by half and spread out a bit, and the 9-acre park went on the state's reservation system. The result is a much nicer campground that's still less than wild, given its location right in downtown Pacific Beach. Still, beachfront campsites are hard to find, and this park's 2,300 feet of shoreline are home to the only campsites in any Washington State Park that offer a true Pacific Ocean view. Some sites are so close to the broad, sandy beach that it's really, really easy to forget you're in a vacation/residential area. Needless to say, it's a very popular

sites	64
🏕️ 🚐	32 electrical hookups, RVs to 45 feet
open	All year
reservations	Up to 9 months in advance; 888/226-7688 or www.parks.wa.gov
contact	Washington State Parks, 360/902-8844; Pacific Beach State Park, 360/276-4297

Beachcombers find plenty of solitude on Pacific beaches.

RV spot. (Tenters, be advised: That four-tree rating above is offered up mostly for the RV crowd; you'll probably lament the park's lack of site privacy and the strong winds, which might conspire to dispatch your rain fly all the way to Humptulips should you fail to make triple knots. You might prefer Ocean City State Park, below.) The park is always popular, but particularly jammed during spring and fall razor-clam seasons. The beach is a noted kite-fly-atorium. The park has an RV dump station and coin-op showers.

Getting there: From Hoquiam, proceed 30 miles northwest (15 miles north of Ocean Shores) on Highway 109 to the campground, well-marked in the town of Pacific Beach.

25 Ocean City State Park 🌲🌲🌲🌲

Tell us if you find a way to keep sand out of the tent. It's never been done at Ocean City State Park, just north of Ocean Shores, one of the area's nicer oceanside campgrounds. The 131-acre park is rich in pine trees and thick shrubbery, which helps cut the persistent wind somewhat. Sites, split into three large loops, are very private, making this the best spot in this area for tenters. Unlike other parks in the area, Ocean City has more than just the ocean competing for attention. You'll find good picnic facilities, as well as a group camp, three primitive, walk-in sites, and a swampy area popular with birdwatchers. The dunes here are also a great place to scope out wildflowers in the spring. And, of course, the Pacific is always a short walk away. Not surprisingly, this is a popular place, especially during sporadic coast razor-clam seasons. Reservations are advised. The campground has an RV dump station and coin-op showers. The water system was recently upgraded.

sites	181
🏕	
🚐	29 full hookups, RVs to 55 feet
open	All year
reservations	Up to 9 months in advance; 888/226-7688 or www.parks.wa.gov
contact	Washington State Parks, 360/902-8844; Ocean City State Park, 360/289-3553

Getting there: From Hoquiam, follow Highway 109 about 16 miles west to Highway 115. Turn left (south) and proceed 1.2 miles to the campground, on the right (about 1.5 miles north of Ocean Shores).

26 Twin Harbors State Park 🌲🌲🌲

Twin Harbors, one of Washington's largest camping areas, is an 1,800-acre behemoth that's a longtime favorite of beach fans. The campground, however, is a significant walk from the beach. Twin Harbors is split in two by Highway 105, with half the sites on wooded lands east of the road, the other half on the windy, more

sites	307
	49 full hookups, RVs to 35 feet
open	Late February through October
reservations	Up to 9 months in advance; 888/226-7688 or www.parks.wa.gov
contact	Washington State Parks, 360/902-8844; Twin Harbors State Park, 360/268-9717

exposed sand dunes on the west side. The hookup sites, like many others installed decades ago for the benefit of visiting anglers, are crammed together, chockablock, on the east side. The park has an RV dump station and coin-op showers. Two trails lead to the ocean, and a nature trail winds through the sand dune area between the campground and the beach. This is an older park, and many of its facilities are showing their age. Some facilities, such as restrooms, were scheduled for upgrades at this writing. Although it's not as crowded as it was during Westport's salmon-fishing heyday of decades past, it's often booked during summer months. Reservations are a good idea.

Getting there: Twin Harbors is 3 miles south of Westport on Highway 105.

㉗ Grayland Beach State Park 🌲🌲🌲🌲🌲

Grayland Beach is the most modern, clean, and comfortable campground in the Grays Harbor area, and it's one of the nicest camping spots on Washington's coast. Like most other beachfront campgrounds, this one is separated from a sprawling, 7,449-foot ocean shoreline by a half mile of sand dunes and scrub grass. But the campsites are more spacious, the facilities more modern, and the entire place much quieter than nearby Twin Harbors (see above), which is closer to the highway. The flat, nicely manicured sites, spread through six compact loops, are well suited to tents, but the plethora of long, level hookup sites makes this a favorite of RVers. Grayland Beach has coin-op showers, but no RV dump station. Call well in advance for a reservation. Note: This campground was scheduled for expansion by 2004.

sites	63
	60 full hookups, RVs to 40 feet
open	All year
reservations	Up to 9 months in advance; 888/226-7688 or www.parks.wa.gov
contact	Washington State Parks, 360/902-8844; Grayland Beach State Park, 360/268-9717

Getting there: Just southwest of the town of Grayland, follow signs on Highway 105 to the park, about 22 miles south of Aberdeen.

Razor-clam digging: An old tradition at Grays Harbor ocean beaches.

㉘ Fort Canby State Park 🌲🌲🌲🌲

It's big. It's historic. It's downright magnificent. Fort Canby, one of the West's truly great campgrounds and one of Washington State's most scenic spots, is a jewel in every sense. The park, sprawled out across 1,882 acres at the southwestern

sites	*250*
🏕️ 🚐	*77 water/electrical hookups, RVs to 45 feet*
open	*All year*
reservations	*Up to 9 months in advance; 888/226-7688 or www.parks.wa.gov*
contact	*Washington State Parks, 360/902-8844; Fort Canby State Park, 360/642-3078*

tip of the state, is marked on the north and south by twin bookend lighthouses, North Head and Cape Disappointment. In between are a massive campground, a sprawling picnic area, 42,600 feet of deliciously clean, flat ocean beach, miles of trails, and a rock jetty jutting into the roiling surf of the Columbia River bar. Like most coastal campgrounds, you can't see the beach from the campsites (it's a short walk away on many sandy trails). But the proud, beautiful North Head Lighthouse is always in view, even when the fog rolls in.

The scenery is only part of the allure here. This wind-blasted land has a rich history. Lewis and Clark ended their long journey here in 1805, plunking their sore feet into the icy Pacific. The park's Lewis and Clark Interpretive Center details the explorers' journey to the Pacific, as well as the history of the two local lighthouses. (When it first blinked on in 1856, the Cape Disappointment Lighthouse became the first in the state, and one of the first on the coast. North Head Lighthouse was added in 1898. The latter has been scheduled for a long-overdue renovation by 2004.)

The campground has an RV dump station, coin-op showers, and 250 sites that are spread in small, oceanfront loops through the sand dunes and in a grassy area farther upland, near swampy Lake O'Neil. They rate only about a "medium" on the privacy and modernization scales, but you can't beat the setting. Several loops offer sites close enough to the beach to constantly hear the roar and feel the salty breeze. Trails lead to the beach, old gun bunkers, local lakes, and elsewhere. Kids love cycling on the miles of roadway. Not long ago, Fort Canby became the first Washington State Park to feature yurts—frame-and-vinyl tentlike structures with wood floors, sleeping futons, electric heat, and lights. The seven extremely convenient buildings open up camping—and Fort Canby—to folks who don't have all the gear. (They've been a success, but lack of money has prevented State Parks from following Oregon State Parks' lead and installing them in oceanfront campgrounds elsewhere.) The yurts are $30 a night, and can be reserved in advance, as can three small cabins. Reservations for these and for any sites here are a must. This campground, the only major public camp on the Long Beach Peninsula, is full all summer, and it's one of only two in Washington to accept reservations all year.

Getting there: From downtown Ilwaco, follow signs on Robert Gray Drive 3.5 miles south to the park.

The sprawling beach at Fort Canby is a Washington camping highlight.

Other Grays Harbor/Long Beach Campgrounds

The Ocean Shores/Westport area has many private beachfront campgrounds. For current information, contact the **Ocean Shores Chamber of Commerce** (800/76-BEACH; www.oceanshores.org); the Copalis-area **Washington Coast Chamber of Commerce** (360/289-4552 or 800/286-4552; www.washingtoncoastchamber.org); or the **Westport-Grayland Chamber of Commerce** (360/268-9422 or 800/345-6223; www.westportgrayland-chamber.org/). The Long Beach Peninsula is dotted by more than a dozen private campgrounds that serve as alternatives to Fort Canby State Park. Contact the **Long Beach Peninsula Visitors Bureau** (800/451-2542; www.funbeach.com) for current information.

A small campground near the town of Humptulips, called **Riverview Recreation Area** (on the banks of the Humptulips River; 360/987-2216), has 14 sites (6 with full hookups). In the Satsop River drainage, **Schafer State Park** (360/902-8844) has 55 tent and 6 RV sites with partial hookups. Campers seeking to spread the long commute to the southwest coast over two days should consider an overnight stop at little-known **Rainbow Falls State Park** (17 miles west of Chehalis on Highway 6; 360/902-8844), with 43 sites and a large group camp, but no hookups.

Eastside Olympics and Hood Canal

㉙ Falls View 🌲🌲🌲

Falls View is a pleasant Olympic National Forest camp just off US 101 near Quilcene. Tenters especially will appreciate the sites in a nice wooded area with

sites	30
🏕️ 🚐	No hookups, RVs to 21 feet
open	May through September
reservations	None
contact	Olympic National Forest, Hood Canal Ranger District, Quilcene office, 360/765-2200

just enough filtered sunshine and the rushing Big Quilcene River in a canyon below to lull you to sleep. A trail leads a short distance to the picturesque falls; it's worth the walk.

Getting there: Falls View is 3 miles south of Quilcene on US 101.

㉚ Seal Rock 🌲🌲🌲🌲🌲

This charming Forest Service camp on beautiful, placid Hood Canal is one of our favorite overnight spots. It's close enough to the Seattle metro area to journey to after work and still reach by dark, but just far enough away to hide most of its

sites	41
🏕️ 🚐	No hookups, RVs to 21 feet
open	Mid-April through September
reservations	None
contact	Olympic National Forest, Hood Canal Ranger District, Quilcene office, 360/765-2200

charms from the inner-city camping hordes. Sadly, the Forest Service abandoned the reservation system here, which had made the park a safer bet for those arriving from the other side of Puget Sound. The campground is large, with sites very well spaced in several wooded upland loops. The choice spots are on the lower loop, where a dozen or more are located right above the rocky

beach. And brace yourself for a rare treat: level, sand-filled tent pads! The waterfront here is a great place to gather shellfish or just sit in the shade of a madrone and scout for harbor seals and that elusive mammoth called Mount Rainier, which sometimes pokes its head from the clouds far to the southeast. The campground, which has flush toilets, but no showers or RV dump station, is fully barrier free, as is a very nicely built boardwalk nature trail on the beach bluff. Keep

A short, barrier-free nature trail skirts the beach at Seal Rock.

your eyes peeled for Trident submarines, which mosey over from the nearby Bangor base to make practice runs in ultradeep Dabob Bay.

Getting there: The campground is on the shore of Hood Canal, about 2 miles north of Brinnon on US 101.

㉛ Dosewallips State Park 🌲🌲🌲🌲

By all means, bring the kids. Dosewallips State Park is the 425-acre toy store of the Washington State Parks system. There's plenty to do here, from hiking and mountain biking to fishing and clamming—or just relaxing on the park's pleasant green lawns. Dosewallips, with waterfront on both sides of the Dosewallips River and a marshy estuary on Hood Canal itself (via a short trail to the other side of US 101) is a big, well-developed park, and undoubtedly the most popular camp in Hood Canal country. The 140 sites are spread in a broad, grassy meadow area, a former homestead site, on the west side of US 101, and in a beach area on the east side. There's little privacy between them, but the cushy grass feels mighty nice under the backs of tent campers. The second-growth forested upland offers 4 miles of trails for hiking or cycling, and

sites	140
🏕️	
🚐	40 full hookups, RVs to 60 feet
open	All year
reservations	Up to 9 months in advance; 888/226-7688 or www.parks.wa.gov
contact	Washington State Parks, 360/902-8844; Dosewallips State Park, 360/796-4415

fishing from the river or Hood Canal is sometimes fruitful. Wildlife lovers often spot elk here in the winter. Book early for summer. Dosewallips has an RV dump station and coin-op showers. Historical note: Check out the remnants of old spur (logging) railroad tracks on the park's southeast side.

Getting there: The park is 1 mile south of Brinnon on US 101.

③② Elkhorn ▲▲▲▲

Campers (particularly tenters) who like what they find in the lower Dosewallips River drainage will love what the river holds in store higher up, where the water is swift and strong and fewer RVs clog the road. Two fine campgrounds are found on the upper river—Elkhorn, a Forest Service camp, and Dosewallips, a national park site (see below). Unfortunately, both were closed to car campers in 2002, when a major washout struck the road a mile below Elkhorn. It hadn't been repaired when this guide went to press; call first to ask about road repairs—or prepare to hoof it a mile up the road for a rustic, walk-in or bike-in camping experience. When the road reopens, the camp is worth the drive: Elkhorn, elevation 600 feet, lies at the Olympic National Park border on the banks of the river beneath thick, shady forest. Most sites are on the river, which is gorgeous any time of the year. The campground has well water and pit toilets, but no garbage service.

sites	20
🏕️ 🚐	No hookups, RVs to 21 feet
open	Mid-May through September
reservations	None
contact	Olympic National Forest, Hood Canal Ranger District, Quilcene office, 360/765-2200

Getting there: From US 101 1.5 miles north of Brinnon, turn west on Dosewallips Road (Forest Road 2610) and proceed 10 miles to the campground.

③③ Dosewallips ▲▲▲▲

Here's the wilder, upstream version of Dosewallips River camping in places like Dosewallips State Park. (See important note on road washout in Elkhorn listing, above.) Dosewallips, an Olympic National Park campground, is a pretty spot, and it's wonderfully located if you're a hiker (the Dosewallips Trailhead is right across the parking lot). That means it's often full with soon-to-be or just-was Dosewallips hikers in summer months. The 30 tent sites are a bit primitive but very nice, with most close to the rushing,

sites	30
🏕️	No hookups; tents only
open	May to early September
reservations	None
contact	Olympic National Park, 360/565-3130

Like the good old days: Hang-drying at Dosewallips State Park.

white-water river. Seasonal note: Forest Road 2610, even when it's in good repair, usually closes just beyond the campground after first snow; it's not maintained inside Olympic National Park borders in the winter.

Getting there: From US 101 1.5 miles north of Brinnon, turn west on Dosewallips Road (Forest Road 2610) and proceed 15 miles to the campground.

34 Collins 🌲🌲🌲

Insomniacs should love the east-slope Olympics. Just about anywhere you camp over here, a small-but-powerful white-water stream lies a short distance away—usually close enough to usher you off to slumberland with the roar of cold, clear

sites	16
🏕	
🚐	No hookups, RVs to 21 feet
open	Mid-May through September
reservations	None
contact	Olympic National Forest, Hood Canal Ranger District, Hoodsport office, 360/877-5254

water in your ears. Collins Campground lies smack in the center of a river group that lines up, north to south: Dungeness, Big Quilcene, Dosewallips, Duckabush, Hamma Hamma, and Skokomish. Like most campgrounds on these wild

mountain streams, this one is small and shady, but it's pretty and worth the drive. Collins, at 200 feet on the Duckabush River, has pit toilets, but you'll need to filter your own water from the stream. Like other national forest camps in this area, there's no longer garbage service: You'll need to pack it out.

Getting there: From US 101 2 miles south of Brinnon, turn west on Forest Road 2510 and proceed 4.8 miles to the campground, on the left.

㉟ Hamma Hamma 🌲🌲🌲🌲

Another pleasant Forest Service camp with many waterfront sites, Hamma Hamma, elevation 600 feet, is on the banks of its namesake, one of the eastern Olympic Peninsula's most gorgeous rivers. It's the primary camping spot in the Hamma Hamma drainage. A short, wheelchair-accessible interpretive trail begins in the campground. Trout fishing in the river can be fun—even if not always productive—during the summer season. The campground has hand-pumped water (not potable) and pit toilets. You'll need to pack out your own garbage.

sites	15
🏕️🚐	No hookups, RVs to 21 feet
open	May through October
reservations	None
contact	Olympic National Forest, Hood Canal Ranger District, Hoodsport office, 360/877-5254

Getting there: From US 101 14 miles north of Hoodsport, turn west on Hamma Hamma River Road (Forest Road 25) and proceed 6.5 miles to the campground, on the left.

㊱ Lena Creek 🌲🌲🌲

This pretty campground on the Hamma Hamma River is similar to Hamma Hamma (above), with one important distinction: it's within a short walk of the starting point of the Lena Lakes Trail, one of the most popular backpacking routes in the Olympics. That brings plenty of lug-soled campers to this quaint riverfront camp at the confluence of Lena Creek and the Hamma Hamma. Lena Lake is 3.2 miles up the trail, and the more remote Upper Lena is about 3.5 miles—and 2,800 vertical feet—beyond. Don't be surprised if you hear the clink of carabiners by firelight at Lena Creek. Lena Lake is also the primary climbers' access route to the summit of The Brothers, the prominent twin-peaked, 6,866-foot summit visible from much of the Puget Sound region. Lena Creek has well water (not potable) and pit toilets. You'll need to pack out your own garbage.

sites	16
🏕️🚐	No hookups, RVs to 21 feet
open	May through September
reservations	None
contact	Olympic National Forest, Hood Canal Ranger District, Hoodsport office, 360/877-5254

Getting there: From US 101 14 miles north of Hoodsport, turn west on Hamma Hamma River Road (Forest Road 25) and drive 8 miles to the campground.

㊲ Lake Cushman State Park 🌲🌲🌲🌲

The North Fork Skokomish River drainage holds a variety of delights for outdoor lovers, including some of the interior Olympics' grander low-valley and high-alpine hiking trails. A Tacoma City Light dam (completed 1926) on the lower river flooded much of what once was a beautiful valley, but the result—Lake Cushman—created many recreation sites. One of them is Lake Cushman State Park, which straddles Big Creek Inlet. One serious caveat: Lake Cushman State Park—at least that's what this property was called at press time—was slated for closure, when in the midst of its ongoing budget crunch, Washington State Parks canceled its lease on the property. The landowner (Tacoma Power), thankfully, vowed to find a way to keep the scenic park open, but likely with a private contractor running the show. So some changes might be in order by the time you get here. Meanwhile, we'll describe the state park as we last knew it:

sites	82
🏕️ 🚐	30 full hookups, RVs to 60 feet
open	April through October; all year for day use
reservations	Up to 9 months in advance; 888/226-7688 or www.parks.wa.gov
contact	Washington State Parks, 360/902-8844; Lake Cushman State Park, 360/877-5491

The North Fork Skokomish, all bottled up: Lake Cushman reservoir.

Tent sites are on the north shore, RV sites and the picnic area on the south. A smooth, fine-gravel beach makes this a popular summer hangout for sunbathers, water skiers, canoeists, and trout anglers (the park also has three paved boat launch ramps). About 4 miles of marked hiking trails wind through the park, although nicer ones are just up the road at Staircase (see below). For day hikers, this is a nice place to camp and ride the mountain bike on up to the Staircase Trailhead. Lake Cushman State Park has an RV dump station and coin-op showers. Winter camping is allowed in the day-use area only. Historical note: The campground is near the site of the former Antlers Hotel, built here in 1895.

Getting there: From US 101 at Hoodsport, turn west on Lake Cushman Road (Highway 119) and follow signs about 7 miles to the park, on the left.

38 Big Creek 🌲🌲🌲

An average Forest Service camp in an above-average place (near Lake Cushman), Big Creek usually serves as an alternative to Lake Cushman State Park (see above) or Staircase (see below), both located in more scenic spots near the lake. Still, it's a good location, particularly for those who plan multiday hikes in the area. Sites in the forested camp are quite private, a plus for tenters. And two creekside walk-in tent sites are a bonus for light travelers. Big Creek is situated amidst several popular hiking trails, Staircase Rapids, the North Fork Skokomish Trail, and Mount Ellinor, to name a few. The latter, accessible from two trailheads nearby, is a popular leeward Olympics day hike that brings the possibility of viewing mountain goats. Big Creek has well water and vault toilets.

sites	25
🏕️🚐	No hookups, RVs to 21 feet
open	May through October
reservations	None
contact	Olympic National Forest, Hood Canal Ranger District, Hoodsport office, 360/877-5254

Getting there: From US 101 at Hoodsport, turn west on Lake Cushman Road (Highway 119) and drive 9 miles to the campground, near the intersection of Lake Cushman Road and Forest Road 24.

39 Staircase 🌲🌲🌲🌲

Staircase, located mere yards from the trailhead of the magnificent Staircase Rapids Trail, along the beautiful North Fork Skokomish River, is a clear-cut winner for folks seeking solace on the peninsula's eastern slopes. The national park campsites are scattered throughout a somewhat dark but peaceful area on the last "wild" stretch of the North Fork Skokomish before it reaches the headwaters of the Lake Cushman reservoir. It's a serene place with moss-draped trees, cool breezes—and hiking to die for. The Staircase Rapids Trail is a delightful 2-mile route that climbs both sides of the river. A nice log bridge a mile upstream that links the two side trails into one long loop was washed out at this writing; if

sites	56
	No hookups, RVs to 21 feet
open	All year; closes during heavy snow
reservations	None
contact	Olympic National Park, 360/565-3130; Staircase Ranger Station, 360/877-5569

it's still washed out when you visit, the two now-separate trails are both worth walking up and back, but the Rapids Trail on the west side of the river is more scenic. Both trails are easy enough for the whole family, and you'll pass through a wonderful patch of old-growth forest along the way.

Getting there: From US 101 at Hoodsport, turn west on Lake Cushman Road (Highway 119) and proceed 18 miles to the campground, at the end of the road.

⑩ Potlatch State Park 🌲🌲🌲🌲

Potlatch, on the site of an old gathering (or "potlatch") spot for the Skokomish and Twanoh tribes, has one of the more extensive day-use areas on Hood Canal, including a bathhouse, kitchen shelter, boat moorage floats, and a wealth of great picnic space. The 9,500-foot expanse of shoreline is a popular scuba-diving, sea-kayaking, clam-digging, and oyster-picking spot. The camping area, located across US 101, is smaller, but sufficient; many of the spaces are large, pull-through sites.

Hood Canal is lake-flat on some summer days at Potlatch State Park.

sites	37
⛺ 🚐	18 full hookups, RVs to 60 feet
open	All year
reservations	None
contact	Washington State Parks, 360/902-8844; Potlatch State Park, 360/877-5361

Potlatch has an RV dump station and coin-op showers. Local trivia: Like many waterfront state parks, this one got its start as a private development, the Minerva Resort, which took over the prime real estate after an old sawmill burned down here.

Getting there: The park is on US 101, 3 miles south of Hoodsport and 12 miles north of Shelton.

Other Eastside Olympic/Hood Canal Campgrounds

Five miles south of Quilcene, **Rainbow Group Camp** (Hood Canal Ranger District, Quilcene office, 360/765-2200) is a pretty Olympic National Forest spot with 9 sites for up to 50 campers; Rainbow Canyon Trailhead and the popular viewpoint at Mount Walker are nearby. On state-owned Olympic foothills between the Hamma Hamma and Skokomish Rivers, campers will find two free, summers-only Department of Natural Resources camps, **Lilliwaup** (13 sites, no piped water) and **Melbourne** (5 sites, no piped water). Both are reached via Forest Road 24 (Jorsted Creek Road), which leaves US 101 about 2 miles south of Eldon. Contact DNR's Enumclaw office (360/825-1631).

A remote Olympic National Forest site on the South Fork Skokomish, **Brown Creek,** has 20 sites in old-growth forest, with access to hiking trails; open all year with no piped water. Nearby **LeBar Horse Camp** has stock facilities, pit toilets, and potable water. Both are found 15 miles northwest of US 101 via the Skokomish Valley Road and Forest Roads 23, 2353, and 2340. In the remote Wynoochee Lake area, north of Montesano, is **Coho** (56 sites), an Olympic National Forest campground with a boat launch and other amenities (beware Jet-ski noise!). Call the Hood Canal Ranger District, Hoodsport office (360/877-5254) for information on these rustic camps.

North Cascades

Around the Judd household, it's so much a part of the family camping lore that it's become a standing joke. Every few years or so, without fail, Dad will be shuffling through photos or flipping through slides when up will pop a dog-eared portrait of one of us kids sitting in a river, tripping over a log, or even—in the case of my older sister—doing something unseemly, such as drinking skanky meltwater directly from the spigot of one of those big, steel-sided Coleman coolers. At which point one of us will ask the inevitable: "Where was THAT?"

Dad, without so much as hesitating, will blurt: "Up above Winthrop." 'Nuff said. The North Cascades, up above Winthrop, down below it, indeed, all around it, are like that: it's the kind of place that holds the key to magical outdoor memories, the kind where the overall feeling is so striking that the moment continues to glow in the fire of memory long after the details are lost. Which is fine, because logistics are largely irrelevant. What you do remember about the North Cascades are all the important things: The unbelievable clarity of a liquid-glass mountain stream. The smell of your first plunge into a forest floor blanketed 3 feet deep with long, soft, pungent pine needles. The adrenaline surge upon hooking a trout longer than your forearm in a mountain stream narrower than a driveway.

Visitors who lug tents and trailers or drive RVs into the North Cascades get to sleep in some of the wildest, least strip-malled places left in Washington. Those who go a bit farther—down long, steep Forest Service roads that would make your mother, or anyone else on the passenger side, blanch, or up some of the thousands of miles of winding trails—can frolic in even greater wilderness, some of the most rugged left in the Lower 48 states.

The North Cascades are one grand entity comprising many select pieces: The sprawling North Cascades National Park complex, which includes a national park, two national recreation areas, and two federal wildernesses. The curvy, potholed—but nonetheless charismatic—Mountain Loop Highway, which serves up real wilderness right in the backyards of millions of Puget Sound residents. Mount Baker, Mount Shuksan, and the unforgettable Heather Meadows area, one of the greatest places on planet Earth that you can drive to in a car. And, of course, Washington's own northern miracle, the North Cascades Highway, along with the stunningly beautiful Methow River valley, which sips clear water from some of the finest highlands up above Winthrop—then spits it out for a roller-coaster downhill river ride all the way to the Columbia River.

Unless you're blindsided by nasty weather—not far out of the question, any time of the year—it's tough to go wrong camping in the North Cascades. We can only hope that a few decades from now you can relax at home with your own grandkids, fishhook scars, tall tales, warm smiles, and faraway looks at the mere mention of the place—you know the place, what was that place?

Up above Winthrop. It's a pretty good place to pitch a tent. And an even better place to lock away in your soul.

① Turlo	⑳ Shannon Creek
② Verlot	㉑ Rockport State Park
③ Gold Basin	㉒ Howard Miller Steelhead Park
④ Boardman Creek	㉓ Goodell Creek
⑤ Red Bridge	㉔ Newhalem Creek
⑥ Monte Cristo	㉕ Colonial Creek
⑦ Bedal	㉖ Lone Fir
⑧ Clear Creek	㉗ Klipchuck
⑨ Squire Creek County Park	㉘ Early Winters
⑩ Buck Creek	㉙ Ballard
⑪ Sulphur Creek	㉚ River Bend
⑫ Silver Lake Park	㉛ Harts Pass
⑬ Douglas Fir	㉜ Meadows
⑭ Silver Fir	㉝ Pearrygin Lake State Park
⑮ Rasar State Park	㉞ Buck Lake
⑯ Horseshoe Cove	㉟ Flat
⑰ Boulder Creek	㊱ Nice
⑱ Panorama Point	㊲ Falls Creek
⑲ Park Creek	

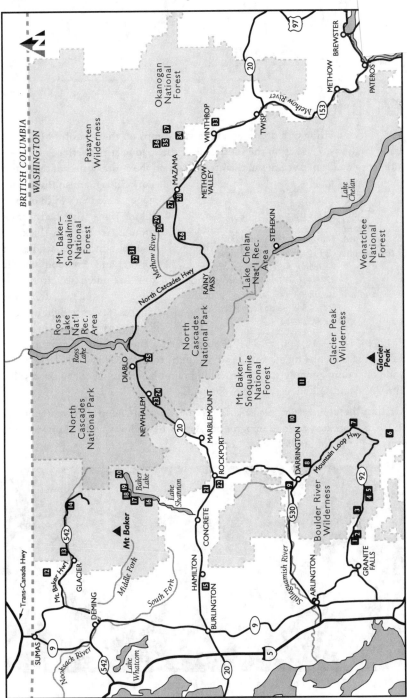

Mountain Loop Highway and Darrington

❶ Turlo 🌲🌲🌲

The first of a string of a dozen Forest Service camps on the beautiful Mountain Loop Highway, Turlo is on the south side of the road near the Verlot Public Service Center. Like most camps in this area, it's set on the crystal waters of the South Fork Stillaguamish River, with good access to a wealth of local hiking trails. The shady campground, set beneath thick firs and western red cedars, has pit toilets, and firewood usually can be purchased from the host. If you're after the choicest places to light up your fire log, set your eyes on sites 1, 3, 12, 14, 15, 17, 18, and 19. They're all on or near the river. If you're in a group with more than one rig, plan on heading up the road to Verlot: Turlo lacks extra-wide or multiple-family spots. The campground has three wheelchair-accessible sites (3, 4, and 5), and all sites have tent pads.

sites	19
🏕️🚐	No hookups, RVs to 31 feet
open	Mid-May through Labor Day
reservations	Up to 240 days in advance; National Recreation Reservation Service, 877/444-6777 or www.reserveusa.com
contact	Mount Baker–Snoqualmie National Forest, Darrington Ranger District, 360/436-1155

Getting there: From Granite Falls, follow the Mountain Loop Highway (Highway 92) 10.8 miles east to the campground, across the highway and a short distance west of the Verlot Public Service Center.

Big Four Ice Caves: A major attraction on the Mountain Loop Highway.

❷ Verlot 🌲🌲🌲

Verlot, just a short waddle up the road from Turlo (see above), is a popular summer hangout for foot soldiers who've either just been, or soon will go, up the Lake Twentytwo and Mount Pilchuck Trails—two of the most popular mountain day hikes within easy reach of the greater Puget Sound area. It's a pleasant campground, and if you want to blast off that trail dust, you'll have both nearby Benson Creek and the icy South Fork Stillaguamish, which gurgles nearby (decent trout and steelhead fishing in season). Half the sites in the easternmost of Verlot's two camping loops are on the river; several on the western loop are on either the river or Benson Creek, with sites 2 and 3 fronting on both. Campers in groups note that Verlot has two double sites (7/8, 15/16). About half the sites in the campground have tent pads. If you're torn between this camp and nearby Turlo, note that this one adds a slight touch of civilization: flush toilets. Verlot is also much sunnier, with a far thinner forest canopy.

sites	25
🏕️ 🚐	No hookups, RVs to 31 feet
open	Mid-May through Labor Day
reservations	Up to 240 days in advance; National Recreation Reservation Service, 877/444-6777 or www.reserveusa.com
contact	Mount Baker–Snoqualmie National Forest, Darrington Ranger District, 360/436-1155

Getting there: From Granite Falls, follow the Mountain Loop Highway (Highway 92) about 11 miles east to the campground, across the road and a short distance east of the Verlot Public Service Center.

❸ Gold Basin 🌲🌲🌲🌲

Gold Basin is by far the most powerful camping magnet in the Mountain Loop corridor, largely because of its unusual size for a Forest Service camp in a relatively remote location. The sites are sprinkled in several loops near the South Fork Stillaguamish River, a great water play and fishing venue. Although it lacks hookups, the campground also is the most RV friendly of all the public campgrounds in this area, with paved sites and more elbow room—not to mention coin-op showers! Expect crowds, and don't hesitate to take

sites	92
🏕️ 🚐	No hookups, RVs to 31 feet
open	Mid-May to late September
reservations	Up to 240 days in advance; National Recreation Reservation Service, 877/444-6777 or www.reserveusa.com
contact	Mount Baker–Snoqualmie National Forest, Darrington Ranger District, 360/436-1155

advantage of the reservation system, which allows about 60 percent of the sites to be booked well in advance. Gold Basin has both pit and flush toilets. A group camp at the west end of the complex can accommodate up to 50 people. Sites 17–19 are wheelchair accessible, and sites 12–16 and 47–51 are walk-in sites for tents only. About half the sites here are equipped with tent pads. The kids will like the large, open playfield, suitable for Frisbee tossing and sister-chasing. If you get bored with the campfire, take a stroll across the highway to Gold Basin Pond, a salmon-fry viewing area with a half-mile-long, wheelchair-accessible boardwalk.

Getting there: From Granite Falls, follow the Mountain Loop Highway (Highway 92) 13.4 miles (2.4 miles east of the Verlot Public Service Center) to the campground, on the left (north) side of the highway.

④ Boardman Creek 🌲🌲🌲

The good news: Sites are nice and spacious at Boardman Creek, near the popular Boardman Lake Trailhead and in the midst of half a dozen other popular hiking trails along the Mountain Loop Highway. The bad news: Sites are scarce and likely to be full much of the summer in this first-come, first-served campground. (It also gets a fair amount of highway-traffic noise, although the rushing river helps alleviate this somewhat.) Boardman Creek has a rustic feel, with pit toilets and no piped water or showers. Water comes from the nearby South Fork Stillaguamish, which also provides good fishing in season. It's a pretty, albeit mildly primitive,

White Horse Mountain looms like a guardian over the Mountain Loop.

sites	*8*
🏕️ 🚐	*No hookups, RVs to 38 feet*
open	*Mid-May to mid-September*
reservations	*None*
contact	*Mount Baker–Snoqualmie National Forest, Darrington Ranger District, 360/436-1155*

spot. RVers, take note: Although it's open to tenters and RVs, this really is a tenter's spot. There's only one long (38-foot) site, and six sites are walk-in, for tents only. You'd be better served at nearby Gold Basin (see above).

Getting there: From Granite Falls, follow the Mountain Loop Highway (Highway 92) about 16.5 miles east (5.5 miles east of Verlot Public Service Center) to the campground, on the left (north) side of the highway.

⑤ Red Bridge 🌲🌲🌲🌲

Another quite pretty but primitive South Fork Stillaguamish River camp, Red Bridge is situated near the river's confluence with Mahardy Creek. The prime sites, numbers 5–15, all front on the South Fork Stilly's broad river bar. The

sites	*15*
🏕️ 🚐	*No hookups, RVs to 31 feet*
open	*Late May to mid-September*
reservations	*Up to 240 days in advance; National Recreation Reservation Service, 877/444-6777 or www.reserveusa.com*
contact	*Mount Baker–Snoqualmie National Forest, Darrington Ranger District, 360/436-1155*

campground's elevation (about 1,300 feet) often causes it to open a bit later and close earlier than other, lower-elevation camps on the Mountain Loop. It's another campground preferred by hikers; sites have good privacy, and all but one (number 13, of course!) are equipped with tent pads. Red Bridge has pit toilets and no piped water or showers. Site number 4 is a double-wide, family spot. Nine sites can be booked in advance.

Getting there: From Granite Falls, follow the Mountain Loop Highway (Highway 92) about 18 miles east (7.1 miles east of Verlot Public Service Center) to the campground, on the right (south) side of the highway.

⑥ Monte Cristo 🌲🌲🌲

Here's a mountain-biking camper's special. From Barlow Pass, at 2,361 feet on the Mountain Loop Highway, an old road (it's quickly turning into trail) proceeds east to the semi-ghost town of Monte Cristo, site of an old mining operation and a major trailhead for routes into some of this country's most prime day-hiking territory: Gothic Basin, Poodle Dog Pass, and Glacier Basin. Near the townsite itself is the small, tents-only Forest Service camp, which makes a good base

sites	8

for hikers who've come this far either by foot or fat-tire cycle. With pit toilets, the campground is primitive. You'll need to pack out your own garbage, backpacker style. But hey, it's free—assuming your car has a Northwest Forest Pass.

open	Late May to late September
reservations	None
contact	Mount Baker–Snoqualmie National Forest, Darrington Ranger District, 360/436-1155

Getting there: From Granite Falls, follow the Mountain Loop Highway (Highway 92) about 31 miles to the parking area at Barlow Pass. Follow the Monte Cristo Road on foot or cycle for about 4 miles to the campground.

⑦ Bedal 🌲🌲🌲

Explorers who venture beyond Barlow Pass onto the north-south (unpaved) section of the Mountain Loop Highway (properly known as Forest Road 20) will happen upon Bedal, an isolated, often chilly site at the confluence of the north

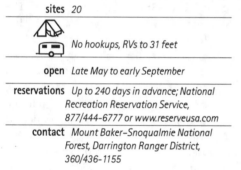

sites	20
	No hookups, RVs to 31 feet
open	Late May to early September
reservations	Up to 240 days in advance; National Recreation Reservation Service, 877/444-6777 or www.reserveusa.com
contact	Mount Baker–Snoqualmie National Forest, Darrington Ranger District, 360/436-1155

and south forks of the scenic Sauk River. The campground is shady, quiet, and remote, set mostly in old-growth forest. Bring plenty of bug dope, and a back-to-nature ethic: Bedal has pit toilets and no piped water or showers. It's very quiet here (aside from the pleasant river noise), and well situated for tenters. Six sites are wheelchair accessible. A notable campground attraction: A large Adirondack shelter in site 18, built entirely of old-growth timber. North Fork Sauk Falls, a true gusher, is only a mile away, and worth a visit.

Getting there: From Darrington, drive about 18 miles southeast on Forest Road 20 (Mountain Loop Highway). From Granite Falls, drive 31.5 miles east to Barlow Pass, and then about 6.5 miles north on Forest Road 20.

⑧ Clear Creek 🌲🌲

It really is. The creek, we mean. The clear waters of Clear Creek meet the equally glassy flow of the beautiful Sauk River near Clear Creek Campground, a rustic site near Darrington, at the northern outlet of the Mountain Loop Highway. It's a pretty area in the summer, but facilities are painfully sparse—and, unfortunately, often unkempt, thanks to the day-tripping partiers who seem to trash the place

sites	13
	No hookups, RVs to 21 feet
open	Mid-May to mid-September
reservations	Up to 240 days in advance; National Recreation Reservation Service, 877/444-6777 or www.reserveusa.com
contact	Mount Baker-Snoqualmie National Forest, Darrington Ranger District, 360/436-1155

occasionally. Clear Creek has pit toilets and no piped water or showers. (It also offers little privacy between sites—"a more open, communal" camping experience, sayeth the Forest Service.) Most sites have tent pads, numbers 12 and 13 are close to the river, and two are wheelchair accessible. The Forest Service recently began collecting fees at this formerly free campground—a questionable move, in our opinion, until the place is spruced up. If you do wind up camping here, though, a wonderful diversion is within walking distance: The Old Sauk River Trail, a great, 6-mile day hike through the forest along the river. It begins a short distance to the south.

Getting there: From Darrington, drive about 2.5 miles south on Forest Road 20 (Mountain Loop Highway) to the campground, on the left (east) side of the highway.

⑨ Squire Creek County Park 🌲🌲🌲

Hankering to explore the wilds of the Mountain Loop Highway or the nearby Glacier Peak Wilderness, but can't stomach the thought of parking your business end on a cold pit-toilet seat? Get thee to Squire Creek, a Darrington-area county

sites	32
	No hookups, RVs to 25 feet
open	All year
reservations	None
contact	Snohomish County Parks, 425/388-6600; Squire Creek County Park, 360/436-1283

park set in old-growth forest and promoting a "family" feel. This 53-acre park offers nicely spaced campsites, two large picnic shelters, an RV dump station, and some nice local hiking trails. Most of the sites are pull-throughs—a bonus to RVers—and several are wheelchair accessible. The park is also close enough to Darrington (3 miles) to pick up supplies by foot or bicycle. Squire Creek, amazingly enough, flows close by, and you'll love the nearby views of White Horse Mountain, which looms over Darrington like a snowcapped guardian angel. Expect the campground to fill up on summer weekends—particularly in July, when the Bluegrass Festival is running at full steam. Note to RVers: If you must have hookups and really want to stay in this area, consider Howard Miller Steelhead Park, about 19 miles north of Darrington in Rockport (see below).

Getting there: The campground is on the left (north) side of Highway 530, 3 miles west of Darrington and 26 miles east of the Highway 530/Interstate 5 junction near Arlington.

⑩ Buck Creek 🌲🌲🌲🌲

You're looking for a forested, wild campground a half-day's drive from Seattle—one that'll make you feel really out there. Look no further than Buck Creek, a spartan-but-beautiful spot so close to roaring, rollicking North Cascades white water that you're likely to get occasional splashes on your rain fly. This delightful camp in tall, tall firs sits just upstream from Buck Creek's confluence with the Suiattle River, which springs from the seldom-trod flanks of 10,540-foot Glacier Peak. The Suiattle truly is a wild and scenic river, emphasis on wild in the winter, when the milky gusher often jumps its banks—and takes part of the access road to Buck Creek and another campground, Sulphur Creek (see below), with it. But when the road's open in the summer (call first to make sure), the Suiattle drainage is a magical spot for campers, hikers, mountain bikers, river rafters, and steelhead anglers. And Buck Creek Campground is a good place to start all those adventures. Although you can fit small RVs inside its confines, this really is one of the

Raging waters and big trees are the stars at Buck Creek Campground.

sites	26

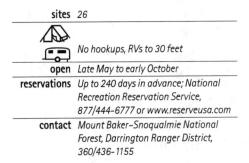

	No hookups, RVs to 30 feet
open	Late May to early October
reservations	Up to 240 days in advance; National Recreation Reservation Service, 877/444-6777 or www.reserveusa.com
contact	Mount Baker–Snoqualmie National Forest, Darrington Ranger District, 360/436-1155

prettier tent-camping spots in the North Cascades. Site 6 and its multiple walk-in offshoots, near the really big rock (believe us, you'll know it when you see it) are particularly charming. Many other sites at the rustic (pit toilets, no piped water) campground are streamfront, and if you visit in the early summer, it's an impressive stream. The trailhead for the Huckleberry Mountain Trail, a strenuous, 14-mile round-trip hike to a former lookout site, is a mile west of the campground.

Getting there: From Darrington, follow Highway 530 about 7.5 miles north to Suiattle River Road (Forest Road 26). Turn right (east) and follow Suiattle River Road about 15 miles to the campground. Use extreme caution on the poorly maintained Suiattle River Road, which is paved, but often pocked with alarmingly severe dips and ruts.

⑪ Sulphur Creek 🌲🌲🌲

Sulphur Creek, high (at about 1,900 feet) in the scenic Suiattle River drainage, isn't technically a tents-only campground. But functionally, it works out that way. Located near the river's Sulphur Creek confluence, the primitive but very pretty

sites	20
open	Late May to early September
reservations	Up to 240 days in advance; National Recreation Reservation Service, 877/444-6777 or www.reserveusa.com
contact	Mount Baker–Snoqualmie National Forest, Darrington Ranger District, 360/436-1155

campground lies at the end of 23 miles of often very rough road. But those who persevere will be rewarded with rugged, but equally rich, wilderness scenery. The campground is basic Forest Service issue (pit toilets, no piped water or showers). Most sites are in riverside vegetation: vine maple and scrubby alder. And all of them, if the winds aren't cooperating, impart the smell of sulfur, which emanates from the creek. Sites 14/15, 16/17, and 19/20 are double sites. Sites 12, 16/17, and 18 are wheelchair accessible. The campground's popularity lies in its proximity to a major trailhead. The Suiattle River Trail begins near here, offering day hikers a wonderful forested walk and backpackers access to the splendors of the wild, seldom-seen Glacier Peak Wilderness. The trail leads on to destinations such as Image Lake (21 miles one way) and beyond to Suiattle Pass and the east-slope Cascades, with access to the Lake Chelan area. If you're feeling more modest, a 1.8-mile trail winds up Sulphur Creek from a trailhead across the road from the camp entrance.

Getting there: From Darrington, follow Highway 530 about 7.5 miles north to Suiattle River Road (Forest Road 26). Turn right (east) and follow Suiattle River Road about 23 miles to the campground, near the end of the road. Use caution on the rough (and sometimes washed out) Suiattle River Road.

Other Mountain Loop Highway/Darrington Campgrounds

Six Forest Service group camps are nicely located near the South Fork Stillaguamish River, along the Mountain Loop Highway, with varying levels of services: **Wiley Creek** (4 miles east of the Verlot Public Service Center) has tent/trailer facilities for up to 100 campers in two separate group sites, equipped with four shelters and a combination of tent/trailer spaces) **Esswine** (5.2 miles east of the Verlot Public Service Center), has facilities for 25 campers; **Tulalip Millsite** (8.2 miles east of the Verlot Public Service Center), has room for 60 campers; **Marten Creek** (9.2 miles east of the Verlot Public Service Center) has tent-camping facilities for 25 campers; **Coal Creek Bar** (12 miles east of the Verlot Public Service Center), near the South Fork Stillaguamish, can accommodate 25 campers; and **Beaver Creek** (13 miles east of the Verlot Public Service Center), near the South Fork Stillaguamish and with views of Big Four Mountain, can fit 25 campers. All six campgrounds must be reserved in advance; all have pit toilets and no piped water or showers. For reservations and information, contact the Mount Baker–Snoqualmie National Forest's Darrington Ranger District (360/436-1155).

The Department of Natural Resources oversees five small, free, primitive campgrounds in the Mountain Loop corridor. Four are hike-in, summer-only sites accessed from the Ashland Lake Trailhead, reached via Forest Roads 4020 and 4021. They are **Beaver Plant Lake** (2.1 miles from the trailhead; 6 sites); **Lower Ashland Lake** (2.5 miles in; 6 sites); **Upper Ashland Lake** (3 miles in; 6 sites); and **Twin Falls Lake** (4.5 miles in; 5 sites). Another remote DNR site, **William C. Dearinger** (on the south bank of the Suiattle River, northeast of Darrington on SW-D-5400 Road) has 12 sites and no piped water. Contact the DNR's Sedro-Woolley office (360/856-3500).

Finally, while it's located a bit west of this area's target boundaries, another Snohomish County Park, **River Meadows** (425/388-6600), is one to put on your long-range planning list. The 200-acre site on Jordan Road near Arlington now offers tent camping along the banks of the Stillaguamish, but someday will expand into an RV-accessible campground. From Highway 530 near Arlington, turn right onto Arlington Heights Road, proceed 2 miles, bear right onto Jordan Road, and continue about 3 miles to the park entrance on the right.

Mount Baker Highway and Baker Lake

⑫ Silver Lake Park ▲▲▲

Not many out-of-towners are aware of 411-acre Silver Lake Park, a wonderful Whatcom County facility at the site of a former private resort and early 1900s homestead. The park, north of Maple Falls along the Mount Baker Highway, is set on a quiet mountain lake with acres of green space. The campground includes a pleasant tent area and 53 RV sites, which can be reserved in bunches for group outings. Fishing, swimming, and canoeing on the calm lake are always fun, and rental pedal boats, fishing boats, and canoes are available. Silver Lake Park also is home to a small

sites	80
	53 water/electrical hookups, RVs to any length
open	All year
reservations	360/599-2776
contact	Whatcom County Parks, 360/733-2900; Silver Lake Park, 360/599-2776

A quiet afternoon on Silver Lake, a North Cascades family favorite.

museum, picturesque lakefront rental cabins, several large kitchen shelters, a day-use lodge with a dining room, and a 28-site horse camp, across the highway and about a quarter-mile north. The horse camp, which has extensive stables and other horse facilities as well as RV hookups, is available (by reservation in summer) to non-horse campers as well; many RVers prefer it because sites are more open to the sun than those in the heavily forested main campground. Wherever you choose to park, kids will love the swimming beach and large playground in the main camp's day-use area—about a 10-minute walk from the camping loops. Note that Whatcom County residents get a price break as well as first dibs each year on reservations, which don't open up to others until April. The campground can feel pretty busy when it's full in the summer, but it's a downright peaceful place in the spring or fall, with only a highly vocal pack of local coyotes conspiring to keep you up at night.

Getting there: From Bellingham, drive about 25 miles east on Mount Baker Highway 542 to Maple Falls. Turn left (north) on Silver Lake Road and follow signs about 3 miles to the park entrance, on the right.

⑬ Douglas Fir 🌲🌲🌲

Douglas Fir and Silver Fir (see below), the Mount Baker Highway's two primary camping spots, are lovely firs, indeed. Douglas, the first encountered on the trek up the Mount Baker Highway (a designated National Scenic Byway), is a gorgeous, shady spot on the North Fork Nooksack, with 30 sites sprinkled between—you guessed it. The facilities are well-used, standard Forest Service issue: pit toilets, piped water. Three of the sites are wheelchair accessible; sites 2, 4, 5, 7, 9, and 12 are riverfront. Most sites lack tent pads, but are flat and open enough for tenters. This isn't the most private campground in the world, with little underbrush to separate many of the sites. But the constant gurgling of the nearby North Fork Nooksack has lulled many a worn-out hiker, angler, photographer, and unabashed camper to sleep over the years. An added touch is a small picnic area with an outdoor kitchen (also reservable). Note: Stop in at the Glacier Public Service Center (summers only) near the campground. It's the best one-stop information source for trail and back-country information in the region.

sites	30
🏕️🚐	No hookups, RVs to 26 feet
open	Mid-May to early October; winters with no services
reservations	Up to 240 days in advance; National Recreation Reservation Service, 877/444-6777 or www.reserveusa.com
contact	Mount Baker–Snoqualmie National Forest, Mount Baker Ranger District, 360/856-5700

Nooksack Falls, a short drive from Douglas or Silver Fir campgrounds.

Getting there: From Bellingham, drive about 33 miles east on Mount Baker Highway 542 to the town of Glacier. Continue 2 miles east to the campground, on the north side of the highway near milepost 36.

⑭ Silver Fir 🌲🌲🌲🌲🌲

This is our favorite campground hideaway on the way to Mount Baker, and one of our favorites in all the lands of the sprawling Mount Baker–Snoqualmie National Forest. Silver Fir is tucked into a bend in the road, and a bend in the beautiful

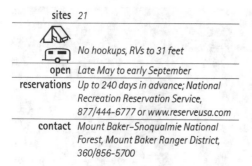

sites	*21*
	No hookups, RVs to 31 feet
open	*Late May to early September*
reservations	*Up to 240 days in advance; National Recreation Reservation Service, 877/444-6777 or www.reserveusa.com*
contact	*Mount Baker–Snoqualmie National Forest, Mount Baker Ranger District, 360/856-5700*

North Fork Nooksack River, just before both get steep and serious on their way up to a drop-dead gorgeous view at Artist Point, between Mounts Baker and Shuksan. The facilities are far from grand—pit toilets—but about half of the spaces here are places you'll plunk your tent and not want to leave for a while. Sites 2–4 are wheelchair accessible; site 1 is a double site, a good choice for families or small groups with two rigs. Most sites are very private—a delight for tenters—and open onto the bouldered bank of the North Fork Nooksack. Although it's close to the Mount Baker Highway, the campground is intimate and often quiet, and extremely peaceful in early fall, just before winter closing time. It's a great base from which to explore the wealth of hiking and outdoor recreation choices in the Nooksack drainage and the Artist Point/Heather Meadows area at the end of Mount Baker Highway. A winner.

Getting there: From Bellingham, drive about 33 miles east on Mount Baker Highway 542 to the town of Glacier. Proceed an additional 14 miles east to the campground, on the right.

Heather Meadows, one of the grandest auto-accessible alpine destinations in the state.

⑮ Rasar State Park 🌲🌲🌲🌲

Washington State Parks, budget-cut to the point of embarrassment by the recreational geniuses in the Washington State Legislature (write them, please), doesn't get a chance to open a new campground very often. Park officials took full advantage of the rare opportunity with Rasar, a sprawling, quiet, Skagit River park that opened in the late 1990s to rave reviews from tenters and RVers seeking solace in the woods without venturing too far from the Puget Sound metro area. Campsites—flat, paved, and tidy—are nicely laid out in salal, huckleberry, and Oregon grape underbrush

sites	49
🏕️ 🚐	20 water/sewer hookups, RVs to any length
open	All year, weather permitting
reservations	None
contact	Washington State Parks, 360/902-8844; Rasar State Park, 360/826-3942

beneath hemlocks and firs. Sites come in the full range: from long pull-throughs with hookups, to eight small, private, walk-in sites for tenters and three "primitive" sites for hikers and cyclists. The walk-ins include a pair of Adirondack shelters, each of which can sleep four people. Two group camps are across the road from the main campground and can be reserved.

Facilities are as new as you'll find in a Washington State Park, and the nearby day-use area, complete with covered picnic shelter and stove (reservable) and playground facilities, is a hit with kids and parents. Short trails lead from the day-use area across a sprawling hay field, where nice views of North Cascades peaks are

The Skagit River swells with summer runoff at Rasar State Park.

seen to the east. About a half mile from the day-use area, trails open onto the slow-rolling Skagit River—often full to its banks and then some in the winter or spring snowmelt seasons. A flat sandbar here (large or small, depending on river flows) provides river access for anglers, sun bathers, and swimmers. (Note, however, that the current is extremely strong; it's probably not a good place to take a dip anywhere beyond ankle deep.)

Getting there: From Burlington, drive 19 miles east on North Cascades Highway 20 to Lusk Road. Turn right (south) and proceed less than a mile to a stop sign at Cape Horn Road. Turn left and proceed about a mile to the park entrance on the right.

⑯ Horseshoe Cove 🌲🌲🌲🌲

Years ago, the people who run Puget Sound Energy (most of us locals grew up knowing it as Puget Power) forever changed the face of the lands south of Mount Baker by damming the Baker River, a northern tributary of the mighty Skagit, for hydropower. The result—good, bad, or indifferent—is the Baker Lake National Recreation Area, a sprawling lowland of mostly second-growth forest and, thanks to the twin concrete dams, a pair of reservoirs known as Lake Shannon (to the south) and Baker Lake (to the north). Baker Lake is prized for sportfishing (kokanee, Dolly Varden, cutthroat trout), monster views of the south face of 10,778-foot Mount Baker—and campgrounds, half a dozen of which ring the lakeshore.

The first encountered on a journey here is Horseshoe Cove, a very pleasant, tidy, shady spot in a mixed fir-and-alder forest just above the Upper Baker Dam. The sites are fairly closely packed but still offer decent privacy for tenters—arguably the best of any of the established Forest Service camps in the Baker Lake region. The campground has the usual Forest Service amenities (pit toilets, no showers), but some bonuses, including for-sale firewood and, during our last visit, rental canoes available from the campground host. A swimming beach and boat launch are close by—very convenient for boaters, canoeists, swimmers, and, regret-

sites	34
🏕️🚐	No hookups, RVs to 34 feet
open	Mid-May to early October; winters with no services
reservations	Up to 240 days in advance; National Recreation Reservation Service, 877/444-6777 or www.reserveusa.com
contact	Mount Baker-Snoqualmie National Forest, Mount Baker Ranger District, 360/856-5700

tably, Jet-ski jockeys, who tend to congregate here in the summer. This is a popular spot; use the reservation system. Note: The campground also has three group sites for up to 25 people each; they must be reserved in advance. Sites 8, 10, 11, and the group sites are wheelchair accessible.

Getting there: From Interstate 5 at Burlington, follow North Cascades Highway 20 east 22.5 miles to Baker Lake Road (just west of Birdsview). Turn left (north) and proceed 14.8 miles to Forest Road 1118. Turn east (right) and drive 2 miles to the campground.

⑰ Boulder Creek 🌲🌲🌲

Boulder Creek, the smallest of the Forest Service camps around Baker Lake, isn't on the shoreline. It's about a mile west, set on the banks of Boulder Creek, just off Baker Lake Road. The campground is small and facilities limited (pit toilets, no piped water or showers). But it's not at all unpleasant, offering two large group sites (one is reservable, for up to 25 people), some peace and quiet (assuming you don't mind the sound of a gurgling, glacier-fed stream), and mountain views from some spaces.

sites	8
	No hookups, RVs to 16 feet
open	Late May to early September
reservations	Up to 240 days in advance; National Recreation Reservation Service, 877/444-6777 or www.reserveusa.com
contact	Mount Baker–Snoqualmie National Forest, Mount Baker Ranger District, 360/856-5700

Getting there: From Interstate 5 at Burlington, follow North Cascades Highway 20 east 22.5 miles to Baker Lake Road (just west of Birdsview). Turn left (north) and proceed 17.5 miles to the campground.

⑱ Panorama Point 🌲🌲🌲🌲

If you have but one night to spend and are fortunate enough to grab an empty spot, Panorama Point is the place to stay at Baker Lake. One of the more picturesque Forest Service camps in the region, the aptly named park sits on a triangular point jutting into the heart of Baker Lake reservoir, with some sites right on the lakeshore. A boat launch and swimming area are nearby. The campground, at about 800 feet in elevation, is densely forested, and cool to the point of cold for much of the season. It's equipped with well water and pit toilets; no showers. Sites 10 and 13 are wheelchair accessible and have tent pads. This is a grand base camp for hiking in the area. Popular trails on the south slopes of

sites	16
	No hookups, RVs to 24 feet
open	Late May to early September
reservations	Up to 240 days in advance; National Recreation Reservation Service, 877/444-6777 or www.reserveusa.com
contact	Mount Baker–Snoqualmie National Forest, Mount Baker Ranger District, 360/856-5700

Mount Baker, such as the Elbow Lake, Park Butte/Railroad Grade, and Mazama Park/Cathedral Pass Trails, are a short drive away. Fishing, for kokanee salmon, rainbow and cutthroat trout, and Dolly Varden, often is productive. Canoeists can paddle across the deep, clear reservoir and embark on a charming hike on the East Bank Baker Lake Trail, and can even add an overnight stop at Maple Grove Campground, on the lake's eastern shore. If you should run out of wieners, Baker Lake Resort, a (cluttered) private campground and store, is about a mile up the road.

Getting there: From Interstate 5 at Burlington, follow North Cascades Highway 20 east 22.5 miles to Baker Lake Road (just west of Birdsview). Turn left (north) and proceed 18.7 miles to the turnoff for the campground, on the right.

⑲ Park Creek 🌲🌲🏕

Park Creek is where many of us have, at least once, roughed it (pit toilets, no piped water) after getting shut out of larger, better-developed campgrounds farther south on Baker Lake. But some people reserve sites at this small, heavily wooded camp on purpose now, because it's a short distance away from the lake and all its accompanying hubbub. It's pretty dark in here, though; not a place you'd like to stay forever unless you're hiding from something or someone.

sites	12
🏕🚐	No hookups, RVs to 22 feet
open	Late May to early September
reservations	Up to 240 days in advance; National Recreation Reservation Service, 877/444-6777 or www.reserveusa.com
contact	Mount Baker–Snoqualmie National Forest, Mount Baker Ranger District, 360/856-5700

Getting there: From Interstate 5 at Burlington, follow North Cascades Highway 20 east 22.5 miles to Baker Lake Road (just west of Birdsview). Turn left (north) and drive 19.5 miles to Forest Road 1144. Turn left (west) and proceed a short distance to the campground.

⑳ Shannon Creek 🌲🌲

It's a long ways out here, and not all that nicely developed, but Shannon Creek is another good alternative for Baker Lake revelers, particularly those pulling boat trailers. This campground on the west shore of the lake is rustic, but is adjacent to a boat launch and swimming area. Although two sites are walk-in camps for tenters, the campground overall is not a great place for tents, with gravelly surfaces and little privacy between sites. Campers in small RVs might find it suitable, however. The campground is equipped with pit toilets and piped water, but no showers.

Little kids, flat water and big mountains mix nicely in Lake Shannon.

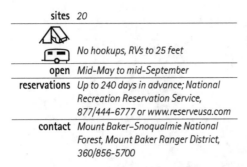

sites	20
	No hookups, RVs to 25 feet
open	Mid-May to mid-September
reservations	Up to 240 days in advance; National Recreation Reservation Service, 877/444-6777 or www.reserveusa.com
contact	Mount Baker–Snoqualmie National Forest, Mount Baker Ranger District, 360/856-5700

Getting there: From Interstate 5 at Burlington, follow North Cascades Highway 20 east 22.5 miles to Baker Lake Road (just west of Birdsview). Turn left (north) and drive 22.8 miles to the campground entrance, on the right.

Other Mount Baker/Baker Lake Campgrounds

Mount Baker–Snoqualmie National Forest camps in the Mount Baker Highway corridor include **Excelsior Group Camp** (6.5 miles east of Glacier on Mount Baker Highway 542; Mount Baker Ranger District, 360/856-5700), which has pit toilets, no piped water, and two group sites accommodating 25 campers each. Farther up the Nooksack drainage, **Hannegan** (at the end of Forest Road 32; 360/856-5700 or 360/599-2714, summers only) is a backcountry campground that doubles as a major trailhead for treks into the western portion of North Cascades National Park. It has one pit toilet and no piped water. In the Baker Lake area, **Bayview Group Camps** north and south (Mount Baker Ranger District, 360/856-5700) offer facilities for tent and RV camping for up to 25 campers each; they're reservable and have pit toilets, but no piped water. Another option is **Grandy Lake Park** (360/336-9414), a small Skagit County Park with rustic sites on a lily-pad covered lake set next to Baker Lake Road, a few miles north of North Cascades Highway 20. The camp, open May through October, has about a dozen sites, mostly flat, level and graveled, set amidst a stand of alder and maple trees. A gravel boat launch/fishing access is found at the lakeshore. **Maple Grove** (Mount Baker Ranger District, 360/856-5700), about midway up Baker Lake on the east shore, is a paddle- or walk-in site along the newly expanded East Bank Baker Lake Trail. The Forest Service campground, 4 miles from the southern East Bank Trailhead, has 6 wooded sites and no other facilities, but it's free. A prominent private campground in the area is **Kulshan** (360/853-8341), operated by Puget Sound Energy. The camp has 79 sites, some with full hookups. Farther up the valley, the energy company also maintains **Baker Lake Resort** (888/711-3033), which has a campground and cabins.

North Cascades Highway and National Park

㉑ Rockport State Park 🌲🌲🌲🌲🌲

Trees so big they'll scare you. Excellent access to the Skagit, a federally designated Wild and Scenic River. Full RV hookups. Hot showers. All within a short distance of a trail leading to the top of Sauk Mountain, one of our favorite spring wildflower hikes. Have we died and gone to heaven? Nah, but as close as you can get to it within spitting distance of Concrete. Rockport, one of Washington's "newish" (i.e., 1960s) state parks, contains a wealth of treats, the grandest of which you can't miss: old-growth Douglas firs, and plenty of them. The large, stately trees are a rarity in this valley, which has been heavily manhandled by loggers and dam builders over the decades. Sites are nicely spaced, and most campers will quickly discover those on the outside of the main camping loops—almost all spacious, level pull-throughs—to be the sites of choice. The 670-acre park has an RV dump station and coin-op showers; the facilities are more modern than any you'll find in the region. Also on the grounds are fine picnic facilities (look for the historical marker with information about botanist David Douglas who "discovered" the fir

Big rigs don't look so big among the really big trees at Rockport State Park.

sites	62
🏕️🚐	50 full hookups, RVs to 45 feet
open	April through October
reservations	None
contact	Washington State Parks, 360/902-8844; Rockport State Park, 360/853-8461

now bearing his name in 1825); 5 miles of trails, including a short, barrier-free trail with a view of the Skagit River; a walk-in group (reservable) campsite for up to 45 people, eight private, walk-in tent sites; and four Adirondack shelters, each fitted with eight bunks. The trees are the grandest attraction, however. When you visit, offer up some thanks to the Sound Timber Company, which opted not to log this stand, selling it to the state for one dollar in 1935. Alpine hikers take note: The Sauk Mountain Trailhead is an 8-mile drive from here via Forest Roads 1030 and 1036. The trail, which gains only about 1,200 feet in elevation on a 2.1-mile walk, tops out at 5,337 feet, with views all around.

Getting there: The park is on the north side of North Cascades Highway 20 near milepost 96, about 7 miles east of Concrete and 1 mile west of Rockport.

22 Howard Miller Steelhead Park 🌲🌲🌲

Go figure. This is the only campground in the North Cascades—and probably one of very few in the state—that's more crowded in winter than summer. The lure won't be obvious by glancing at the frosty ground or frozen mud puddles. Peer

sites	59
🏕️🚐	30 electrical hookups, 19 water/electrical hookups; RVs to any length
open	All year
reservations	Up to 10 months in advance; 360/853-8808
contact	Howard Miller Steelhead Park, 360/853-8808

down the banks of the Skagit River, however, and all becomes clear: spawning chum salmon, splashing near shore, and hundreds of bald eagles swooping after them. The Skagit, particularly the stretch between Rockport and Marblemount, is home to one of the largest wintering bald eagle populations in the Lower 48 states. Howard Miller Steelhead Park, a county-run campground and gathering spot near the riverbank, is as good a place as any to see them. The Forest Service operates a staffed lookout site near here, and many bird clubs and other eagle fans congregate at the campground for float trips or delightfully simple, crisp days standing along the road with binoculars. Bird-watching activity, which begins in December, peaks around the first week of February, when Rockport hosts its annual Bald Eagle Festival. But the campground gets plenty of use by anglers, as well. The Skagit is a notable steelhead stream, and the park is named for an avid angler and former Skagit County commissioner who not only supported public fishing access on the river—but did something about it, acquiring these formerly private lands for the county. The campground is well-equipped for

A riverside retreat at Howard Miller Steelhead Park.

winter or any season, with flush toilets, showers, a covered picnic area, a playground, Adirondack shelters (each sleeping up to eight campers), an RV dump, and other niceties. Call well in advance for reservations.

Getting there: From the North Cascades Highway 20/Highway 530 junction at Rockport, turn south on Highway 530 and proceed a short distance to the campground, on the right.

㉓ Goodell Creek 🌲🌲🌲

This small, rustic site along the upper Skagit River near the Seattle City Light village of Newhalem is the first North Cascades National Park campground encountered as you head east along the North Cascades Highway (for more on the national park, see Colonial Creek, below). The facilities are sparse (pit toilets, gravel roads and sites), but it's a nice spot that also serves as a popular stopover for Skagit River rafters. Nearby is the small, rustic Goodell Creek Group

sites	21
🏕️🚐	No hookups, RVs to 22 feet
open	All year; winter with no services
reservations	None
contact	North Cascades National Park Headquarters, Sedro-Woolley, 360/856-5700

Camp, available only by reservation through the Marblemount Ranger Station (360/873-4590 ext. 17, summers only).

Getting there: Watch for signs along North Cascades High-way 20, just west of Newhalem.

㉔ Newhalem Creek 🌲🌲🌲🌲

The town of Newhalem, a Seattle City Light administrative town turned tourist attraction, looks like an artificial Mayberry RFD dropped into the jaws one of the most awesome river canyons—the upper Skagit—in the North Cascades. It's all a little disarming, at least until you get off the "downtown" streets and explore the patches of forest along the river. There you'll find Newhalem Creek, one of two major campgrounds in North Cascades National Park, and thus a major summertime stopover. After touring Newhalem (it's less than a mile's walk away), the campground is a pleasant plunge back into the woods, with very clean, tidy, nicely spaced sites (a boon for tenters, in particular) tucked beneath sweet-smelling fir trees. The three loops are well spread out, each offering a wheelchair-accessible site. The campground has ample running water and an RV dump station, but, like every other national park we've ever visited, no showers: the only thing keeping this otherwise-dandy campground from five-tree status! The campground also has two group sites accommodating 24 campers each. One is equipped with a large sheltered area. (To reserve a group site, call 360/873-4590 ext. 17.) The North Cascades Visitors

sites	107
🏕️🚐	No hookups, RVs to 32 feet
open	Mid-May to mid-October
reservations	None
contact	North Cascades National Park Headquarters, Sedro-Woolley, 360/856-5700

Newhalem Creek flows through its namesake campground.

Center is within walking distance, making this a perfect first-day's stop on your tour of the North Cascades.

Family camping planners, take note: A number of very scenic nature trails (such as the Trail of the Cedars, at the foot of Main Street in Newhalem, and the don't-miss spectacle of Ladder Creek Falls, hidden behind the nearby Gorge Powerhouse) begin near the campground. But with no lake nearby for fishing and boating, there's probably not as much to do here as at Colonial Creek, the other major national park stopover just up Highway 20. Then again, there isn't as much hubbub here, either.

Getting there: Newhalem Creek is just west of the town of Newhalem. Follow signs from milepost 120 on North Cascades Highway 20.

㉕ Colonial Creek 🌲🌲🌲🌲

How spectacular are the North Cascades for mountain fun lovers? It takes not just a national park, but a national park complex to contain and protect them. The North Cascades complex includes the national park, the Lake Chelan National Recreation Area, and the Ross Lake National Recreation Area. Each stands on its own as a premiere wild spot; together the complex comprises some of the most rugged, unpeopled terrain in the Lower 48 states. The North Cascades are wickedly rugged and savagely beautiful, with rocky, glaciated peaks interlaced with deep, lush valleys. Even the best efforts of industrialized man—Seattle City Light's hydropower project, which lights the Emerald City—have failed to steal the charm from these 684,000 acres of wild lands. In 1988, 93 percent of the complex was designated as the Stephen Mather Wilderness. Unlike most national parks, this one is mostly inaccessible to autos, with Highway 20, the North Cascades Highway, serving as the only transportation link through its core.

sites	162
🏕️🚐	No hookups, RVs to 32 feet
open	Mid-May to mid-October
reservations	None
contact	North Cascades National Park Headquarters, Sedro-Woolley, 360/856-5700

Near the middle of a west-to-east trek on that scenic highway, most of the park's half-million annual visitors will encounter Colonial Creek Campground, the largest and most popular camping spot in the complex. (You can't miss it: The campground actually straddles the highway.) Nestled near a creek mouth on the banks of frigid, aqua-blue Diablo Lake, Colonial Creek is a gorgeous spot with towering firs that provide solace and blank out most noise from the nearby highway. The campground's boat launch provides great small boat/canoe access to Diablo Lake (beware strong winds), not to mention a chance to test your true mettle by plunging into the icy cold waters for 3.5 seconds or until you turn blue, whichever comes first. A large wooden fishing platform was being constructed

Boats awaiting boaters in the icy waters of Diablo Lake.

here during our last visit in the fall of 2002. The sites rate about a medium on the privacy scale; some are wheelchair accessible.

Colonial Creek's natural charms aren't the only reason it's so popular. It's also centrally located, a big plus for hikers and Highway 20 day-trippers. In the campground is the trailhead to the Thunder Creek Trail, one of the longest hiking corridors in the park, with access to numerous side trails that climb steadily to the top or shoulders of rugged North Cascades peaks. Stop at the visitors center near Newhalem (206/386-4495), for more trail information.

Getting there: Colonial Creek is at North Cascades Highway 20 milepost 130, 10 miles east of Newhalem and 4 miles east of the Diablo Lake turnoff.

Other North Cascades Highway /National Park Campgrounds

On the west side of North Cascades Highway 20, Cascade Road leaves the highway at Marblemount and leads to three relatively remote campgrounds. **Cascade Island** (360/902-1000), a Department of Natural Resources camp, has 15 sites (no hookups), no fees, and is open all year. The next two campgrounds are rustic national forest camps, offering few services (vault toilets, but no piped water): **Marble Creek** (8 miles east of North Cascades Highway 20) is open from mid-May to late September, with 23 sites, no hookups, RVs to 31 feet, and no piped water. **Mineral Park** (16 miles east of North Cascades Highway 20), is open from mid-May to mid-September, with 5 primitive sites, no hookups, RVs to 15 feet, and no piped water. The latter is used mainly as a staging area for hikes into the Glacier Peak Wilderness. Note: Both of these campgrounds were free until recently—a status befitting their bare-bones public services. Now, they not only both charge fees, but accept reservations through the Forest Service's National Recreation Reservation Service (877/444-6777 or www.reserveusa.com). For more details, call the Mount Baker Ranger District (360/856-5700).

Eagle-watchers or steelhead anglers who get shut out at Rockport's Howard Miller Steelhead Camp can try the private **Clark's Skagit River Resort** (800/273-2606), which has campsites with hookups, as well as rental cabins. North Cascades National Park visitors, particularly tenters, should check out **Gorge Creek** (360/856-5700), a tiny, peaceful riverfront campground near the town of Diablo. It's a quieter alternative to the more bustling Colonial Creek.

Hikers and boaters are in for a treat on **Ross Lake,** the behemoth body of water behind Ross Dam: a string of 20 national park campgrounds accessible only by boat or on foot. Hikers can begin the trek to these campgrounds by following all or part of the 31.5-mile East Bank Ross Lake Trail, reached by hiking the Panther Creek Trail (the trailhead is near Panther Creek Bridge, near milepost 138 on North Cascades Highway 20) about 3 miles to its junction with the East Bank Ross Lake Trail. A water route is also available. Although the only boat launch on the lake is at Hozomeen Campground, accessible only through British Columbia, and the only way to get a kayak or canoe to the lake is to haul it a couple miles down a steep trail, there is another option. Visitors can rent kicker boats from Ross Lake Resort (206/386-4437), which floats on the lake behind Ross Dam and is itself an adventure to reach, and then go campground hopping. The free campsites, most of which have mooring docks, are beautifully located on bluffs or in old-growth forest near the banks of the lake. They're open summers only. Because they're so hard to reach, sites usually are available. They're primitive, with pit toilets and no piped water. But it's hard to imagine a more peaceful setting anywhere in Washington State. They are **Green Point** (1 mile from Ross Dam via boat; 7 sites); **Cougar Island** (2 miles; 2 sites); **Roland Point** (4 miles; 1 site); **Big Beaver** (4 miles; 7 sites); **McMillan** (5.5 miles; 3 sites); **Spencer's Camp** (6 miles; 2 sites); **May Creek** (6.5 miles; 1 site); **Rainbow Point** (7.5 miles; 3 sites); **Devils Junction** (10.5 miles; 1 site); **Ten Mile Island** (11 miles; 3 sites); **Dry Creek** (11.5 miles; 4 sites); **Ponderosa** (12 miles; 2 sites); **Lodgepole** (12.5 miles; 3 sites); **Lightning Creek Horse Camp** (13 miles; 3 sites); **Lightning Creek Boat Camp** (13.5 miles; 6 sites); **Cat Island** (14.5 miles; 6 sites); **Little Beaver** (17 miles; 6 sites); **Boundary Bay** (17.5 miles; 3 sites); **Silver Creek** (21 miles; 4 sites). At the head of the lake, **Hozomeen** (23 miles; 122 sites) is accessible by auto, but only through British Columbia. Three other boat-in sites are found on nearby Diablo Lake. They are **Hidden Cove** (1 site), **Thunder Point** (3 sites), and **Buster Brown** (3 sites). Call the national park (360/856-5700) for details.

Methow Valley

26 Lone Fir 🌲🌲🌲🌲

Lone Fir, a quiet, pretty, subalpine camp on Early Winters Creek, marks the progression into the dry-side Okanogan National Forest for North Cascades Highway travelers. The campground facilities are basic—pit toilets—and sites are too small for larger road-hog RVs. But it's a pleasant, quiet tent spot in a lovely alpine area, with nicely spaced sites offering peekaboo views of a series of stunning, craggy North Cascades peaks such as the Early Winters Spires. The campground also offers easy access to hiking trails; Lone Fir Trail begins right in the campground and winds along—and over, via four very stylish wood bridges—Early Winters Creek. It's a great family walk. The popular Washington Pass Overlook on Highway 20 is about 6 miles west. Note: Lone Fir is at 3,640 feet, so expect this to be a chilly stopover in the shoulder seasons.

sites	27
🏕️ 🚐	No hookups, RVs to 20 feet
open	June through September
reservations	None
contact	Okanogan National Forest, Methow Valley Visitors Center, 509/996-4000

Getting there: Lone Fir is near milepost 168 on North Cascades Highway 20. It's about 27 miles northwest of Winthrop.

Fat tires and the Old West meld in the town of Winthrop.

㉗ Klipchuck 🌲🌲🌲

Another scenic spot on crystal-clear Early Winters Creek, Klipchuck is the largest campground in the upper Methow Valley, on the downhill (east) side of the North Cascades Highway. It's equally popular with dry-side forest fans and hikers, who can depart from the camp in any of a number of directions for short, medium, or long treks into the Okanogan National Forest. (A nice day-hiking trail follows the creek for 2 miles from the campground.) If you're not a hiker and just want to experience the drier slope of the North Cascades, you'd be hard pressed to find a better spot than this lovely campground nestled in a stand of majestic, sweet-smelling pines. Six of the nicely spaced, semiprivate sites are for tents only, and are nice ones, at that. Trout fishing in the stream can be productive. Keep your eyes peeled for rattlesnakes in this area, however. The campground, which has pit toilets, is at 2,920 feet. It can be downright hot in the summer, but wonderfully bright and crisp in the spring and fall. Note: This is a major departure point for backpackers and horse packers. The Driveway Butte Trailhead is adjacent to the campground.

sites	46
🏕️ 🚐	No hookups, RVs to 34 feet
open	June through September
reservations	None
contact	Okanogan National Forest, Methow Valley Visitors Center, 509/996-4000

Getting there: On North Cascades Highway 20 about 19 miles northwest of Winthrop (near milepost 175), turn north on Forest Road 300 and go 1 mile to the campground.

㉘ Early Winters 🌲🌲🌲

This is as close as you can camp to the, um, bustling downtown core of Mazama. Actually, it's getting closer to "bustle" status all the time, with the upper Methow Valley's increasing popularity as a year-round recreation getaway for hikers, mountain bikers, and cross-country skiers. The drip-by-drip development of Arrowleaf Resort, a cross-country ski/mountain bike/golf mecca at the site of the oft-proposed, ultimately rejected Early Winters ski area, has changed this area slowly, but not in a bad way, we trust. A sip of the old ways can still be enjoyed at Early Winters, an average Forest Service camp at the confluence of the Methow River and Early Winters Creek. Facilities are standard federal-government issue: pit toilets. The campground also is fairly exposed to the sun, making

sites	13
🏕️ 🚐	No hookups, RVs to 24 feet
open	June to early October
reservations	None
contact	Okanogan National Forest, Methow Valley Visitors Center, 509/996-4000

Early Winters, on the dry side of the North Cascades, is a tenter's favorite.

it downright hot and dusty during the dog days of summer. And it's a bit too close to Highway 20 to pretend like you're away from it all. Still, it's cheap, as far as campgrounds go. The location is also quite good—straight across the valley from Goat Wall, smack in the middle of access points to the Methow Community Trail system, near roads leading to some of the area's excellent backcountry hiking and ski trails. It's a nice place to camp in late September, when the skies cool as fall begins early and in earnest, and the kids are all home at school, where they belong. Note that this is where Highway 20 closes on the east side for winter.

Getting there: Early Winters straddles North Cascades Highway 20 milepost 177, just north of the turnoff to the town of Mazama and a stone's throw from Wilson's Ranch.

㉙ Ballard 🌲🌲

Methow Valley campers who really want to get out there (and, after all, isn't that why you came to the Methow in the first place?) can do so in the Lost River/Harts Pass area. Harts Pass Road, which begins near Mazama and turns into Forest Road 5400, leads to four national forest camps on the upper Methow River, all within walking distance of grand trout streams and backcountry trailheads. Ballard is the first, but not the best, unless you like to pitch your tent atop fresh horse cookies (nearby Robinson Creek Trailhead is a major horse-packing jump-off point to places such as Ferguson Lake). But it'll do in a pinch. Sites are fairly primitive: pit toilets, no piped water, and no garbage service. Pack out what you bring in. Plus a little extra.

Getting there: From Mazama, about 14 miles west of Winthrop via North Cascades Highway 20, follow Harts Pass/Lost River Road (County Road 1163) northwest for about 7 miles until the pavement ends and the road becomes Forest Road 5400. Continue about 2 miles to the campground.

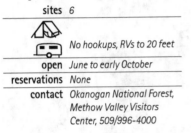

sites	6
	No hookups, RVs to 20 feet
open	June to early October
reservations	None
contact	Okanogan National Forest, Methow Valley Visitors Center, 509/996-4000

30 River Bend 🌲🌲🌲

River Bend, the second of four national forest camps on the upper Methow River via the Harts Pass Road, is another small camp favored by horse packers and hikers, most bound for destinations such as the West Fork Methow Trail (an anglers' favorite) or nearby Driveway Butte (a steep, dusty, 8-mile round-trip hike with sweeping views). It's also primitive, with pit toilets, no piped water, and no garbage service. Be prepared to rough it here.

Getting there: From Mazama, about 15 miles west of Winthrop via North Cascades Highway 20, follow Harts Pass/Lost River Road (County Road 1163) northwest for about 7 miles, where the pavement ends and the road becomes Forest Road 5400. Continue about 2.5 miles to Forest Road 5400-060. Turn west and proceed less than a half mile to the campground on the left. Note: The road is rough and usually not suitable for RVs or trailers past Ballard Campground (see above).

sites	5
	No hookups, RVs to 16 feet
open	June to early October
reservations	None
contact	Okanogan National Forest, Methow Valley Visitors Center, 509/996-4000

31 Harts Pass 🌲🌲🌲🌲

Harts Pass is a thin-air special. Located on the way to the Slate Peak overlook, which at about 7,200 feet is the highest place you can drive to in Washington, this campground is as high (6,198 feet) as any auto-accessible camp we're aware of. OK, so it's almost a tie with Meadows (see below). In any case, bring your warm

Pack horses are frequent visitors to the upper Methow drainage.

sites	*5 walk-in*
open	*Mid-July to late September*
reservations	*None*
contact	*Okanogan National Forest, Methow Valley Visitors Center, 509/996-4000*

jammies, even in the summertime. The campground sits in wild, beautiful alpine country, just on the cusp of the remote 500,000-acre Pasayten Wilderness in the northern Okanogan National Forest. The sites are a short walk from the parking area. The Pacific Crest Trail passes nearby, making this a popular staging area for hikers and backpackers. Note: Beware the horse flies, particularly in early summer!

Getting there: From Mazama, about 15 miles west of Winthrop via North Cascades Highway 20, follow Harts Pass/Lost River Road (County Road 1163) northwest for about 7 miles until the pavement ends and the road becomes Forest Road 5400. Continue just under 13 miles to the campground. Note: The road is rough and not suitable for RVs or trailers past Ballard Campground (see above).

㉜ Meadows ▲▲▲

The highest of the high Methow Valley camps, Meadows is really out there; the oft-treacherous road access makes it a site that's used as often by starters, enders, or through-hikers on the Pacific Crest Trail as car campers. But it's a magnificent base camp for roaming the true majestic heart of the North Cascades. The nice thing about hiking from the Meadows/Harts Pass area is that you start out high, so getting up above tree line is rarely a problem. The same warnings for other upper Methow campgrounds apply here: pit toilets, no piped water, no garbage service. Lots of biting flies. But for most of us, the thin air here often seems to mask the hardships. The area is especially spectacular in early summer, when wildflowers burst onto the scene.

sites	15
open	Mid-July to late September
reservations	None
contact	Okanogan National Forest, Methow Valley Visitors Center, 509/996-4000

Getting there: From Mazama, about 15 miles west of Winthrop via North Cascades Highway 20, follow Harts Pass/Lost River Road (County Road 1163) northwest for about 7 miles until the pavement ends and the road becomes Forest Road 5400. Continue about 13 miles to Forest Road 500. Turn south and continue about a mile to the campground. Note: This road is rough and not suitable for RVs or trailers past Ballard Campground (see above).

㉝ Pearrygin Lake State Park ▲▲▲▲

Pearrygin Lake, an RVers favorite, is the primary camping venue near Winthrop, the mid–Methow Valley Western-kitsch town that began its "civilized" life as a trading outpost for trappers and miners, then reverted largely into a mecca for polar-fleece–clad hikers, skiers, mountain bikers, anglers, and campers. The campground earns top honors not only because of its relatively high number of sites and amenities, but for a pleasant atmosphere. The Methow Valley's summertime weather—dry, but not quite as hot as lower central Washington climes—makes this 580-acre lakefront park a magnet for anglers (the lake produces hefty trout), boaters, and sun worshippers.

The campground, not surprisingly, is full most of the summer. Reservations are a good idea. Sites on the grass lawn are a bit uncomfortably close together,

sites	83
	30 full hookups, RVs to 60 feet
open	April through October
reservations	Up to 9 months in advance; 888/226-7688 or www.parks.wa.gov
contact	Washington State Parks, 360/902-8844; Pearrygin Lake State Park, 509/996-2370

particularly for tenters' tastes. But the facilities make up for that. Like most state parks (but unlike other Methow camping areas), Pearrygin Lake has piped water, flush toilets, coin-op showers, and an RV dump station. A group camp is suitable for 48 campers. Kids will love the swimming beach (with bathhouse), sprawling lawns, and play facilities. Adults will love the shade of the old willows, boat launch, and dock. The great picnic sites will suit the whole family. Wildflowers can be grand if you time your springtime trip right. Best of all, it's an easy mountain-bike ride to downtown Winthrop for a bigger-than-your-head burrito at the Duck Brand Inn.

Historical note: Most of the park is on acreage originally cleared and settled by Winthrop-area homesteaders in the 1890s, many of whom left after the town's mining "boom" fizzled by 1900.

Getting there: From Winthrop, follow Bluff Street (it becomes East Chewuch Road) about 2 miles north to County Road 1631. Turn right (east) and proceed less than 2 miles to the park entrance, on the right.

Pearrygin Lake State Park is a green oasis in the rough, rocky Winthrop area.

㉞ Buck Lake 🌲🌲🌲

A small camp on a scenic lake northwest of Winthrop, Buck Lake is a favorite of mountain bikers, who kick up much summertime dust on county and Forest Service roads in this area. Like its Forest Service cousins in the Chewuch River drainage north of Winthrop, facilities at Buck Lake are primitive: pit toilets and no piped water, showers, or garbage service. But it's definitely off the beaten path, and fishing can be productive in Buck Lake. The elevation is 3,250 feet.

sites	9
	No hookups, RVs to 16 feet
open	June through September
reservations	None
contact	Okanogan National Forest, Methow Valley Visitors Center, 509/996-4000

Getting there: From North Cascades Highway 20 just west of Winthrop, follow County Road 1231 (it becomes West Chewuch Road) about 6.5 miles, until it becomes Forest Road 51. Proceed about 2.5 miles north to Forest Road 5130 (Eightmile Creek Road). Turn left (northwest) and drive about a half mile to Forest Road 100. Turn left and go about 2 miles to the campground.

㉟ Flat 🌲🌲🌲

Flat, in a multiway tie for the shortest and possibly dumbest campground name in the state, is the first, and most heavily used, of four Forest Service sites along Eightmile Creek, a gorgeous, clear tributary of the Chewuch River. Summer trout fishing in the creek can be very productive, and even if it's not, the cool waters feel ooh, so good on those gritty, sunburned, and Teva-scraped feet. Flat is small and primitive, with tidy sites and few amenities (pit toilets, no piped water, showers, or garbage service). But it's in a lovely, pine-forested valley, and first-time visitors lulled to sleep by the creek often become repeat customers. The campground is at 2,855 feet.

sites	12
	No hookups, RVs to 18 feet
open	June through September
reservations	None
contact	Okanogan National Forest, Methow Valley Visitors Center, 509/996-4000

Getting there: From North Cascades Highway 20 just west of Winthrop, follow County Road 1213 (it becomes West Chewuch Road) about 6.5 miles, until it becomes Forest Road 51. Drive about 2.5 miles north to Forest Road 5130 (Eightmile Creek Road). Turn left (northwest) on it and drive 2 miles to the campground.

36 Nice 🌲🌲🌲

Well, gee. It sort of is. Nice pretty much lives up to its name. It's a cozy little spot on Eightmile Creek, offering the same angling opportunities as other camps in this river drainage. But that's about it. The campground is really not much more than a roadside pullout, with three sites that seem to get their fair share of use in spite of the primitive amenities (pit toilets, no piped water, showers, or garbage service). The campground sits at 2,728 feet, and is just up the road from Flat (see above). Although one site is officially open to RVs, we don't think they make rigs small enough to fit in here anymore. And there's no turnaround space for trailers. Note: Even higher on Eightmile Creek (farther than most people are willing to go for the resulting payoff) are two additional Forest Service camps, Ruffed Grouse (4 sites) and Honeymoon (6 sites). Both are primitive, with no piped water or other services. Call the contact number above for information.

sites	3
🏕️ 🚐	No hookups; 1 site, maximum length 12 feet
open	June through September
reservations	None
contact	Okanogan National Forest, Methow Valley Visitors Center, 509/996-4000

Getting there: From North Cascades Highway 20 just west of Winthrop, follow County Road 1231 (it becomes West Chewuch Road) about 6.5 miles, until it becomes Forest Road 51. Proceed 2.5 miles north to Forest Road 5130 (Eightmile Creek Road) and turn left (northwest). Drive 4 miles to the campground.

37 Falls Creek 🌲🌲🌲🌲

It's the water. Dozens of beautiful, crystal-clear streams drain the rocky reaches of wilderness around and above the Methow Valley, often breaking into raucous white water or plunging over rock formations. It's one of the most alluring natural features of this valley, which has so many rocky peaks, stone faces, pine trees, and flowing streams, it seems more like high, dry Montana or Colorado country than Washington. This silvery grace is on fine display at Falls Creek Campground, near the confluence of Falls Creek and the Chewuch River, a major northern tributary of the Methow. The river and stream are gorgeous in their own right, but Chewuch Falls, a short walk from the campground on a barrier-free trail, is worth the trip alone. Falls Creek is small and somewhat remote but

sites	7
🏕️ 🚐	No hookups, RVs to 18 feet
open	June through September
reservations	None
contact	Okanogan National Forest, Methow Valley Visitors Center, 509/996-4000

Mountain bikers take over where skiers leave off as summer sweeps the Methow.

charming. Note: This campground, at 2,100 feet, is the closest to Winthrop (and most developed) of three Forest Service camps along the Chewuch. Chewuch (4 tent-only sites) and Camp Four (5 tent-only sites) are both higher in the Chewuch Valley and serve primarily as staging areas and horse camps for hikers headed into the Pasayten Wilderness. Call the contact number above for information.

Getting there: From North Cascades Highway 20 just west of Winthrop, follow County Road 1213 (it becomes West Chewuch Road) about 6.5 miles, until it becomes Forest Road 51. Drive just over 5 miles north to the campground, on the right.

Other Methow Valley Campgrounds

Peace, solitude, white water, and pit toilets abound in the Twisp River drainage, midway down the Methow Valley west of the town of Twisp. A series of small, rustic Forest Service camps are found here, all with pit toilets, but no piped water, showers, garbage, or other services. They're popular with anglers, hikers, horse packers, and backpackers headed up and over Sawtooth Ridge, through the

Sawtooth Wilderness, to the Stehekin area of Lake Chelan in North Cascades National Park. Most of these rustic camps are open to tents or RVs to 22 feet from May to September and are accessed from the Twisp area via Twisp River Road and Forest Road 44. From east to west up the valley, they are **War Creek** (14.5 miles east of North Cascades Highway 20; 10 sites); **Mystery** (19.5 miles; 4 sites); **Poplar Flat** (20.5 miles; 16 sites); **South Creek** (22 miles; 4 sites); and **Road's End** (24.5 miles; 4 sites).

Other remote Twisp-area campgrounds are **Black Pine Lake** (via Twisp River Road and Forest Road 43; 23 sites); **Foggy Dew** (via Highway 153, Gold Creek Road, and Forest Road 4340; 13 sites); and **Twisp River Horse Camp** (via Twisp River Road 9114 and Forest Roads 44 and 4430; 12 sites). East of Twisp, just off Highway 20, are **Loup Loup** (25 sites) and **JR** (6 sites). All of these campgrounds charge a nominal fee. For more information, call the Methow Valley Visitors Center (509/996-4000). Northeast of Winthrop and Twist, a number of Forest Service campgrounds also are maintained by the Okanogan National Forest's Tonasket Ranger District. For a list, see the Okanogan Valley and Highlands section in the Northeast Washington chapter.

Central Cascades

Never underestimate the importance of a very wide back door. That might be the best moral to the story of camping in Washington's Central Cascades, a true rear exit for Puget Sound families seeking relief from summertime blazing heat—not to mention the thousands of meandering Nebraskan tourists clogging the aisles at Pike Place Market.

Our longstanding indifference to the hills out back illustrates an odd truth about Washington summer getaways: When it comes to camping out, many of us think first of Puget Sound or the ocean coast, spread right out in our front yards. Intuitively, we know what's out back. Many miles of rock, alpine lakes, dirt roads, and indefatigable mosquitoes. We know it's big, wild, high, pleasant, and even—gasp—occasionally uncrowded. But it's also foreign and a bit scary. So many of us insist on heading the other direction or, worse, repeatedly drive right through the Central Cascades without stopping to pitch a tent and say hello. Even campers who make annual pilgrimages to the hot, dry, lake-studded lands of eastern Washington often err by treating this region as a land to be passed through in the middle of a long drive to someplace else.

Trust us: Those who take heed of the brown "camping" signs along Interstate 90 and US 2 often will be richly rewarded.

The main east-west highways in Washington are the top and bottom layers of a sandwich of the gods, of sorts. The meaty filling, thousands of square miles of wild mountain lands, offers overnight experiences ranging from truly gnarly, hike-in wilderness to comfy splendor on the shores of manmade reservoirs.

Make no mistake: The Central Cascades are hardly bursting at the seams with good campgrounds, or even convenient ones. For an area so vast and so wild, in fact, it's disturbing that the intrepid traveler is limited to what's there. Blame the topography: When it comes to camping, these mountains are a victim of their own wild nature. The Alpine Lakes Wilderness spreads across a huge chunk of this land, leaving it—thank heavens—off-limits to vehicle traffic, camping, and just about everything else except silent walking. And portions of the region under no such restrictions throw up their own, natural barriers to large-scale Winnebago invasion. Winter weather is wicked here, with many feet of rain and tons of snow closing the region to all but the most determined small mammals in the off-season. As any Forest Service planner will tell you, washouts, forest fires, avalanches, and mud slides make it tough to keep existing Central Cascades campgrounds on the map from one season to the next.

Still, some of our favorite, quick escapes from Seattle are found in these hills. The close-to-home quiet pine forest of Lake Kachess, streamside campgrounds on the upper Cle Elum River, and the always-convenient, pull-in ease of Lake Easton State Park, all in the heart of the hills on Interstate 90. The diverse recreation lures of campgrounds on, around, and above Lake Wenatchee, off US 2. The quiet majesty and crystal-clear waters of the Icicle River drainage near Leavenworth. And those easy-to-find places near the major highways are just for starters. Determined campers who can live without a lot of amenities will find a wealth of gorgeous, if rough-around-the-edges, Forest Service camps on high, gravel roads throughout this area.

Contrary to popular myth, the Central Cascades aren't all clear-cut wastelands. And they're too close to home to ignore. This summer, resist the call of the salt water and spend some time in your high-altitude backyard. Find a favorite corner. Call it your own.

① Wallace Falls State Park	⑯ Rock Island
② Troublesome Creek	⑰ Blackpine Creek Horse Camp
③ San Juan	⑱ Tinkham
④ Money Creek	⑲ Denny Creek
⑤ Beckler River	⑳ Crystal Springs
⑥ Nason Creek	㉑ Kachess
⑦ Lake Wenatchee State Park	㉒ Lake Easton State Park
⑧ Glacier View	㉓ Wish Poosh
⑨ Goose Creek	㉔ Cle Elum River
⑩ Tumwater	㉕ Red Mountain
⑪ Eightmile	㉖ Salmon La Sac
⑫ Bridge Creek	㉗ Owhi
⑬ Johnny Creek	㉘ Beverly
⑭ Ida Creek	㉙ Mineral Springs
⑮ Chatter Creek	㉚ Swauk

Central Cascades Map

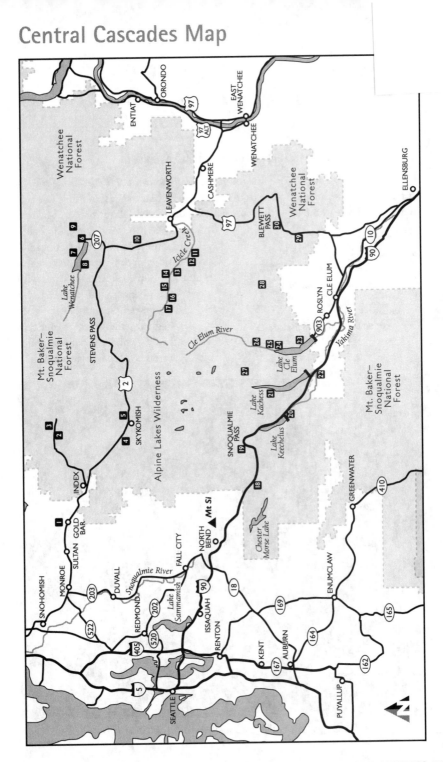

Stevens Pass Corridor and Lake Wenatchee

❶ Wallace Falls State Park 🌲🌲⛺

Let's face it: Very few people come to Wallace Falls to camp. It's the 7-mile round-trip hike to the scenic falls—one of the most spectacular in Washington's Cascade Range—that draws most visitors to this state park. The half-dozen walk-in tent spaces are easy to miss, scattered as they are amidst the trees near the trailhead. A short stroll from the car, the sites are not unpleasant and are quite private, with gravel floors, beneath tall alders and a few firs. A newer picnic shelter could provide a great emergency bivouac in bad weather. The hike is a definite don't-miss. The trail is steep in places, but well

sites	6
open	All year; closed for camping Sundays, Mondays and Tuesdays in winter
reservations	None
contact	Washington State Parks, 360/902-8844; Wallace Falls State Park, 360/793-0420

A modern shelter is a great weather escape at Wallace Falls State Park.

traveled. The falls, a 265-foot cascade of the South Fork Wallace River, can be viewed from below, or above, where a sweeping view of the Skykomish Valley is added incentive. Unlike most state parks, this one has no coin-op showers. Local trivia: The name Wallace is a misnomer. It was applied to the turn-of-the-century townsite of Wallace (now Startup) and is believed to be derived from the name of a native couple, Joe and Sarah Kwayaylsh.

Getting there: From Interstate 5 at Everett, follow US 2 east 28 miles to Gold Bar. Turn left at the "Wallace Falls" sign at First Street, proceed a half mile to May Creek Road, turn right, and follow signs an additional 1.5 miles to the park entrance, on the left.

❷ Troublesome Creek 🌲🌲🌲

Campers headed east on US 2 can get far, far away from the highway noise—and just about everything else—at either of two Forest Service camps high on the North Fork Skykomish. Troublesome Creek is the larger and better developed (the other is San Juan, see below), and makes a shady resting spot for road-weary travelers who don't mind a jaunt up a sometimes bone-jarring Forest Service road. Six of the sites are walk-ins for tenters; the rest are all back-ins that will accommodate smaller RVs. Sites 3, 4, and 24 are wheelchair accessible. About half the sites front a large gravel bar on Troublesome Creek or the river, where fishing is always fun, though not always productive. A short nature trail begins in the campground and leads into the forest across the road, and a number of major trailheads are a short drive away. The campground has pit toilets.

sites	30
🏕️🚐	No hookups, RVs to 24 feet
open	Mid-May to mid-September
reservations	Up to 240 days in advance; National Recreation Reservation Service, 877/444-6777 or www.reserveusa.com
contact	Mount Baker–Snoqualmie National Forest, Skykomish Ranger District, 360/677-2414

Getting there: From US 2 at Index, turn north on Index-Galena Road and drive 12 miles northeast to the campground, on the right.

❸ San Juan 🌲🌲🌲

A small site on the North Fork Skykomish northeast of Index, San Juan is a viable, albeit primitive, alternative to the more popular Troublesome Creek (see above), which, due to its reservation status, is more likely to be full in the summer. Fishing and hiking in the area are the primary draws. The campground, set amidst old-growth Douglas fir and western red cedars, has pit toilets, but no piped water

sites	9
🏕 🚐	No hookups, RVs to 21 feet
open	Mid-May to mid-September
reservations	None
contact	Mount Baker–Snoqualmie National Forest, Skykomish Ranger District, 360/677-2414

or showers. Most sites are on the river. Note to previous visitors: San Juan, for years a free campground, is free no more.

Getting there: From US 2 at Index, turn north on Index-Galena Road and drive 14 miles northeast to the campground, on the right.

④ Money Creek 🌲🌲🌲🌲

PE #7, 10, 11, 12°

Railroads come to life at Money Creek. Too much to life for the liking of some, particularly those who don't appreciate being wakened from a sound sleep by a lumbering freight train. The Burlington Northern line runs a stone's throw from this pretty campground. If evidence of railroads, present tense, makes you crazy, a grand place to examine railroads, past tense, is a short drive away—the Iron Goat Railroad Trail, an increasingly popular (and easy) hike along a former Stevens Pass railroad corridor. Money Creek, in fact, is as good a place as any to make a base camp for exploring the entire upper Skykomish drainage along US 2. The camp sits at the confluence of Money Creek and the Skykomish, in a

sites	24
🏕 🚐	No hookups, RVs to 21 feet
open	Memorial Day to Labor Day
reservations	Up to 240 days in advance; National Recreation Reservation Service, 877/444-6777 or www.reserveusa.com
contact	Mount Baker–Snoqualmie National Forest, Skykomish Ranger District, 360/677-2414

rare stand of old-growth firs that are drop-dead beautiful any time of the year. As an added bonus, both the east and west loops of the campground were renovated in 2002, with new pavement, pit toilets, tent pads, and other facilities. It's vastly improved from its former self. Strongly consider making a reservation before heading out here on weekends. The camp's location right on US 2 makes it too visible to be ignored or missed by camping travelers. (Try for site 6 or 7, riverfront in the west loop.)

Getting there: The campground is 4 miles west of Skykomish on US 2, just before milepost 46.

⑤ Beckler River 🌲🌲🌲🌲

It's a bit rough around the edges, probably due to the occasional riotous flooding of the Beckler River, upon which (and alas, in which, during the winter) many of the campsites sit. But something about Beckler River keeps beckoning us back. Maybe it's the rushing white water, right at your feet as you sit at a campfire and soak up the good life. Or the fact that it's just far enough from civilization to feel wild, but close enough to run into Skykomish for fresh—well, reasonably fresh—marshmallows. It's a pretty site in second-growth forest, with typical Forest Service amenities: piped water, pit toilets, and picnic tables built to last. This is a good place to bring the mountain bikes; lots of seldom-traveled Forest Service roads stretch out from here. Note: 7 of the sites are for tents only; sites 4 and 12 are wheelchair accessible. The even numbered sites 4–14—all pull-throughs—are the most highly sought riverfront locales. Reservations generally are a good idea.

sites	27
	No hookups, RVs to 21 feet
open	Memorial Day to Labor Day
reservations	Up to 240 days in advance; National Recreation Reservation Service, 877/444-6777 or www.reserveusa.com
contact	Mount Baker–Snoqualmie National Forest, Skykomish Ranger District, 360/677-2414

Getting there: From US 2 just east of Skykomish, turn north on Forest Road 65 and drive 1.5 miles to the campground.

The Beckler River, a Skykomish tributary north of US 2.

⑥ Nason Creek 🌲🌲🌲

By all rights, Nason Creek should have an inferiority complex. As Forest Service campgrounds go, this one is large and well equipped. But it's also right on the access road to Lake Wenatchee State Park, and many campers err in cruising right past it in the rush to land a site at the more popular lakeside campground. Nason Creek can't compete with the state park's reputation. But it's almost as close to the lake, and in many respects offers a nicer camping experience to the cramped, heavily shaded, somewhat claustrophobic sites at the state park. Many of the sites in this campground (it's bigger than it looks; note the three separate entrances off the access road) are creekfront and very spacious, making them even more popular among RVers than the oft booked-up state park. But don't bet on finding open spaces here in the dead of summer, either. For good reason, the campground is extremely popular with boaters, anglers, and other Lake Wenatchee vacationers. Unlike many Forest Service camps, this one has flush toilets and piped water. No showers, but you'll find them a short walk down the road at the state park.

sites	73
🏕️ 🚐	No hookups, RVs to any length
open	May through October
reservations	None
contact	Wenatchee National Forest, Lake Wenatchee Ranger District, 509/763-3103

Getting there: From US 2 at Cole's Corner (about 19 miles northeast of Leavenworth), turn north on Highway 207, following signs for Lake Wenatchee State Park. At about 3.5 miles, turn left on Cedar Brae Road and look for campground entrances on both sides of the street, and a third across the creek on the right.

A shady spot in the high, dry forest of Nason Creek.

⑦ Lake Wenatchee State Park 🌲🌲🌲🌲

Long before man invented the Winnebago—or the collapsible tent, for that matter—native campers flocked to the shores of Lake Wenatchee to fish, relax, and meet the neighbors from the west side. That tradition continues today in the camping community at Lake Wenatchee State Park, a large gathering spot appropriately bringing together the best of eastern and western Washington. One of the few Washington State Parks in a true alpine-lake setting, Lake Wenatchee is a favorite of boaters, anglers, hikers, cyclists, and, in the winter, cross-country skiers and snowmobilers.

sites	197
🏕️ 🚐	No hookups, RVs to 60 feet
open	All year
reservations	Up to 9 months in advance; 888/226-7688 or www.parks.wa.gov
contact	Washington State Parks, 360/902-8844; Lake Wenatchee State Park, 509/763-3101

Extending across both sides of the Wenatchee River's outlet from the lake, the park is actually two separate campgrounds: The south area comprises sites 1–100, tightly spaced, smallish sites in dense forest. Some people prefer this area because it's a close walk to a horse-rental facility and the park's sprawling beach swimming area. But RVers or privacy lovers will likely be more happy in the north area (entrance: 1 mile down the road beyond the south entrance at Cedar Brae Road), where sites 101–197 are more well spaced, many of them pull-throughs. Both camping areas have coin-op showers, flush toilets, and piped water. Most are a short walk from the Lake Wenatchee shoreline. In addition to the nearly 200 campsites, you'll find 10 group campsites for up to 80 people, a boat launch, 60 picnic sites with three covered shelters, two RV dump stations, an amphitheater, 3.5 miles of trails for horses, and 7.5 miles of trails for humans. Boat and horse rentals also are available.

Lake Wenatchee, elevation 1,900 feet, is a great base camp for exploration of the east side of the Glacier Peak Wilderness. Forest Service roads follow the Little Wenatchee, White, and Chiwawa Rivers—all Wenatchee tributaries—and climb high into the beautiful east-slope Cascades and some of the most treasured alpine country in the state.

The park stays open all winter, when staff members groom 30 kilometers of trails for cross-country skiing. Campground loops are closed then, but one heated restroom is open, and camping is allowed in the lakeside day-use area for those with Sno-Park permits.

Getting there: From Cole's Corner on US 2 (about 19 miles northeast of Leavenworth), turn east on Highway 207 and follow signs 3.5 miles to the south campground and day-use entrance, or 4.5 miles to the north entrance.

⑧ Glacier View 🌲🌲🌲

It can't match the facilities of nearby Lake Wenatchee State Park or the easy access of Nason Creek, but Glacier View, a small, lovely Forest Service camp, has location on its side. Tucked into the southwest shore of the lake, this is primarily a tenter's haven (very small RVs or campers can get in here, but turnaround space is very limited). Most of the sites are walk-ins on the lakeshore, making this a very popular boater/angler camp during the summer (a gravel boat launch is on the premises). Some of our favorite sites are the walk-ins (numbered 1a, 1b, 1c, and 1d) on the west (left) side as you enter: Privacy is somewhat limited, but the pay-offs—fantastic lake and mountain views, and, in some cases, a gurgling stream waterfall right in your site—are well worth it. The campground has piped water and pit toilets, most of them upgraded in the summer of 2002. The trailhead to popular Hidden Lake is located a short distance shy of the campground.

sites	20
🏕️ 🚐	No hookups, RVs to 16 feet
open	May through September
reservations	None
contact	Wenatchee National Forest, Lake Wenatchee Ranger District, 509/763-3103

Getting there: From Cole's Corner on US 2 (about 19 miles northeast of Leavenworth), turn north on Highway 207 and proceed 3.5 miles to Cedar Brae Road. Turn left, drive a half mile, veer left at the Lake Wenatchee State Park entrance, and continue about 5 curvy miles to the campground, which is about 1.5 miles beyond the end of the pavement.

Swimmers can dip in the cold, clear waters of Lake Wenatchee.

⑨ Goose Creek 🌲🌲

Goose Creek, a typical Forest Service campground in typical east-slope Cascades forest, is a decent alternative to Lake Wenatchee State Park, which often is over-crowded. But it's not a great destination on its own. Noisy ORVs bound for roads in the Entiat drainage often make this portion of the Wenatchee National Forest noisier than most non-ORV campers would prefer. The elevation is 2,900 feet, and the campground has pit toilets and piped water.

sites	29
🏕️ 🚐	No hookups, RVs to 30 feet
open	May to mid-October
reservations	None
contact	Wenatchee National Forest, Lake Wenatchee Ranger District, 509/763-3103

Getting there: From Highway 207 near Lake Wenatchee State Park, follow Forest Road 62 northeast for 4.5 miles, around Fish Lake, to Forest Road 6100. Turn right and drive 1 mile southeast to the campground.

Other Stevens Pass Corridor/Lake Wenatchee Campgrounds

A popular westside Stevens Pass group campground is Mount Baker–Snoqualmie National Forest's **Miller River** (south of Skykomish via Old Cascade Highway and Forest Road 6410; Skykomish Ranger District, 360/677-2414), with 17 back-in tent/RV sites for up to 100 campers. It's open summers only. Lake Wenatchee–area campers seeking a more remote experience can seek out three small, primitive (pit toilets, no piped water) Forest Service camps in the shadow of Glacier Peak on the Little Wenatchee River, northwest of the lake. The tent camp-grounds, all on Forest Road 6500 (off Lake Wenatchee's North Shore Drive) are **Soda Springs** (5 sites), **Lake Creek** (8 sites), and **Little Wenatchee Ford** (3 sites). The latter is the staging area for many Glacier Peak Wilderness expeditions, such as the pop-ular Cady Creek/Little Wenatchee backpacking loop. All three campgrounds are open summers only and are free. Call the Wenatchee National Forest, Lake Wenatchee Ranger District (509/763-3103).

One river valley to the north of the Little Wenatchee lies the White River, another major Glacier Peak drainage. It's the site of three more small, primitive (pit toilets, no piped water) Forest Service campgrounds on Forest Road 6400 (White River Road). The first, **Napeequa Crossing** (5 sites) is close to the popular Twin Lakes Trailhead, with trails into the Glacier Peak Wilderness. The second, **Grasshopper Meadows** (5 sites) is only about a mile from the third, **White River Falls** (5 sites), which is set near the impressive falls of the same name. All three camps are free and open summers only. Call the Wenatchee National Forest, Lake Wenatchee Ranger Dis-trict (509/763-3103).

A similar string of campgrounds is found on the remote Chiwawa River Road (Forest Road 6200), northwest of Lake Wenatchee, along the eastern border of the spectacular Alpine Lakes Wilderness. From lower river to upper, they are: **Alder Creek Horse Camp** (24-horse capacity); **Grouse Creek Group Camp** (reservation-only); **Finner Creek** (3 sites); **Riverbend** (6 sites); **Rock Creek** (4 sites); **Chiwawa Horse Camp** (21 sites); **Schaefer Creek** (10 sites); **Atkinson Flats** (7 sites); **19 Mile** (4 sites); **Alpine Meadows** (4 sites); and **Phelps Creek** (7 sites) and **Phelps Creek Equestrian** (6 sites), both near Trinity. All are primitive, with pit toilets and no piped water. Most charge no camping fee, but require a Northwest Forest Pass trailhead parking permit. Contact the Wenatchee National Forest, Lake Wenatchee Ranger District (509/763-3103).

Four other small, free, primitive Forest Service camps are found in the upper Wenatchee drainage: **Theseus Creek** (Forest Road 6701; 3 sites); **Meadow Creek** (Forest Road 6300; 4 sites); **Deep Creek** (Forest Road 6100; 3 sites); and **Deer Camp** (Forest Road 6101; 3 sites). Call the Wenatchee National Forest, Lake Wenatchee Ranger District (509/763-3103).

Leavenworth and Icicle Canyon

⑩ Tumwater 🌲🌲🌲

Tumwater Canyon is a stunner, period. Motorists plunging down through the canyon, on the upper Wenatchee River along US 2, are treated to a jutting rock and swirling white-water spectacle as grand as any along a major highway in the United States. This gorgeous slice into the center of the Central Cascades surely was the main reason this route was designated a National Scenic Byway. In the upper reaches of this shady, cold-water bit of heaven is Tumwater, a large Forest Service campground. It's not exactly as spectacular as the surrounding scenery, but it'll do as a decent overnight spot for weary US 2 travelers and hikers bound for the gorgeous Alpine Lakes Wilderness highlands above this river and in the Icicle Creek drainage. (The Hatchery Creek and Chiwaukum Creek Trailheads both are nearby, leading into areas burned in the massive Hatchery Creek wildfire of 1994.) The campground is fairly average, with private, shrub-walled sites OK

Ghostly trees stand as reminders of a massive 1994 wildfire in the Icicle Canyon.

sites	84
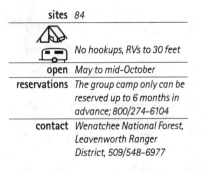	No hookups, RVs to 30 feet
open	May to mid-October
reservations	The group camp only can be reserved up to 6 months in advance; 800/274-6104
contact	Wenatchee National Forest, Leavenworth Ranger District, 509/548-6977

for tents and still large enough to accommodate medium-sized RVs. A group camp is available for up to 84 campers. Bonus: Horseshoe pit! Site 41 is a group site for up to five vehicles. Note: Bring that fleece sweater along. It's usually shady and quite cool in the shoulder seasons here at 2,050 feet.

Getting there: Tumwater is 10 miles northwest of Leavenworth on US 2.

12, 14, 15, 20, 23, 24, 26   7,8
62, 35, 37, 39, 40, 34, 5, 6 Double

⓫ Eightmile 🌲🌲🌲

The Icicle Canyon, one of the Central Cascades' loveliest collisions of high, ominous mountains and low, peaceful streams, is graced by seven Forest Service campgrounds, each and every one popular with the hordes of hikers, horse

sites	45
	No hookups, RVs to 21 feet
open	Mid-April to late October
reservations	The group camp only can be reserved up to 6 months in advance; 800/274-6104
contact	Wenatchee National Forest, Leavenworth Ranger District, 509/548-6977

packers, backpackers, rock climbers, wildlife watchers, and others who flock here each summer. With more than 8,000 feet separating the floor from the highest peak, the canyon is one of the deepest in Washington. Bordered on the north by Icicle Ridge and on the south by the Stuart Range, the Icicle drains much of the Alpine Lakes Wilderness, a truly Alps-like highland heaven. The first campground encountered is Eightmile, which fronts on Icicle and Eightmile Creeks. It has piped water and pit toilets, and is tough to get into during much of the summer. Trailheads to Stuart/Colchuck and Eightmile Lakes, both popular backpacking destinations, are nearby. Several sites are double-sized, family sites. The elevation is 1,800 feet.

Getting there: From US 2 at the west end of Leavenworth, drive about 7 miles southwest on Icicle Road (County Road 76)—the campground is named for Eightmile Road, which is found about a mile beyond.

⓬ Bridge Creek 🌲🌲🌲

A tiny camp about a mile up the road from Eightmile Creek (see above), Bridge Creek is the domain of tenters only—a welcome relief, if you're a tenter. The campground, with all dirt roads and camping sites, can be dusty and hot in the summer, but all sites are peaceful places on the banks of Icicle Creek. Facilities are

sites	6

🏕️

open	Mid-April through October
reservations	The group camp only can be reserved up to 6 months in advance; 800/274-6104
contact	Wenatchee National Forest, Leavenworth Ranger District, 509/548-6977

primitive, with hand-pumped water and pit toilets. The campground also has one group site. The elevation is 1,900 feet.

Getting there: From US 2 at the west end of Leavenworth, drive 9.4 miles southwest on Icicle Road (County Road 76).

Lower
15, 14, 9, 3ᶜ, 2ᶜ
upper:
18, 19ᵇ, 20ᵇ, 22ᵈ, 46, 49, 50, 53, 35ᵈ

⑬ Johnny Creek 🌲🌲🌲🌲

This is the biggest, most diverse, and in many ways nicest campground in the Icicle Creek drainage, centrally located and always popular. (Those whose rigs can't stomach much washboarding might also note that this is the last

sites	65

🏕️ 🚐

	No hookups, RVs to 30 feet
open	May through October
reservations	None
contact	Wenatchee National Forest, Leavenworth Ranger District, 509/548-6977

campground on this road before the pavement ends.) The camp, with sites along both Johnny and Icicle Creeks, is set in pine forest and has hand-pumped water and pit toilets. Sites are split into upper and lower loops, and eight sites are walk-in, tent-only sites that afford nice privacy to the fabric-walled crowd. Some

sites have nifty stone fireplaces with cooking surfaces and chimneys. Several sites are double-sized, family sites. Those in the upper loop, away from the river, have

One of many waiting campsites along the Icicle River.

views of the upper Icicle Valley. In spite of the campground's size, finding a site here on summer weekends can be tough. Be prepared to be flexible, and find some friends to sit around your campfire and lament the fact you didn't call far enough in advance (about a year) to get an overnight backcountry permit for the nearby Enchantment Lakes. The elevation is 2,300 feet. Note that sites in the lower loop are a buck more than those across the road, in the upper.

Getting there: From US 2 at the west end of Leavenworth, drive 12.4 miles southwest on Icicle Road (County Road 76).

⑭ Ida Creek 🌲🌲🌲

sites	10
🏕️🚐	No hookups, RVs to 21 feet
open	May through October
reservations	None
contact	Wenatchee National Forest, Leavenworth Ranger District, 509/548-6977

This is your next stop if Johnny Creek (see above) is full. It has similar amenities (hand-pumped water and pit toilets) but it's quieter for tenters, and half the spaces can accept a very small RV or trailer. A wealth of good day-hiking trails are within 2 miles of the campground. The elevation is 2,800 feet.

Getting there: From US 2 at the west end of Leavenworth, drive 14.2 miles southwest on Icicle Road (County Road 76).

⑮ Chatter Creek 🌲🌲🌲

If you're looking for one campground to put you smack dab in the midst of everything Icicle Canyon has to offer, this is it. Chatter Creek's sites are small, making it best for tenters. And they come here in droves, using the camp as a bivouac spot for backpack trips on the Chatter Creek, Icicle Gorge, Jack Creek, and Trout Creek Trails. The campground has pit toilets and hand-pumped water. The campground also has one large group site. The elevation is 2,800 feet.

sites	12
🏕️🚐	No hookups, RVs to 21 feet
open	May through October
reservations	The group camp only can be reserved up to 6 months in advance; 800/274-6104
contact	Wenatchee National Forest, Leavenworth Ranger District, 509/548-6977

Getting there: From US 2 at the west end of Leavenworth, drive 16.1 miles southwest on Icicle Road (County Road 76).

The Icicle River, one of Washington's grandest mountain streams.

⑯ Rock Island 🌲🌲🌲

sites	*22*
🏕️ 🚐	*No hookups, RVs to 21 feet*
open	*May through October*
reservations	*None*
contact	*Wenatchee National Forest, Leavenworth Ranger District, 509/548-6977*

A pretty spot in the upper Icicle Canyon, Rock Island offers 12 tent sites and 10 tent/RV slots. The campground has hand-pumped water and pit toilets. A wealth of good day hikes and backpack routes are nearby. The elevation is 2,900 feet.

Getting there: From US 2 at the west end of Leavenworth, drive 17.7 miles south-west on Icicle Road (County Road 76).

⑰ Blackpine Creek Horse Camp 🌲🌲🌲

The end of the road in Icicle Canyon is a starting point for many Alpine Lakes Wilderness–bound hikers and horse packers: Blackpine Creek Horse Camp. The campground is the site of the Icicle Creek Trailhead, which leads to the popular French Creek drainage and connects to the French Ridge, Snowall Creek, and Meadow Creek Trails to the south. The campground is not exclusively for the horse enthusiast, but the 10 pull-through sites are helpful if you're hauling a horse trailer. This is the only campground in the valley with horse-loading facilities. Tenters are thus left with the added challenge of setting up the tent without

sites	10
⛺ 🚐	No hookups, RVs to 21 feet
open	Mid-May through October
reservations	None
contact	Wenatchee National Forest, Leavenworth Ranger District, 509/548-6977

landing squarely atop a road apple or two. The campground has hand-pumped water, pit toilets, and, as usual, no showers, unless you're man or woman enough to shower under the pump while a buddy keeps it running. The elevation is 3,000 feet.

Getting there: From US 2 at the west end of Leavenworth, drive 19.2 miles southwest on Icicle Road (County Road 76).

Other Leavenworth/Icicle Canyon Campgrounds

For RVers who want to explore the Bavarian-kitsch village of Leavenworth but are not interested in roughing it at the multitude of no-hookup Forest Service camps in the region, try **Pine Village Resort/KOA** (on River Bend Drive, just east of town; 509/548-7709). It offers all the extras: full hookups, cable TV, laundry facilities, hot showers—even a hot tub or two. Another option for RVers in search of hookups is the large **Icicle River RV Resort** (3 miles up Icicle Road; 509/548-5420).

Snoqualmie Pass Corridor: North Bend to Easton

⑱ Tinkham 🌲🌲

It's not exactly gorgeous, but as one of only two Interstate 90 campgrounds west of Snoqualmie Summit, it'll have to do. Tinkham, still hanging in there in spite of repeated flood damage in recent years, offers sites set beneath shady (OK, flat-out dark), second-growth trees not nearly far enough from the roar of Interstate 90 and the South Fork Snoqualmie River. But it is centrally located, amidst a half-dozen popular (too popular!) day-hiking trails. The campground has pit toilets and hand-pumped water. Sites 20–22 are wheelchair accessible. The truth: It's not a place we'd go to spend a relaxing weekend. But it makes do as a decent overnight stopover, with the added plus of 28

sites	47
🏕️ 🚐	No hookups, RVs to 35 feet
open	Late May to mid-September
reservations	Up to 240 days in advance; National Recreation Reservation Service, 877/444-6777 or www.reserveusa.com
contact	Mount Baker–Snoqualmie National Forest, Snoqualmie Ranger District, North Bend office, 425/888-1421

Mountain bikers roll down the John Wayne Trail near Snoqualmie Summit.

reservable sites. Bonus points to anyone who can figure out what happened to campsite 12.

Getting there: From Interstate 90 about 8 miles east of North Bend, take exit 42 (Tinkham), turn right (south) under the freeway, and follow signs about 1.5 miles east on Tinkham Road 55.

⑲ Denny Creek 🌲🌲🌲🌲

Campers seeking a quick night's sleep on the west side of Snoqualmie Pass will find Denny Creek their best option—certainly the most amenity-packed. Located in a deep canyon in the South Fork Snoqualmie River drainage below Interstate 90, the campground's sites are set amidst shady trees along the gurgling creek, which tends to help drown out the increasingly annoying freeway noise. The campground, named for prominent Seattle settler David Denny, has hand-pumped water and, unlike many Forest Service camps, flush toilets (recently upgraded to wheelchair accessible). It's located near several very popular day hikes, including the family-friendly Franklin Falls Trail and the spectacular Denny Creek Trail. The latter path leads to Keekwulee and Snowshoe Falls, then on to Hemlock Pass and ultimately Melakwa Lake (4.5 miles) in the Alpine Lakes Wilderness. The paved frontage road leading northeast from the campground—the old Snoqualmie Pass highway—takes mountain bikers to Snoqualmie Summit, where the Pacific Crest Trail, the Iron Horse State Park cross-state trail, and the Snoqualmie Tunnel can be

Denny Creek Campground has received numerous upgrades.

sites	*33*
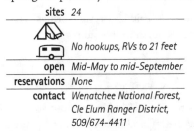	*11 electrical hookups, RVs to 35 feet*
open	*Mid-May to early October*
reservations	*Up to 240 days in advance; National Recreation Reservation Service, 877/444-6777 or www.reserveusa.com*
contact	*Mount Baker-Snoqualmie National Forest, Snoqualmie Ranger District, North Bend office, 425/888-1421*

accessed easily. The campground also has a group site for up to 35 campers. Note: The road to the campground is often flood damaged in the winter. Call before heading here in the spring.

Getting there: From Interstate 90 about 13 miles east of North Bend, take exit 47, drive north under the freeway, and turn right at the T intersection. Drive a quarter mile, then turn left on Denny Creek Road 58. Proceed 2 miles to the campground entrance on the left.

⑳ Crystal Springs 🌲🌲🌲

Hidden in a forested cove behind the Keechelus Dam, which has made a big ol' lake out of what once was the high headwaters of the Yakima River, Crystal Springs is probably better known for its wintertime use—as a major Sno-Park

sites	*24*
	No hookups, RVs to 21 feet
open	*Mid-May to mid-September*
reservations	*None*
contact	*Wenatchee National Forest, Cle Elum Ranger District, 509/674-4411*

trailhead for cross-country skiers and snowmobilers—than for summertime escapes. But—surprise!—all that snow melts away in May to reveal a quaint little campground, with decent sites for tents and very small RVs. Its proximity to noisy Interstate 90 is a big drawback, but it's a prime location for recreation.

Hikers and mountain bikers can set out from here across the Keechelus Dam and connect with the Iron Horse State Park cross-state trail to the south, and Snoqualmie Summit and the 2-mile-long Snoqualmie Tunnel (dress warmly and have a good flashlight) to the west. Another good cycling side trip is Lake Kachess, the next major reservoir north (see below). The campground has pit toilets, but no piped water. The elevation is 2,400 feet—about 600 feet below, and east of, Snoqualmie Summit.

Getting there: The campground is just off Interstate 90 exit 62, 10 miles east of Snoqualmie Summit, 20 miles west of Cle Elum.

㉑ Kachess 🌲🌲🌲🌲

You're in luck. Kachess, one of the largest Forest Service campgrounds in the state, also is one of the niftiest in the Central Cascades, with a wealth of nicely

sites	*120*
🏕️ 🚐	*No hookups, RVs to 32 feet*
open	*Late May through September*
reservations	*Up to 240 days in advance; National Recreation Reservation Service, 877/444-6777 or www.reserveusa.com*
contact	*Wenatchee National Forest, Cle Elum Ranger District, 509/674-4411*

spaced campsites in second-growth pine forest along the banks of Lake Kachess (a reservoir) northeast of Easton. This is an active place in the summer, with plenty to keep the whole family busy. The sprawling, cold reservoir has a swimming area and boat launch, and rentals are available in summer. The campground, which has pit toilets and piped water, also features 30 double-sized, family sites, a group camp for 50 people, a pleasant, barrier-free nature trail, a picnic area with grand views of the lake, and a host of other features. It's also a good base for heading out on some of the local Alpine Lakes Wilderness trails (the Rachel Lake Trailhead is nearby). The lone drawback: All that boat and water-sport activity can make it a bit noisy here, especially in early summer, when the reservoir is full. If you're seeking solitude, try camping here in late August or September, after the reservoir is drawn down far enough to drive the boaters off and turn the swimming beach into a big mudflat. For peak summer weeks, use the reservation system; 42 sites can be reserved in advance.

Getting there: From Interstate 90 eastbound, take exit 62 (Crystal Springs), cross over the freeway, and follow signs about 5 miles north to the campground.

㉒ Lake Easton State Park 🌲🌲🌲🌲

It looks an awful lot like a pretty, natural alpine lake. Well, it isn't. But so what? You're the only one in the crowd who knows better, and nobody else will figure it out. Lake Easton actually is a reservoir, part of the same upper Yakima River

sites	*135*
🏕️ 🚐	*45 full hookups, RVs to 60 feet*
open	*Late April to mid-October for camping; all year for day use*
reservations	*Up to 9 months in advance; 888/226-7688 or www.parks.wa.gov*
contact	*Washington State Parks, 360/902-8844; Lake Easton State Park, 509/656-2586*

water-storage system that created nearby Lake Kachess to the north. But the 516-acre state park on its northern shores is a lovely place, with campsites spread through loops wooded with stately firs on bluffs above the lakeshore. The park also has group sites for up to 50 people. The waterfront picnic/swimming area is particularly nice, and the lake becomes a decent rainbow trout fishery late in the summer, when the water warms. A boat ramp and 20-foot dock complete the water-sports picture. Don't forget the mountain bikes: Plenty of local backroads beckon, and connections to the Iron Horse State Park cross-state trail can be made easily (see Crystal

The dammed headwaters of the Yakima River form Lake Easton.

Springs, above). The main drawback: freeway noise. The campground is quite close to Interstate 90, and the roar of trucks seems to bounce off the valley walls here all night long. The park stays open in winter for day use, primarily by cross-country skiers and snowmobilers. You'll need a Sno-Park permit to access the 37 miles of ski trails that begin here.

Getting there: From Interstate 90 eastbound, take exit 70 (15 miles east of Snoqualmie Pass; about a mile west of Easton) and follow signs a short distance to the park.

Roslyn and Cle Elum River Valley

23 Wish Poosh 🌲🌲🌲🌲

Lots of people hike many, many miles, carrying many, many pounds on their backs, to rub shoulders and boot soles with the Alpine Lakes Wilderness, one of the most spectacular alpine areas in the Lower 48. Others do it the easy way—by

sites	39
🏕️	
🚐	No hookups, RVs to 21 feet
open	Mid-May through September
reservations	None
contact	Wenatchee National Forest, Cle Elum Ranger District, 509/674-4411

car, up the Cle Elum and Teanaway River valleys. The Cle Elum River valley, which juts north toward—and ultimately into—the Alpine Lakes Wilderness from its start near the Northern Exposure TV series backdrop of Roslyn, offers some of the most "wild"-feeling camping in the state, and it's easy to reach from the Seattle area. The price you pay for that

luxury is lack thereof; most campgrounds in the Cle Elum River valley are fairly spartan Forest Service camps, high on pine trees, clear water, blue skies, and wild-flowers, low on amenities. But two of these camps, Wish Poosh, the first encountered along Highway 903 (Salmon La Sac Road), and Salmon La Sac (see below), are comfortable enough to let you have it both ways.

Wish Poosh is on the shores of Lake Cle Elum, actually a large reservoir on the lower river. It's extremely popular with boaters, who can launch here and ply the wide, flat waters. Note: The lake moves farther and farther away from the camp-ground as summer progresses! The camping area is quite nice, with four double-wide sites, large enough to accommodate two RVs or two cars with tents—perfect for families camping together. Seventeen sites are designated for tents, 22 for trailers and RVs. The campground has pit toilets and piped water.

Getting there: From Interstate 90, take exit 80, follow signs about 4 miles to downtown Roslyn, then follow Highway 903 (Salmon La Sac Road) 6.5 miles north to the campground, on the left.

24 Cle Elum River 🌲🌲🌲

Cle Elum River, the next in line (after Wish Poosh, above) on a drive up the Cle Elum River valley, is the alternate campground on Lake Cle Elum, a reservoir on the lower river. It's a standard Forest Service camp, with 23 sites designated as RV spaces and two for tents, although tenters would be fine with most of them. The

sites	23
🏕️🚐	No hookups, RVs to 21 feet
open	Mid-May through September
reservations	None
contact	Wenatchee National Forest, Cle Elum Ranger District, 509/674-4411

campground, at 2,200 feet near the head of the lake (it turns to a large meadow in late summer and fall), has pit toilets and hand-pumped water. The gravel roads give it a rustic feel. Note that the large (up to 100 people) group camp to the immediate right inside the entrance recently was developed (at the expense of some individual sites) to replace the former group site at Salmon La Sac, farther up Highway 903.

Getting there: From Interstate 90, take exit 80, follow signs about 4 miles to Roslyn, then follow Highway 903 (Salmon La Sac Road) 11.5 miles north to the campground, on the left.

25 Red Mountain 🌲🌲🌲

Tired of being surrounded by behemoth Winnebagos? They'd be hard pressed to follow you here. Red Mountain, a mile north of Cle Elum River Campground (see above), is classic, old-time Forest Service–style camping: fire pits, an occasional picnic table, and not much else (the campground has no piped water, not to mention showers). But it does allow you to pitch a tent within spitting distance of the gurgling, ultra-clear Cle Elum River, which will lull you to sleep in a heartbeat. We've seen this campground become home to far more than nine groups of

sites	10
🏕️	
open	Mid-May through October; winters with no fees or services
reservations	None
contact	Wenatchee National Forest, Cle Elum Ranger District, 509/674-4411

overnight campers; tenters tend to spread out north and south of here along the river. Note: Unlike other campgrounds on this stretch, Red Mountain isn't gated at the end of September. You can continue to camp here—for free—through the fall, until snows block access. Bring your own water, toilet paper, and garbage bags.

Getting there: From Interstate 90, take exit 80, follow signs about 4 miles to Roslyn, then follow Highway 903 (Salmon La Sac Road) 13 miles north to the campground, on the left.

26 Salmon La Sac 🌲🌲🌲🌲

It's not quite paradise. But you can hike there from here. Salmon La Sac, the largest and most popular campground in the Cle Elum River valley, is one of the

sites	99
	No hookups, RVs to 21 feet
open	Late May to mid-September
reservations	Up to 240 days in advance; National Recreation Reservation Service, 877/444-6777 or www.reserveusa.com
contact	Wenatchee National Forest, Cle Elum Ranger District, 509/674-4411

very nicest tent-plunking or RV-parking spots in the Central Cascades. Spread out on a plateau above the crisp, clear river, the campground's sites are great for either tenters or small-scale RVers, making this a prime summertime destination for hikers, anglers, mountain bikers, nature lovers, and unapologetically lazy campers. The campground lies at the end of the pavement on Salmon La Sac Road, but much of the greater natural wonders in this area are found farther up the valley, reached via the winding, gravel road that continues beyond the campground. Cycle or drive up this road to stunning upper-river alpine meadows, chock full of wildflowers in spring and majestic colors in autumn. The road also leads to a string of trailheads leading to beloved Alpine Lakes Wilderness destinations: French Creek to Paddy Go Easy Pass (6 miles round-trip), Jolly Mountain (12.5 miles round-trip), and the Deception Pass Loop (15 miles), to name just a few. But you don't need to venture far to find great hiking from Salmon La Sac. Trailheads right near the campground put you on the

The crystal waters of the Cle Elum River at Salmon La Sac.

path to Waptus Lake (16 miles round-trip) near Mount David, one of the more spectacular overnight destinations in the Alpine Lakes Wilderness (permits required; call the ranger station number listed). Day hikers can hoof it 5 miles to Cooper Lake, where you'll find a gorgeous walk-in campground (Owhi, see below), plus another trailhead for hikers bound for Pete Lake (15 miles round-trip).

If all that sounds a bit ambitious, stay "home" at your campsite and fish; the Cle Elum River offers a chance to hook into a rainbow, although fishing has been fairly slow here in recent years (it's usually more productive downstream in Lake Cle Elum, or upstream at (hike-in) Hyas Lake). Salmon La Sac is a large, active campground, equipped with piped water, flush toilets, and Cayuse Horse Camp (15 sites, 3 horsies each). Some sites are barrier free. The main drawback is that many sites are bone-dry and quite dusty in the summer. But the campground makes up for that with some truly gorgeous, riverfront sites, many equipped with niceties such as campfire benches and stone cooking stoves, complete with chimneys. It's a very busy spot; take advantage of the reservation system, which allows 26 sites to be booked in advance. The elevation is 2,400 feet.

Getting there: From Interstate 90, take exit 80, follow signs about 4 miles to Roslyn, then follow Highway 903 (Salmon La Sac Road) 15.5 miles north to the campground, across the bridge on the left.

㉗ Owhi ▲▲▲▲

It's not easy to find, but for tent campers, Owhi is a true hidden gem, worthy of the journey. The campground sits on the wooded shore of Cooper Lake, an absolutely stunning, clear-water lake near the edge of the Alpine Lakes Wilderness.

sites	22
open	Mid-June through October; winters with no fees or services
reservations	None
contact	Wenatchee National Forest, Cle Elum Ranger District, 509/674-4411

The sites are all walk-ins, some quite private, others in a group setting. From some campsites, and especially from canoes in the middle of the lake, the view of the snow-clad Three Queens peak is spectacular. It's a great spot for tenters with canoes or small boats (no motors, internal combustion or electric); fishing can be good after the lake warms in midsummer. Options for further exploration on local trails abound. One trail from the campground leads 5 miles to Pete Lake, and beyond to Spectacle Lakes, both popular backpacking destinations (permits required; call the Cle Elum Ranger District for details). The campground has pit toilets, but no piped water or showers. The elevation is 2,800 feet.

Getting there: From Interstate 90, take exit 80, follow signs about 4 miles to Roslyn, then drive 21 miles northwest to the campground via Highway 903 (Salmon La Sac Road) and Forest Road 46.

Fishing in Cascade Mountain lakes can be a cross-generational experience.

Other Cle Elum River Valley Campgrounds

Beyond Salmon La Sac, the road up the Cle Elum River turns to (steep, rough) gravel, and campsites get downright rustic—although you'd be surprised at the size of RVs that somehow make it up here. The road eventually opens into a wide, green valley near the Cle Elum River's headwaters. Campers take advantage of all this space, popping up tents in many "unofficial" campsites, such as **Scatter Creek** at the south end of Tucquala Lake (this kind of camping is allowed in the national forest). The Forest Service lists only one official, established camp on the upper Cle Elum: **Fish Lake** (about 29 miles north of Roslyn, on Forest Road 4330; 509/674-4411), at the north end of the same marshy valley. Camping in the three sites is free but primitive, with pit toilets but no picnic tables, piped water, or other services. In addition, primitive **backcountry camps** on the shores of Hyas Lake are an easy 4 miles from the trailhead at the end of Forest Road 4330. Note: Forest Road 4330 can be treacherous; trailers and RVs aren't recommended. In addition, Scatter Creek crosses the road in a concrete basin in the upper valley. To reach Fish Lake and the end of the road, you must drive across it, which can be a risky proposition during spring melt-off.

Blewett Pass and Ellensburg

28 Beverly ▲▲▲

To many Washingtonians, the Teanaway River valley northeast of Cle Elum is as close as you can come to Montana without ever leaving the Evergreen State. This dry, scenic, east-slope forest is filled with secret little camping spots, the locations of which occupants guard fiercely. But you can camp in established sites here as well. One such place is Beverly, a remote camp on the North Fork Teanaway. It's out there, peaceful, and primitive (pit toilets, no piped water or showers). The campground is popular with stream anglers and, especially, hikers. A nearby trail, Esmerelda Basin, is one of the most popular in the Alpine Lakes Wilderness. Another, the Beverly-Turnpike Trail, is often used by Stuart Range mountain and rock climbers. It's also the primary western access to the Ingalls Creek Trail, a popular backpack route along the southern edge of the Stuart Range, between the North Fork Teanaway and the Blewett Pass area to the east. The campground elevation is 3,100 feet.

sites	16
	No hookups, RVs to 21 feet
open	June through October
reservations	None
contact	Wenatchee National Forest, Cle Elum Ranger District, 509/674-4411

Getting there: From Cle Elum, follow County Road 970 about 8 miles northeast to Teanaway River Road. Turn left (northwest) and drive to the end of the paved road, about 13 miles. Bear right and continue north on Forest Road 9737 to the campground, about 4 miles.

29 Mineral Springs ▲▲

One of a handful of Forest Service camps along winding, occasionally washed-out US 97 (the Blewett Pass Highway), tiny, cramped Mineral Springs offers a dozen tent/small RV sites at the confluence of Medicine and Swauk Creeks. It's close enough to the highway to feel the big trucks roll by. You'll probably want to camp here only if you can't get into Swauk, another 3.5 miles up US 97. Mineral Springs gets plenty of use in the fall, when hunters take over, and in winter, when snowmobilers and cross-country skiers

sites	7
	No hookups, RVs to 21 feet
open	Mid-May to late September; winters with no fees or services
reservations	None
contact	Wenatchee National Forest, Cle Elum Ranger District, 509/674-4411

move in. A group site for up to 50 campers is available by reservation only. The elevation is 2,700 feet.

Getting there: From Interstate 90 near Cle Elum, follow County Road 970 about 12 miles northeast to the junction with US 97. Continue straight on US 97, proceeding another 6.3 miles north to the campground, on the left (west) side of the highway.

㉚ Swauk 🌲🌲🌲

Swauk, set along the gushing waters of Swauk Creek, near US 97, is many campers' favorite spot in the Blewett Pass corridor—a mountain pass that connects Interstate 90 near Cle Elum with US 2 near Leavenworth. The camp's mixed pine and fir forest hosts some truly cozy sites, such as our favorite, number 18, down on the end. A nice picnic shelter is found in the day-use area. The main drawback: highway noise. Still, it's a nice spot, and the camp is a popular summer stopover for hikers, and a winter haunt for snowmobilers, snowshoers, and cross-country skiers visiting the Swauk Sno-Park for adventures around Swauk and Blewett Passes. The old Blewett Pass Highway intersects US 97 about 1.5 miles south of the campground. The campground has pit toilets, but no piped water or showers. The elevation is 3,200 feet.

sites	22
🏕	
🚐	No hookups, RVs to 21 feet
open	Mid-April to late September
reservations	None
contact	Wenatchee National Forest, Cle Elum Ranger District, 509/674-4411

Convenient day hikes begin in Swauk Campground.

Getting there: From Interstate 90 near Cle Elum, follow County Road 970 about 12 miles northeast to the junction with US 97. Continue straight on US 97, proceeding another 9.8 miles north to the campground, on the right (east) side of the highway.

Other Blewett Pass/Ellensburg Campgrounds

A slate of remote, backcountry campgrounds operated by the Cle Elum Ranger District offer alternatives to the more popular campsites listed above. Most of these are horse camps in the high, dry alpine areas of the Wenatchee National Forest, but they also make suitable camps for backcountry camping enthusiasts. They are **Ken Wilcox Campground** at Haney Meadows (8 miles off US 97 on Forest Road 9712; 19 sites), a campground/horse camp at 5,500 feet; **Red Top** (near the end of Forest Road 9702, 28 miles northeast of Cle Elum; 3 sites); **Buck Meadows** (24 miles west of Ellensburg on Forest Road 3100; 5 sites); **Rider's Camp** (25 miles west of Ellensburg on Forest Road 3100), a dispersed camp area for groups; **Quartz Mountain** (33 miles west of Ellensburg on Forest Road 3100; 3 sites); **Manastash Camp** (26 miles west of Ellensburg on Forest Road 3104; 26 sites); **Tamarack Spring** (25 miles south of Cle Elum on Forest Road 3120; 3 sites); **Taneum** (18 miles south of Cle Elum on Taneum Road 33; 13 walk-in sites); **Icewater Creek** (20 miles south of Cle Elum on Taneum Road 33; 17 sites); **Taneum Junction** (20 miles south of Cle Elum on Taneum Road 33; group site for 75 people/15 vehicles); **Lion Rock Spring** (23 miles north of Ellensburg on Forest Road 35; 3 sites); and **South Fork Meadow** (25 miles south of Cle Elum on Forest Road 3300, spur 119; 3 sites). All are primitive, with pit toilets, but no piped water or other services. Some of these campgrounds are free. Call the Wenatchee National Forest, Cle Elum Ranger District (509/674-4411).

Another remote, free campground in the area is the Department of Natural Resource's **Indian Horse Camp** (19 miles northeast of Cle Elum on Middle Fork Teanaway Road; DNR Ellensburg office, 509/925-8510), with 9 tent sites. Finally, if you're stuck in windy Ellensburg visiting the kid in college, your best bet is the **Ellensburg KOA** (32 Thorp Highway S; 509/925-9319).

South Cascades

You might want to seriously consider packing a few signal flares along with the s'mores fixings. A person could get lost out here. For many Washington campers, the South Cascades, a sprawling sea of deep, dark forests, ancient and contemporary volcanoes, silvery rivers, and indefatigable mosquitoes, are like that long-neglected storage room: You know there's stuff in there you want to see, but you have no idea how to even start wading through it.

Well, we know the feeling. Been there, done that, got high-centered on the Forest Service road. We've spent more time than we care to admit kicking around in the deep woods of Mount Rainier National Park, the Gifford Pinchot and Wenatchee National Forests, the Mount Adams Wilderness, and the Columbia River Gorge, looking for those rare slices of Cascade alpine heaven.

We have but one thing to report: Man, are they ever out there. In droves.

Just get a good map, and try not to confuse one bit of heaven with another. This portion of the state, from Mount Rainier south to the Bridge of the Gods and east to Goldendale, contains by far the highest concentration of campsites in Washington. The vast majority of them are small, somewhat remote national forest sites, reached by driving 20 or more miles on Forest Service roads, which more often than not are washboarded gravel. You know the type: roads you still feel in your large intestine a day later.

That should suggest something right off the bat: With some notable exceptions, these generally aren't the kinds of places you'll find your great aunt and uncle taking the Minnie Winnie for a couple weeks. Vast stretches of this undeveloped land are left to the rest of you infidels in tents and small RVs. Many of the very best tent sites in the state, if not all of the West, are found in this area—on alpine lakes in the Goat Rocks Wilderness south of White Pass, on high-mountain streams near the Indian Heaven Wilderness, and on the rocky slopes of barely dormant volcanoes named Adams and St. Helens.

One thing is certain: You'll never get bored. They are a work in progress, these South Cascades. Think you've seen it all? Go back next week. Nature, in its own charming and destructive way, likely will have changed things around since the last visit. Truly knowing these lands is a lifelong project. And yours is getting shorter by the minute.

1. Ipsut Creek
2. Mowich Lake
3. Sunshine Point
4. Cougar Rock
5. White River
6. Ohanapecosh
7. The Dalles
8. Silver Springs
9. Corral Pass
10. Lodge Pole
11. Pleasant Valley
12. Hell's Crossing
13. Cedar Springs
14. Soda Springs
15. Cougar Flat
16. Bumping Crossing
17. Upper and Lower Bumping Lake
18. Little Naches
19. Kaner Flat
20. Crow Creek
21. Sawmill Flat
22. Halfway Flat
23. Cottonwood
24. Big Creek
25. La Wis Wis
26. Summit Creek
27. Soda Springs
28. Walupt Lake
29. White Pass Lake
30. Dog Lake
31. Clear Lake North
32. Clear Lake South
33. Indian Creek
34. Peninsula
35. South Fork
36. Hause Creek
37. Willows
38. Windy Point
39. Lewis and Clark State Park
40. Mayfield Lake Park
41. Ike Kinswa State Park
42. Mossyrock Park
43. Taidnapam Park
44. Iron Creek
45. Tower Rock
46. North Fork
47. Seaquest State Park
48. Lower Falls Recreation Area
49. Beaver
50. Panther Creek
51. Paradise Creek
52. Moss Creek
53. Oklahoma
54. Peterson Prairie
55. Goose Lake
56. Cultus Creek
57. Tillicum
58. Morrison Creek
59. Blue Lake Creek
60. Adams Fork
61. Horseshoe Lake
62. Takhlakh Lake
63. Beacon Rock State Park
64. Horsethief Lake State Park
65. Brooks Memorial State Park
66. Maryhill State Park

South Cascades Map

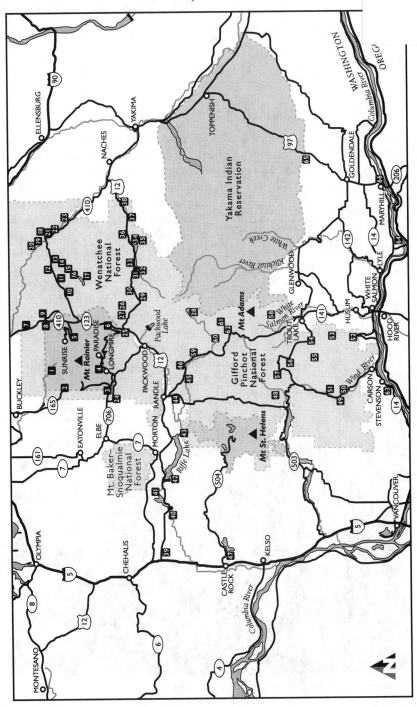

Mount Rainier National Park

❶ Ipsut Creek 🌲🌲🌲

Ipsut Creek, one the more remote of six campgrounds in Mount Rainier National Park, also is one of its most peaceful. From its location near the end of Carbon River Road, visitors can fan out on a number of Mount Rainier hiking trails leading to some of the park's prime attractions, including the Wonderland Trail, Spray Park, Seattle Park, Mystic Lake, Tolmie Peak, Carbon Glacier, and the Northern Loop Trail. Sites are small and wooded, best suited for tents. Which is good, because the rough-and-tumble access road (when it's open) isn't exactly RV-friendly. The Park Service, in fact, would like to make this a hike-in-only campground in the future. The campground has two group sites, pit toilets, and no piped water, showers, or other services. But it's worth the trouble. In our experience, every stay at Ipsut Creek is a memorable one. The elevation is 2,300 feet. Note: Stays are limited to 14 days at all Mount Rainier National Park campgrounds during July and August.

sites	31
open	All year, weather permitting
reservations	None
contact	Mount Rainier National Park, 360/569-2211

A classic Washington view: Mount Rainier from Paradise.

Getting there: From Puyallup, drive 13 miles east on Highway 410 to Buckley. Turn right (south) on Highway 165. Proceed to the bridge over the Carbon River Gorge, then bear left to Mount Rainier National Park's Carbon River entrance. Drive 5 miles on Carbon River Road to the campground at the end of the road. Note: The upper 5 miles of Carbon River Road can be quite rough and often are washed out by flooding. Check with the national park before traveling.

❷ Mowich Lake 🌲🌲🌲

Mowich Lake, Mount Rainier's other remote mountain camp (see Ipsut Creek, above), is a walk-in campground in the northwest corner of the park, near some of Rainier's most scenic day-hiking trails. Campers who haul their stuff a short distance to the loosely organized sites here are in for a treat—waterfront camping on a picturesque lake, with Rainier looming in the distance. From here, hikers can set out on the Spray Falls Trail, which leads to the falls, Spray Park, Seattle Park, the Carbon Glacier,

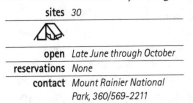

sites	30
open	Late June through October
reservations	None
contact	Mount Rainier National Park, 360/569-2211

and other, more distant destinations on the Wonderland Trail, which stretches 93 miles all the way around Mount Rainier. The campground is primitive, with chemical vault toilets and tables, but no piped water or other services. Campfires are not allowed. Note that Mowich Lake Road does not open until early summer, and usually remains rough and washboarded all summer. The campground elevation is 4,929 feet. Note: Stays are limited to 14 days at all Mount Rainier National Park campgrounds during July and August.

Getting there: From Puyallup, drive 13 miles east on Highway 410 to Buckley. Turn right (south) on Highway 165 and proceed through Carbonado. Just beyond the Carbon River Gorge bridge, bear right onto Mowich Lake Road. Follow the road about 17 miles to its end. Note: The road is unpaved beyond its junction with the Carbon River Road.

❸ Sunshine Point 🌲🌲🌲

This isn't the largest, most scenic or most-anything-else campground in Mount Rainier National Park—except for one thing: It's most convenient. The small campground, just inside the Nisqually entrance, is handy for travelers hoping to spend a day or more exploring the Longmire/Paradise area on the south side of the mountain. Sites are a bit exposed—both to weather and other campers—in an open, grassy area on a gravel bench above the milky Nisqually River. Because of its relatively low elevation (2,000 feet), this is the only campground inside the

sites	18
	No hookups, RVs to 25 feet
open	All year
reservations	None
contact	Mount Rainier National Park, 360/569-2211

national park accessible all winter. It offers pit toilets but no other services. Note: Stays are limited to 14 days at all Mount Rainier National Park campgrounds during July and August.

Getting there: From Tacoma, drive south on Highway 7 to Elbe and continue 12 miles east on Highway 706 to the Mount Rainier National Park's Nisqually entrance. The campground is a quarter mile ahead on the right.

❹ Cougar Rock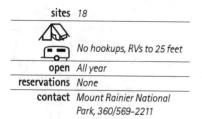

Cougar Rock, the main campground for southside (Paradise-area) visitors to Mount Rainier National Park, is a victim of its own success. It's so scenic, and so popular in a park that's often overcrowded, you must have a reservation to get in

sites	188
	No hookups, RVs to 35 feet
open	Late May to mid-October
reservations	Required from late June through Labor Day; 800/365-CAMP or http://reservations.nps.gov/
contact	Mount Rainier National Park, 360/569-2211

here between late June and Labor Day. Sites are first-come, first-served before and after that window. In our experience, the campground is full at times during the peak period; other times it isn't. Which, frankly, makes us strongly question the fairness of a "mandatory reservation" system that makes every arriving camper go through the hassle and expense of making an on-site "reser-

vation" upon arrival—even if the campground isn't full. (Park rangers don't seem to like the system, either, and have trouble defending it to campers.) This reservation system also takes an unusually heavy bite out of your prepaid total if you have to cancel.

That said, lucky campers who do land one of the sites here will find a small camping city, with great access to all of Rainier's summertime delights, including some of the best day hiking in the state (weather permitting). Sites, set in small, subalpine trees, have medium privacy, and are suitable for both tents and RVs. Don't expect tent pads, though, and be warned that not all sites can accommodate a Super Jumbo Colossus Costco tent. The campground has piped water, flush toilets, an RV dump station, an amphitheater, and other niceties. Group sites for 12 or more are available. The elevation is 3,180 feet. Note: Stays are limited to 14 days at all Mount Rainier National Park campgrounds during July and August.

Getting there: From Tacoma, drive south on Highway 7 to Elbe, and continue 12 miles east on Highway 706 to the Mount Rainier National Park Nisqually entrance. Proceed 6 miles to Longmire and another 2.3 miles to the campground entrance.

❺ White River 🌲🌲🌲

White River, an older campground in a pleasant locale near the river sharing its name, serves a dual purpose: It sucks in many of the tourist hordes heading up to the spectacular Sunrise day-use area for hiking, picnicking, and photography, and it doubles as a trailhead for backpackers and climbers headed to some of the park's most spectacular backcountry sites. Needless to say, it all adds up to large crowds, which often push the limits of this campground. Take the RV size limit literally: Most campsites here are tiny, and many are cramped together, with only miminal, small-tree cover for privacy between sites. It's best enjoyed by tenters who don't mind being around many other tenters, particularly during peak season.

sites	112
🏕️🚐	No hookups, RVs to 20 feet
open	Late June through September
reservations	None
contact	Mount Rainier National Park, 360/569-2211

Fortunately, that's often the primary clientele: White River is the launching point for a trail to a viewpoint of the snout of the Emmons Glacier, then on up the White River to Glacier Basin, a popular backpack destination. The route extends beyond to Camp Schurman, a bivouac site for climbers headed up the Emmons Glacier route to the mountain's 14,411-foot summit. Another very popular trail to the Summerland/Panhandle Gap area begins nearby, at Fryingpan Creek. The campground has an RV dump station. The elevation is 4,400 feet.

A woman hikes along Sunrise Rim.

Note: Stays are limited to 14 days at all Mount Rainier National Park campgrounds during July and August. If this campground, as is often the case, is full, nearby Silver Springs (see below) is a great alternative, with far more spacious and livable campsites.

Getting there: From Enumclaw, drive 43 miles east on Highway 410 to the Mount Rainier National Park White River entrance. Proceed 5 miles west to the campground.

⑥ Ohanapecosh 🌲🌲🌲🌲

Ohanapecosh is the premier camping area at Mount Rainier, and one of the finest in the state, thanks to its location along the stunningly clear, beautiful Ohanapecosh River, which drains the eastern flanks of the mountain, where few glaciers are active enough to dispense glacial flour. Trails leading from the campground up the river have it all: old-growth trees, an awesome river gorge spanned by a log bridge, a thundering waterfall, and access to the park's fabled Shadow of the Sentinels Trail, which leads between some massive, 1,000-year-old western red cedars and Douglas firs. This river valley truly is one of the more beautiful, memorable spots in a state that's chock full of outdoor delights. A visitors/interpretive center in the campground is a nice added touch, particularly for families. The campground is also strategically located: Stevens Canyon Road, the park's drive-through scenic showcase between here and the Paradise area on the south side of the mountain, begins just to the north. Or proceed north on Highway 123 up the east side of the mountain to Chinook Pass and more jaw-dropping views along Highway 410.

sites	205
🏕️ 🚐	No hookups, RVs to 32 feet
open	Late May to mid-October
reservations	Required from late June through Labor Day; 800/365-CAMP or http://reservations.nps.gov/
contact	Mount Rainier National Park, 360/569-2211

The shady campground itself is pleasant, with spacious sites in a wooded area on both sides of the river. Privacy is somewhat lacking, but you probably won't mind in the plum riverfront sites, where the rushing Ohanapecosh always seems to make everything seem all right. Not surprisingly, campsites are tough to come by here in the summertime. Reservations are required between late June and Labor Day weekend. (See the note about this perplexing reservation scheme in the listing for Cougar Rock, above.) Make sure you're on your best behavior at this camp: The staff here has earned a reputation for being, shall we say, a little excessively protective of the grounds. We've seen senior citizens shooed away for picnicking in the wrong place. And we personally received a major tongue-lashing here recently for committing the mortal sin of using a solar shower in the campground. You've been warned! The campground elevation is 1,914 feet. Note: Stays

The Ohanapecosh River surges through a deep gorge below Silver Falls.

An alpine stream in Mount Rainier National Park.

are limited to 14 days at all Mount Rainier National Park campgrounds during July and August. If Ohanapecosh is full, a good alternative is La Wis Wis, a Forest Service campground 7 miles to the south, near Packwood (see the White Pass Corridor section below).

Getting there: The campground is 5 miles north of the Highway 123/US 12 junction near Packwood. During summer months, visitors from the Seattle area also can reach the campground via Highway 706 (Stevens Canyon Road) from the west, or Highway 410 (Chinook Pass Highway) from the north.

Chinook Pass Corridor

⑦ The Dalles ▲▲▲

Like nearby Silver Springs (see below), The Dalles is a Forest Service camp outside the northern boundary of Mount Rainier National Park. The campground, situated in a stand of old-growth forest (which qualifies as rare anywhere in the Mount Baker–Snoqualmie National Forest), is quite pleasant, particularly on warm summer days, when the dense overhead canopy keeps the area cool. Sites on the west side are along the White River; east-side sites are set in the woods below Highway 410. A bonus for trip planners: About 60 percent of the sites here can be reserved. Saving a site in advance is a good idea in the summer. This park, as well as Silver Springs, below, gets plenty of overflow from Mount Rainier's over-taxed campgrounds, two of which

sites	44
	No hookups, RVs to 21 feet
open	Memorial Day through Labor Day
reservations	Up to 240 days in advance; National Recreation Reservation Service, 877/444-6777 or www.reserveusa.com
contact	Mount Baker–Snoqualmie National Forest, Snoqualmie Ranger District, White River office, 360/825-6585

require reservations between late June and Labor Day (see Cougar Rock and Ohanapecosh, above). Crystal Mountain and the national park's spectacular Sunrise day-use area are short drives from here. The campground has pit toilets and piped water. The picnic area is a nice rest stop for road-weary summer Rainier visitors.

Getting there: The Dalles is 26 miles southeast of Enumclaw on Highway 410 (7 miles northwest of Mount Rainier National Park).

⑧ Silver Springs ▲▲▲▲

Silver Springs, one of four Snoqualmie Ranger District campgrounds scattered in the forests north of Mount Rainier, is a good secret weapon for Mount Rainier–area explorers who don't want to fight the camping crowds within the national park itself. The campground is lovely, in a rare stand of old-growth forest along the White River. Sites, remodeled and repaved in recent years, are extremely spacious, offering privacy for tenters and room to stretch out for RV or trailer owners. Some double-sized, family sites are an added feature for groups. Management practices here add a bit of flexibility to your itinerary: Spaces can be reserved here in the summertime, but, unlike the more popular camps at Mount Rainier, reservations aren't required. Crystal Mountain and Sunrise both are

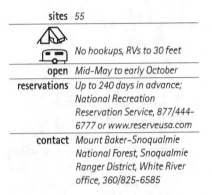

sites	55
	No hookups, RVs to 30 feet
open	Mid-May to early October
reservations	Up to 240 days in advance; National Recreation Reservation Service, 877/444-6777 or www.reserveusa.com
contact	Mount Baker–Snoqualmie National Forest, Snoqualmie Ranger District, White River office, 360/825-6585

short day trips from the campground, which has pit toilets and piped water. It's one of the better campgrounds you'll find in or around Mount Rainier National Park—with a fraction of the crowds.

Getting there: Silver Springs is 32 miles southeast of Enumclaw on Highway 410 (1 mile west of the Mount Rainier National Park boundary).

⑨ Corral Pass 🌲🌲

Corral Pass, a high (5,600-foot) camp in the Mount Baker–Snoqualmie National Forest northeast of Mount Rainier, often is used by hikers and horse packers as a base for exploring the nearby Norse Peak Wilderness. Day hiking can be fun right

sites	20
open	20 July through September
reservations	None
contact	Mount Baker–Snoqualmie National Forest, Snoqualmie Ranger District, White River office, 360/825-6585

from this campground, providing you don't mind dodging a few horse pucks here and there. The campground itself is set in the forest and is quite primitive, with pit toilets but no piped water or showers. It does have a horse-loading ramp, however—handy both for loading horses into trailers and

Dad into the Mercury Navigator after a long trek into the mountains. There is no camping fee, but you'll now need a Northwest Forest Pass parking permit to stay here.

Getting there: From Highway 410, 31 miles southeast of Enumclaw, turn east on Forest Road 7174 and proceed 6 miles to the campground. Note: The gravel road is rough and not suitable for trailers or RVs.

⑩ Lodge Pole 🌲🌲🌲

Note the sweet smell of high, dry, mixed forest. Highway 410 explorers will notice a marked difference as they follow the American River toward the east-slope Cascades. A string of Forest Service camps are found along the river, serving as great stopovers for long-distance travelers, or destinations for Seattle-area campers in need of a quick wilderness fix. All these campgrounds border the 51,000-acre Norse Peak Wilderness, which stretches between the Chinook and Naches Passes in the Wenatchee National Forest. For the west-to-east traveler, the first campground on

sites	33
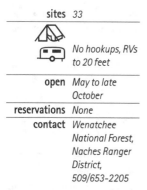	No hookups, RVs to 20 feet
open	May to late October
reservations	None
contact	Wenatchee National Forest, Naches Ranger District, 509/653-2205

this stretch is Lodge Pole, which has campsites scattered among pines, hand-pumped water, and pit toilets. Recent renovations to this camp make it much more pleasant, and for hikers, it's strategically located: The Norse Peak Wilderness lies due north, the 166,000-acre William O. Douglas Wilderness due south. The campground elevation is 3,500 feet.

Getting there: Lodge Pole is 45 miles northwest of Naches (about 8 miles east of the Mount Rainier National Park boundary), near milepost 76 on Highway 410.

⑫ Pleasant Valley 🌲🌲🌲

Like nearby Lodge Pole (above) and several other campgrounds, Pleasant Valley is a, well, pleasant Forest Service site on the American River in the Wenatchee National Forest, near the Norse Peak and William O. Douglas Wildernesses.

sites	16
	No hookups, RVs to 32 feet
open	Mid-May through November
reservations	None
contact	Wenatchee National Forest, Naches Ranger District, 509/653-2205

Unlike its neighbors, though, this campground has longer, more modern spaces that are better able to accommodate lengthy RVs. A recent renovation spiffed the place up considerably. The campground also has an RV dump station, as well as hand-pumped water and pit toilets. A trailhead at the campground leads up Kettle Creek to the American

A pleasant day at Pleasant Valley, on the American River.

Ridge Trail, a 26.5-mile ridgetop path in the William O. Douglas Wilderness. The camp is very popular with RVers, and, unfortunately, you no longer can get a campsite reservation here. The campground elevation is 3,300 feet.

Getting there: Pleasant Valley is 41.5 miles northwest of Naches, at milepost 80.2 on Highway 410.

⑫ Hell's Crossing 🌲 ▲▲▲

Another in the string of Wenatchee National Forest camps along the American River, Hell's Crossing is most popular among tent campers (most sites are too small for RVs) who like the dry, pine forests. Three sites are double-sized, family camps. Like most campgrounds in this area, this one offers great access to day-hiking and backpacking trails, particularly to American Ridge and Goat Peak, a William O. Douglas Wilderness summit with a memorable fire lookout. The campground has pit toilets and well water (at the west end only). The elevation is 3,250 feet.

sites	*18*
	No hookups, RVs to 16 feet
open	*May to early November*
reservations	*None*
contact	*Wenatchee National Forest, Naches Ranger District, 509/653-2205*

Getting there: The campground is 38 miles northwest of Naches, at milepost 83.4 on Highway 410.

Bunchberry or Canadian dogwood, a common Cascades wildflower.

⑬ Cedar Springs 🌲🌲🌲🌲

The first of several Wenatchee National Forest camps in the scenic Bumping River drainage, Cedar Springs is set along the river, where trout fishing is allowed during the summer. This is also a popular picnic spot for day-trippers headed for Bumping Lake, 11 miles farther southwest on Bumping Lake Road. Many good hiking trails are found a short distance down Bumping Lake Road. The campground has hand-pumped water and pit toilets. The elevation is 2,800 feet.

sites	15
🏕️ 🚐	No hookups, RVs to 22 feet
open	Late May to late November
reservations	None
contact	Wenatchee National Forest, Naches Ranger District, 509/653-2205

Getting there: From Enumclaw, drive 47 miles east on Highway 410 to Chinook Pass and proceed another 19 miles east (about 33 miles northwest of Naches) to Bumping Lake Road (Forest Road 18), at milepost 88.4. Turn right (south) and drive about half a mile to the campground.

⑭ Soda Springs 🌲🌲🌲

Soda Springs is a well-known camp in the Bumping River drainage, and probably the best RV camp in the valley. It also provides an interesting lesson in geology. Soda Springs really is a spring—located nearby, it keeps pumping out minerals from deep inside the earth, a reminder of the geologic forces that created this South Cascades outdoor adventure land. Some of that geology lesson is described on an interpretive trail across the river from the campground; the rest you'll absorb on your own by hiking local trails and driving the scenic Chinook Pass and White Pass Highways. The campground has piped water, pit toilets, an RV dump station, and some nice picnic shelters for day-trippers headed for Bumping Lake (or for bike campers caught in a rainstorm). Elevation at this campground on the Bumping River is 3,100 feet.

sites	26
🏕️ 🚐	No hookups, RVs to 30 feet
open	May to late November
reservations	None
contact	Wenatchee National Forest, Naches Ranger District, 509/653-2205

Getting there: From Enumclaw, drive 47 miles east on Highway 410 to Chinook Pass and proceed another 19 miles east to Bumping Lake Road (Forest Road 18), at milepost 88.4. Turn right (south) and continue 5 miles to the campground.

⑮ Cougar Flat 🌲🌲🌲

Another pleasant campground along the Bumping River, Cougar Flat is close to a wide range of good day-hiking and backpacking trails, such as the gut-busting Mount Aix Trail, and the more pleasant Bumping Lake Trail (see Upper and Lower Bumping Lake, below). The small campground has hand-pumped water, pit toilets, and an RV dump station. The elevation is 3,100 feet.

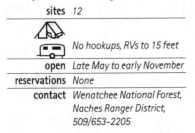

sites	12
🏕️	
🚐	No hookups, RVs to 20 feet
open	Late May to mid-September
reservations	None
contact	Wenatchee National Forest, Naches Ranger District, 509/653-2205

Getting there: From Enumclaw, drive 47 miles east on Highway 410 to Chinook Pass and proceed another 19 miles east to Bumping Lake Road (Forest Road 18), at milepost 88.4. Turn right (south) and continue about 6 miles to the campground, on the left.

⑯ Bumping Crossing 🌲🌲🌲

Bumping Crossing, the only campground in this valley not located directly on Bumping Lake or the Bumping River, isn't a bad consolation prize. The river runs nearby, and it's a lot quieter than the lakefront campground. Also more primitive.

sites	12
🏕️	
🚐	No hookups, RVs to 15 feet
open	Late May to early November
reservations	None
contact	Wenatchee National Forest, Naches Ranger District, 509/653-2205

Bumping Crossing has pit toilets but no piped or pumped water, so bring your own. Watch for elk here and throughout the Bumping River valley in the evenings. The camp is free, but you'll need a Northwest Forest Pass.

Getting there: From Enumclaw, drive 47 miles east on Highway 410 to Chinook Pass and proceed another 19 miles east to Bumping Lake Road (Forest Road 18), at milepost 88.4. Turn right (south) and go about 10 miles to the campground, on the right.

⑰ Upper and Lower Bumping Lake 🌲🌲🌲🌲

This is the main attraction in the Bumping River drainage—the place most campers, particularly those with boats, go to first in search of a place to set up shop. It's easy to see why. The 23-site lakefront (lower) campground has launching and moorage facilities, and even a handful of sites directly on the lake. Its longer sites are preferred by RVers. The 45-site upper camp, recently refurbished, is a pleasant tent/RV area. The campground's popularity is reflected in its status as

sites	68
	No hookups, RVs to 50 feet
open	Mid-May to late November
reservations	Up to 240 days in advance; National Recreation Reservation Service, 877/444-6777 or www.reserveusa.com
contact	Wenatchee National Forest, Naches Ranger District, 509/653-2205

only one of two in the Naches Ranger District still on a national reservation system. Use it to your advantage. Waterskiing and fishing are the primary activities here (the lake is stocked with trout; boat rentals are available at a private resort on the lake nearby), but don't overlook the great hiking trails in the valley. One, the Bumping River Trail, is an increasingly popular backpacking route, which can be hiked as a 20-mile, one-way hike between two separate trailheads. Watch for elk along the route. The campground has hand-pumped water and pit toilets. Several sites are wheelchair accessible. The elevation is 3,400 feet.

Getting there: From Enumclaw, drive 47 miles east on Highway 410 to Chinook Pass and continue another 19 miles east to Bumping Lake Road (Forest Road 18), at milepost 88.4. Turn right (south) and drive 11.5 miles to the campground, on the right.

18 Little Naches 🌲🌲🌲

A small Forest Service camp near the confluence of the Little Naches and American Rivers, Little Naches isn't very peaceful; it's near a major gateway for ORV riders (see notes on Kaner Flat, below), and some sites are within sight of the

sites	21
	No hookups, RVs to 32 feet
open	Late May to early November
reservations	None
contact	Wenatchee National Forest, Naches Ranger District, 509/653-2205

highway. Still, if you catch it during a quiet time, kids will love short day trips north to Horsetail Falls on the Little Naches, or south (via Forest Road 1706) to Boulder Cave, a 350-foot-long natural tunnel equipped with interpretive signs—and occupied by the rare, big-eared bat! Fishing in nearby streams also is a prime summer activity. The campground has hand-pumped water and pit toilets. The elevation is 2,562 feet.

Getting there: Little Naches is 26.5 miles northwest of Naches on Highway 410.

19 Kaner Flat 🌲🌲

Kaner Flat, with nice sites on the Naches River, has a lot going for it: great scenery, spacious campsites, good location. It also has a lot going against it, namely, dirt bikes and ORVs, which flock here to take advantage of the Naches Trail, an old

sites	41
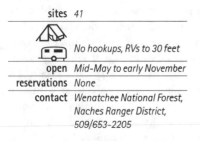	No hookups, RVs to 30 feet
open	Mid-May to early November
reservations	None
contact	Wenatchee National Forest, Naches Ranger District, 509/653-2205

wagon-train route that winds through the mountains. For campers, this campground marks a transition, of sorts, between the hiker-oriented wilderness experience to the west and the blue-smoke and loud-noise hubbub of lands in this area and to the east. Tent campers will probably wish they'd chosen a more western destination for the night. The campground, 2.5 miles off Highway 410, has hand-pumped water and pit toilets. The elevation is 2,678 feet.

Getting there: The campground is 30 miles northwest of Naches via Highway 410 and Forest Road 1900.

20 Crow Creek

sites	15
	No hookups, RVs to 30 feet
open	Mid-April to early November
reservations	None
contact	Wenatchee National Forest, Naches Ranger District, 509/653-2205

Like nearby Kaner Flats, Crow Creek is popular with dirt bikers and ORV jockeys, to which the Wenatchee National Forest dedicates large chunks of its forest. The campground has hand-pumped water and pit toilets. It's 3 miles off Highway 410, at an elevation of 2,900 feet.

Getting there: The campground is 32 miles northwest of Naches via Highway 410 and Forest Roads 1900 and 1904.

21 Sawmill Flat

This is another good hiker's base camp for trails leading into the Wenatchee National Forest. Sawmill Flat, set near the Naches River, also offers good fishing access. Dirt bikers and ORV drivers like it too. It's a standard-issue Forest Service

sites	24
	No hookups, RVs to 24 feet
open	April through November
reservations	None
contact	Wenatchee National Forest, Naches Ranger District, 509/653-2205

camp, with small sites in a pine forest, hand-pumped water, and pit toilets. Like some neighboring campgrounds, this one has a handful of family sites, double-wide spaces able to accommodate two vehicles. Whether you like the place or not might largely depend on your neighbors: When the ORV crowd hasn't taken it over, this is a popular family campground, thanks to its proximity to Boulder Cave and other natural attractions. The elevation is 2,500 feet. Halfway Flat, another Wenatchee National Forest campground, is nearby (see below).

Getting there: The campground is 25 miles northwest of Naches on Highway 410.

㉒ Halfway Flat 🌲🌲

For years, we thought this campground's biggest claim to fame was the correct answer to the Jeopardy question: How does Coke taste if you leave it sitting open on the counter for four hours? But a recent visit showed us this is a pleasant, although primitive, campground on the Naches River, with good hiking trails and stream fishing in the immediate area. Did you just get a new, totally self-contained motorhome and want to go far, far away from the neighbor's barking dogs? Halfway Flat might fit the bill. But you might just be trading pesky Fido for blue smoke. Beware the noise from ORVs which often seem to arrive here in

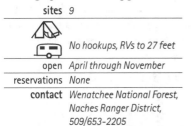

sites	9
	No hookups, RVs to 27 feet
open	April through November
reservations	None
contact	Wenatchee National Forest, Naches Ranger District, 509/653-2205

A ground squirrel standing guard over a campsite.

great droves. The spaces are large enough for most RVs, and most were recently renovated. The campground has pit toilets but no piped water, showers, or other services. The elevation is 2,050 feet.

Getting there: The campground is 28.5 miles northwest of Naches via Highway 410 and Forest Road 1704.

㉓ Cottonwood 🌲🌲🌲

This camp on the banks of the Naches River is a grand place to visit in the fall, when the hordes of summer campers—and mosquitoes—have returned to wherever it is they hide out for the winter. It's a shady, scenic spot, with good river access for fishing and sore-feet soaking. The campground has piped water, vault toilets, and an RV dump station. The elevation is 2,300 feet.

sites	16
🏕️ 🚐	No hookups, RVs to 22 feet
open	April through November
reservations	None
contact	Wenatchee National Forest, Naches Ranger District, 509/653-2205

Getting there: The campground is 22 miles northwest of Naches on Highway 410, at milepost 99.5.

Other Chinook Pass Corridor Campgrounds

One small Wenatchee National Forest campground, **American Forks** (milepost 88.4 on Highway 410; 12 sites) was being renovated at press time and could not be reviewed. Call the Naches Ranger District (509/653-2205) for details. Two group camps also operated by the Wenatchee National Forest are found along the Highway 410 corridor. They are **Pine Needle** (31 miles northwest of Naches on Highway 410; 6 group sites, RVs to 21 feet), and **Indian Flat** (24 miles northwest of Naches on Highway 410; 11 group sites, RVs to 30 feet). Reservations are required for both camps. Contact the Naches Ranger District (509/653-2205).

White Pass Corridor

㉔ Big Creek 🌲🌲🌲

Big Creek, a small campground near the western entrance to Mount Rainier National Park, is a good alternative for those summer weekends when you just

sites	29
🏕️🚐	No hookups, RVs to 22 feet
open	Late May to early September
reservations	Up to 240 days in advance; National Recreation Reservation Service, 877/444-6777 or www.reserveusa.com
contact	Gifford Pinchot National Forest, Cowlitz Valley Ranger District, Packwood office, 360/497-1172

know the national park will be packed. Sites are nicely spaced, and offer privacy that appeals to tent campers. Most RVers will find the campground's corners and narrow passages—between large hemlock, fir, and maple trees—difficult to negotiate, although the camp does have some pull-through sites. This is a good place to come tent camping with the in-laws (if there indeed is such a place): four of the sites here are double-wide, family spots, able to accommodate two vehicles. All the wonders of Mount Rainier's southwest side, including the Paradise day-use area, are a short drive away. The campground has pit toilets and piped water. The elevation is 1,800 feet.

Getting there: Big Creek is 4 miles south of Ashford (about 23 miles north of Packwood) via Highway 706 and Forest Road 52.

㉕ La Wis Wis 🌲🌲🌲🌲

This pretty Forest Service campground, set beneath a gorgeous, partially old-growth forest near the confluence of the Ohanapecosh and Cowlitz Rivers, is one of the nicest in the US 12 corridor, and right up there on the list of great places to

sites	90
🏕️🚐	No hookups, RVs to 24 feet
open	Mid-May to late September
reservations	Up to 240 days in advance; National Recreation Reservation Service, 877/444-6777 or www.reserveusa.com
contact	Gifford Pinchot National Forest, Cowlitz Valley Ranger District, Packwood office, 360/497-1172

camp in the South Cascades. The sites are particularly popular with tent campers; most are too small for RVs, but have the unique, private feel that tent campers love. Not that overnighting RVers won't fit in here. Some sites are convenient, paved pull-throughs, others are double-wide, family sites, able to fit two vehicles. The premium spots here are on the riverfront Hatchery Loop, which offers a handful of gorgeous, walk-in tent sites. The campground has pit and flush toilets, piped water, a picnic area, and good river-fishing access. Best of all, the Ohanapecosh area of Mount Rainier National Park is a mere 7 miles up the road. Warning: This campground often serves as an overflow area for nearby Ohanapecosh, where reservations are required from late June through Labor Day. Reservations here are a good idea, any time in the summer. The elevation is 1,400 feet.

Getting there: From Packwood, drive about 6.5 miles east on US 12. Turn north on Forest Road 1272 and proceed a half mile to the campground.

26 Summit Creek 🌲🌲🌲

We've driven by Summit Creek several times on trips up (bumpy, rocky, occasionally torturous) Forest Road 4510. So far, we've never found a great reason to camp here. Which isn't a slam on the campground, a tidy, if primitive, spot along Summit Creek. It's actually quite pretty. But there's not a lot to do here except stare at the bottom side of your big blue tarp for hours on end. But hey, if you're reading this during a management seminar and that thought sounds pretty

Tenters love the intimate, private sites at La Wis Wis.

sites	6
open	Mid-June through Labor Day
reservations	None
contact	Gifford Pinchot National Forest, Cowlitz Valley Ranger District, Packwood office, 360/497-1172

enticing, have at it. The campground has pit toilets, but no piped water or other facilities. Bring your water filter for the creek. Camping here is a bargain, if nothing else. At this writing, it's one of those (increasingly rare) free Forest Service camps. The elevation is 2,400 feet.

Getting there: From Packwood, drive about 9 miles east on US 12 to Forest Road 45. Turn left (north) and proceed about 2.5 miles on Forest Roads 45/4510 to the campground.

㉗ Soda Springs 🌲🌲🌲

It's tough to get to, and once you arrive, there's not much there. But the primitive campsites at Soda Springs, north of US 12 between Mount Rainier and Rimrock Lake, might seem plush to trekkers who stagger into camp after weeklong forays

sites	8
open	Mid-June to late October
reservations	None
contact	Gifford Pinchot National Forest, Cowlitz Valley Ranger District, Packwood office, 360/497-1172

into the Dumbbell Lake area. That region, part of the beautiful William O. Douglas Wilderness, which lies just to the east, is typical of this high-Cascades, Mount Rainier rain shadow country: endless chains of scenic lakes and mountain peaks formed by ancient, violent volcanism, chock-a-block with modern, insatiable mosquitoes in the summer.

Soda Springs is an "end-of-the-road" camp used largely by backcountry hikers. But it's definitely a quiet escape for the tent camper who's just looking to get far, far away from it all. The campground has pit toilets, but no piped water. Nearby Summit Creek is the water source; bring a filter. And don't complain: As of this writing, at least, the campground is free—if you have a Northwest Forest Pass parking permit. The elevation is 3,200 feet.

Getting there: From Packwood, drive about 10 miles east on US 12 to Forest Road 45. Turn left (north) and proceed about 5 miles on Forest Roads 45/4510 to the campground, near the end of the road.

㉘ Walupt Lake 🌲🌲🌲🌲

A pretty alpine lake with a ban on big motors. A boat launch. A sandy beach and clear views into the majestic Goat Rocks Wilderness. What's the catch? About 20 miles of gravel roads, that's what. Walupt Lake, a central Gifford Pinchot National

sites	51
	No hookups, RVs to 22 feet
open	Mid-June to early September
reservations	Up to 240 days in advance; National Recreation Reservation Service, 877/444-6777 or www.reserveusa.com
contact	Gifford Pinchot National Forest, Cowlitz Valley Ranger District, Packwood office, 360/497-1172

Forest camp well south of US 12, is a worthy reward for those who make the trek all the way down here. The campground is popular both with lake-fishing, -swimming, and -gazing fans and hikers bound for the Goat Rocks. One trail that begins right in the campground, in fact, leads to the upper end of the lake and beyond to the Goat Rocks Wilderness, home of some of the most scenic mountain vistas and valleys in the Northwest. Many Walupt Lake visitors head that way on horseback; an adjacent horse camp has space for nine equestrian families. This is also a nice campground for canoe enthusiasts. The shallow launch and a ban on large motors on the lake (it's trolling motors only) makes for calm, peaceful waters with great views. The main campground has 39 single campsites (28 reservable), three double or family sites, pit toilets, and piped water. The elevation is 3,900 feet. Reservations are a good idea in July and August.

Getting there: From US 12 about 2.5 miles west of Packwood, turn south on Forest Road 21, proceed about 16.5 miles, turn east on Forest Road 2160, and continue about 4 miles to the campground.

Casting for trout in Walupt Lake in the South Cascades.

㉙ White Pass Lake 🌲🌲🌲

Talk about your multiple uses. The Forest Service gets twelve full months of duty out of this handy area along pretty little White Pass Lake. In the winter, it's White Pass Ski Area's local cross-country venue, with trails that fan out around the (then-frozen) lake. But after the big thaw, the area reverts to White Pass Lake Campground, a small, scenic spot that's a handy stopover for US 12 travelers. The campground, best suited for tents and small RVs, gets a fair amount of use from hikers as well. The Pacific Crest Trail passes very near here, offering great day-hiking opportunities in the William O. Douglas Wilderness to the north and the Goat Rocks Wilderness to the south. A worthy day hike can be made at the ski area across the road. Just follow the cat track (gravel road) up the main slope and keep climbing. You'll wind up on the ridgetop, with splendid views south into the Goat Rocks, within a couple miles. However: Beware the killer mosquito hordes during summer! The campground has pit toilets, but no piped water or showers. The lake, a decent trout fishery once the water warms, is reserved for fly fishers only. An adjacent horse camp has six campsites, hitching rails, and other equestrian facilities. The elevation is 4,500 feet.

sites	16
	No hookups, RVs to 20 feet
open	May to late October
reservations	None
contact	Wenatchee National Forest, Naches Ranger District, 509/653-2205

Getting there: The campground is 19 miles east of Packwood at the White Pass summit, directly across US 12 from the White Pass Ski Area.

㉚ Dog Lake 🌲🌲🌲

sites	11
	No hookups, RVs to 20 feet
open	May to late October
reservations	None
contact	Wenatchee National Forest, Naches Ranger District, 509/653-2205

How in the world did they squeeze a campground in here? That's what you'll be wondering as you drive the short access road to Dog Lake, a small national forest campground on a tiny lakeshore bench, squeezed between water and mountain in a rugged, rocky area east of White Pass. It's a pretty little lake, and not a bad place to camp, especially for hikers. A number of trails fan out into the William O. Douglas Wilderness north of here. However, RVers may find the place a bit rustic. The campground has pit toilets, but no piped water, showers, or other services. The elevation is 3,400 feet.

Getting there: The campground is on US 12, about 21 miles east of Packwood (about 2 miles east of White Pass Ski Area).

③ Clear Lake North 🌲🌲🌲

Clear Lake North sits on the shores of one of the more fascinating waterways along the east slope of US 12. The lake actually is a portion of Rimrock Lake, a massive reservoir formed by the dammed-up headwaters of the Tieton River. The

sites	33
🏕️ 🚐	No hookups, RVs to 22 feet
open	Mid-April through November
reservations	None
contact	Wenatchee National Forest, Naches Ranger District, 509/653-2205

water level varies dramatically from month to month. When it's full, the reservoir is a stunningly beautiful lake, reflecting the rugged peaks of the Goat Rocks Wilderness. But when it's dry, the entire place turns to a giant mudflat, riddled with channels and populated by dirt-bike and ATV riders. Needless to say, aim for spring or early summer, when the reservoir is full. Clear Lake North, the first of two camps at the western end of this aquatic monstrosity, is by far the more primitive. It thus gets much less use than Clear Lake South (see below). The campground has pit toilets, but no piped water or showers. It does offer good bird-watching and fishing access to the lake. Watch for nesting bald eagles and ospreys. An interpretive trail along the lake offers wildlife-viewing information, and the North Fork Tieton, which flows out of the lake, is a great place to watch spawning kokanee (landlocked salmon; they'll

An afternoon boat jam on Clear Lake, in the North Fork Tieton drainage.

be bright red). Note: Because this is a public water resource, no swimming is allowed in the lake; fishing only. The elevation is 3,100 feet.

Getting there: From US 12 at the west end of Rimrock Lake (about 35 miles west of Naches), follow signs a short distance south on Forest Road 1200.

32 Clear Lake South ▲▲▲▲

sites	23
	No hookups, RVs to 22 feet
open	Mid-April to early November
reservations	None
contact	Wenatchee National Forest, Naches Ranger District, 509/653-2205

This is the more developed of two campgrounds set near one another at Clear Lake, a waterway connected to Rimrock Lake to the east. (See Clear Lake North, above, for recreation information.) Clear Lake South has hand-pumped water and pit toilets. The elevation is 3,100 feet.

Getting there: From US 12 at the west end of Rimrock Lake (about 35 miles west of Naches), follow signs a short distance south on Forest Road 1200.

33 Indian Creek ▲▲▲

RVers looking for a nesting spot on the east slope of US 12 often wind up at Indian Creek, one of the most developed of the handful of Forest Service campgrounds on this side of White Pass. The camp, near Rimrock Lake (see Clear Lake

sites	39
	No hookups, RVs to 32 feet
open	Mid-May to mid-September
reservations	Up to 240 days in advance; National Recreation Reservation Service, 877/444-6777 or www.reserveusa.com
contact	Wenatchee National Forest, Naches Ranger District, 509/653-2205

North, above), has pit toilets, piped water, and an RV dump station. A private marina and resort are nearby, providing a store for major firewood and bug-dope purchases. Boaters camp here in the early summer, when the reservoir is full and boating and waterskiing commence at nearby Rimrock Lake. Reservations are a good idea during those months. The elevation is 3,000 feet.

Getting there: The campground is 31 miles west of Naches on US 12.

③④ Peninsula 🌲🌲

Peninsula is one of two rustic Forest Service camps off the beaten path in the Rimrock Lake area. Like nearby South Fork (see below), Peninsula is on the southeastern

sites	Dispersed camping
🏕️	
🚐	No hookups, RVs to 20 feet
open	Mid-April to late November
reservations	None
contact	Wenatchee National Forest, Naches Ranger District, 509/653-2205

shore of the big reservoir, the water level of which goes up and down dramatically throughout the year. It's a fairly primitive site, with pit toilets and no piped water or showers. But the views from the lakeshore of the incredible, volcano-hewn rocky peaks in this area are flat-out staggering. This is one of those places worth visiting and snapping a few photos even if you're not prepared to camp. The campground has a boat launch, which is the main draw for boaters (particularly water-skiers) in the summertime. The camp also gets some wintertime use by snowmobilers and cross-country skiers, thanks to a Sno-Park nearby. The elevation is 3,000 feet. Note: Campers pay either a minimal fee, or must possess a Northwest Forest Pass parking permit.

Getting there: From US 12, about 22 miles west of Naches, turn south on Forest Road 1200 (Tieton Reservoir Road), proceed 3 miles, then follow signs a short distance west on Forest Road 711 to the camp.

③⑤ South Fork 🌲🌲🌲

Welcome to the Land of the Lost. Fans of that cheesy 1970s dinosaur show will feel right at home at South Fork, a remote spot on the South Fork Tieton River, which runs through a valley so rugged and rocky it often looks like another

sites	9
🏕️	
🚐	No hookups, RVs to 20 feet
open	Late May to mid-October
reservations	None
contact	Wenatchee National Forest, Naches Ranger District, 509/653-2205

planet. The South Fork Tieton valley contains some of the most dramatic evidence you'll ever find of the unimaginably violent volcanic forces that forged this region. Explorers willing to rough it on questionable Forest Service roads can set out from this camp for days or weeks of discovery: massive landslides, giant waterfalls, lava flows, and other gargantuan natural features (witness the notable Blue Slide, a large landslide area farther upstream on the South Fork, or the aptly named Goose Egg Mountain, which you'll pass along Forest Road 1200 on the way in) all are within reach. The campground itself has your basic Forest Service offerings: pit toilets and a dump station, but no other services. The term "site" is a bit of a misnomer for the camping spots. This is actually just a large parking area, mostly frequented by small RVs and campers. The elevation at South Fork, about a mile upstream from the river mouth at Rimrock Reservoir, is 3,000 feet.

Getting there: From US 12, about 22 miles west of Naches, turn south on Forest Road 1200 (Tieton Reservoir Road), proceed about 4 miles, then follow Forest Road 1203 a short distance south to the campground.

36 Hause Creek 🌲🌲🌲🌲

Bring your wet suit and helmet. Like most nearby campgrounds along the Tieton River, west of Naches, this one is river-rafting central in the fall, when the scheduled release of water from the Tieton Dam (just upstream) grabs the attention of the entire Northwest rafting community. Two reasons: (1) The Tieton drainage provides a gorgeous, clear-water-over-big-boulders ride; and (2) it's the only river in the state running at more than half speed in the fall, the traditional river-rafting downtime. Fall is a good time to visit even if you're not rafting, as local aspens, alders, and larches turn a splendid gold and the canyon takes on an early-season bite of cold in the evening. It's hot and drier, but still nice, in the summertime. Hause Creek is the most developed campground on the Tieton below Tieton Dam, and the best RV campground in the area. It has flush toilets (!) and an RV dump station. One campsite is barrier free. The elevation is 2,500 feet.

sites	42
🏕️ 🚐	No hookups, RVs to 30 feet
open	Late May to late November
reservations	None
contact	Wenatchee National Forest, Naches Ranger District, 509/653-2205

Getting there: The campground is 22 miles west of Naches on US 12.

37 Willows 🌲🌲🌲

Here's a nice spot along the Tieton River, especially for nature lovers. During the spring and fall, the Tieton drainage is one of the loveliest alpine river valleys in Washington, with vegetation and topography more reminiscent of higher, rockier places like the Colorado Rockies than the Evergreen State. It's particularly beautiful in the fall, when the river reaches full throttle as Rimrock Lake is drawn down, and local larch, alder, and aspen trees (and yes, willow bushes) put on a goldenrod color show. Watch for wapiti in this area; the largest herd of Rocky Mountain elk in the state winters

sites	16
🏕️ 🚐	No hookups, RVs to 20 feet
open	April through November
reservations	None
contact	Wenatchee National Forest, Naches Ranger District, 509/653-2205

over in this valley, where a feeding station at Oak Creek is a popular wintertime tourist attraction. The campground has hand-pumped water and pit toilets. The elevation is 2,400 feet.

Getting there: The campground is about 19 miles west of Naches on US 12.

㊳ Windy Point 🌲🌲🌲

It opens early in the season, closes late, and provides great access to the scenic Tieton River. That's enough to keep faithful campers coming back to this small national forest camp a short drive west of Naches. The campground has hand-pumped water and pit toilets. The elevation is 2,000 feet. See Willows, Hause Creek, South Fork, Peninsula, and Clear Lake North and South, above, for local recreation information.

sites	15
🏕️	
🚐	No hookups, RVs to 22 feet
open	April through November
reservations	None
contact	Wenatchee National Forest, Naches Ranger District, 509/653-2205

Getting there: Windy Point is about 13 miles west of Naches on US 12.

Other White Pass Corridor Campgrounds

While they're not technically in the White Pass Corridor, two Tacoma Power campgrounds near Elbe on the utility's Nisqually River Project can be good first-night stops for Seattle-area campers headed for US 12 via the Highway 7 route from Pierce County. They are **Alder Lake Park** (139 sites, 52 with full or partial hookups; showers, RV dump, and other amenities) and **Rocky Point** (24 water/electrical hookup sites). Both are open all year; contact Tacoma Power (360/569-2778). On the west side of White Pass, campers stuck on a mid-August night with no sites open at Ohanapecosh or La Wis Wis might resort to the private **Packwood RV Park** (on US 12 at Packwood; 360/494-5145). A private alternative in the Rimrock Lake area is **Silver Beach Resort** (about 30 miles west of Naches; 509/672-2500), with plentiful full hookup sites and other amenities.

Mount St. Helens

㊴ Lewis and Clark State Park 🌲🌲🌲

Something about this place smells old. Actually, most of the star attractions here truly are. Lewis and Clark, a short drive east of Interstate 5 south of Chehalis, contains a patch of old-growth forest, ancient volcanic caverns (now used to store natural gas), historic buildings, and a stretch of the old north spur of the Oregon Trail from the Cowlitz River Landing to Tumwater. The old-growth forest—one of the last lowland stands of ancient trees in western Washington—is worth a visit all on its own. Legend has it that downed trees in the local stand of Douglas fir, western hemlock, and western red cedar were so huge—6 to 9 feet in diameter—that wagon-road builders had to build ramps over them because they had no saws large enough to saw through. Although the horrific Columbus Day storm of 1962 blew nearly half of the remaining trees down, many still stand. Also worth a visit are the park's Civilian Conservation Corps-constructed buildings and the John R. Jackson House (tours available), an 1845 pioneer log cabin that was the first north of the

sites	25
🏕️🚐	No hookups, RVs to 60 feet
open	April through September
reservations	None
contact	Washington State Parks, 360/902-8844; Lewis and Clark State Park, 360/864-2643

Hoofing it up the ridge to the crater rim of Mount St. Helens.

Columbia River. Also on the premises is a Mount St. Helens visitors center, where the volcano crater is visible on clear days.

The small campground is in a wooded area, with thick underbrush separating the sites. The 620-acre park also has a nature trail, wading pool, picnic sites with shelters, horseshoe pits, and two group campsites for up to 150 campers. A horse stable and riding trails are found on the east side of Jackson Highway, the park access road. You'll find 5 miles of horse trails and 8 miles of hiking trails nearby. Note: Although this campground is accessed via US 12, we include it and most other camps in the campground-starved Mount St. Helens section because all are frequented by Mount St. Helens–area recreators.

Getting there: From the US 12/Interstate 5 junction south of Chehalis, proceed about 2.5 miles east on US 12 to Jackson Highway. Turn right and drive about 1.5 miles to the park entrance.

40 Mayfield Lake Park 🌲🌲🌲

It's not spectacular, large, or all that well-known to US 12 travelers or Mount St. Helens visitors, but this 50-acre park, a longtime county facility now run by Tacoma Power, is a good alternative to Ike Kinswa State Park for lake lovers, and

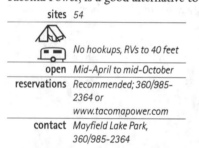

sites	54
	No hookups, RVs to 40 feet
open	Mid-April to mid-October
reservations	Recommended; 360/985-2364 or www.tacomapower.com
contact	Mayfield Lake Park, 360/985-2364

to Lewis and Clark and Seaquest State Park for campers heading toward Mount St. Helens. The campground, with some waterfront sites on the 2,250-acre Mayfield Lake, has a dump station, an expansive picnic and swimming area, a boat launch, flush toilets, and coin-op showers. Sites are nicely spaced, with average to above-average privacy. The park also has a 25-site group camp, available by reservation. Fishing in the lake can be good for planted trout or coho. Note: This is one of three popular parks now operated by Tacoma Power, as part of its Cowlitz River Project, which includes Mayfield and Mossyrock Dams and their resulting reservoirs, Mayfield and Riffe Lakes. The others are Mossyrock Park and Taidnapam (both below). Note that each of the beachfront campgrounds might cease to be beachfront when the reservoirs are drawn down. For recorded lake and river-level information, call 888/502-8690.

Getting there: From Interstate 5 south of Chehalis, take exit 68 (US 12) and drive about 17 miles east to Beach Road. Turn left (north) and drive about a quarter mile to the park.

⑪ Ike Kinswa State Park 🌲🌲🌲

This scenic 454-acre park lies on the north shore of 14-mile-long Mayfield Lake, a Cowlitz River impoundment created by Tacoma Power's Mayfield Dam. It's a summer water-recreation heaven, packed to the gills in warm months with water-

sites	*103*
🏕️ 🚐	*41 full hookups, RVs to 60 feet*
open	*All year*
reservations	*Up to 9 months in advance; 888/226-7688 or www.parks.wa.gov*
contact	*Washington State Parks, 360/902-8844; Ike Kinswa State Park, 360/983-3402*

skiers, anglers, swimmers, and sunbathers. A boat launch, located on the west side of the bridge providing access to the main park area, gets heavy use. The campsites, in three wooded loops, are quite nice—a combination of back-in and pull-through—all near restrooms with flush toilets and coin-op showers. The park also has two primitive walk-in sites (a good bet for cycle travelers), a picnic area near the mouth of the Tilton River, a nonpatrolled swimming area, an RV dump station, and 46,000 feet of shoreline. Reservations are recommended, assuming the present reservation system continues at this park.

Stay-tuned note: When this guide went to press, Ike Kinswa was one of a dozen parks on leased land—mostly owned by the federal government or public utilities—threatened with closure by the state, which said it was forced to cancel property leases to meet a budget crisis. Early indication was that Ike Kinswa's owner,

Picnic space at Ike Kinswa State Park, on 14-mile-long Mayfield Lake.

Tacoma Power, planned to cooperate with the state to co-manage the park and keep it open—with an eye toward "maximizing revenues." We're not sure what that means, but expect changes here.

Historical note: The park occupies a site that once served as a Cowlitz Indian settlement. Several Cowlitz graves were removed from an area near the park's bridge before the area was flooded by the creation of Mayfield Dam. Two marked graves were left at the site and fenced for protection in 1974. The park, formerly Mayfield Lake State Park, was renamed in 1971 to honor the late Ike Kinswa, a Cowlitz who owned property in the area.

Getting there: From Interstate 5 south of Chehalis, take exit 68 (US 12) and drive 14 miles east to Silver Creek Road. Turn north and follow signs 3.5 miles to the park.

42 Mossyrock Park 🌲🌲🌲🌲

Mossyrock, the second of Tacoma Power's triad of lakefront parks in this area, is the power company's camping powerhouse. A big, diverse park developed on the southwest shore of Riffe Lake in 1971, it has a little something for everybody—particularly if they're anglers. The lake is open year-round, and stocked with coho, steelhead, and rainbow trout. Other fishing venues in the area include the North Shore Fishing Access behind Mossyrock Dam, and Swofford Pond, which is stocked with rainbow and brown trout, largemouth bass, channel catfish, and bluegill. The campground is equally diverse, with a lakeside main camping loop featuring 24 water/electrical hookups and a wealth of pull-through sites. Also on hand are a 20-site reservable area with hookups, a 30-site "overflow" camp with no hookups, another 33-site overflow area with water/electrical hookups and showers, a 60-site group camp with a big kitchen shelter, a dozen walk-in tent sites, and an additional 10-site group camp. (We detect a theme here. By all means, get a group together.) The camp, a great family place, also has a store, playfields, and playground equipment, and just about everything else you'll need—except for solitude. It's a busy place in summer.

sites	203
🏕️ 🚐	77 water/electrical hookups, RVs to 40 feet
open	All year, except December 20 to January 1
reservations	Recommended; 360/983-3900 or www.tacomapower.com
contact	Mossyrock Park, 360/983-3900

Getting there: From Interstate 5 south of Chehalis, take exit 68 (US 12) and drive about 21 miles to Williams Street. Turn right and continue several blocks to a T intersection in the town of Mossyrock. Turn left on State Street and proceed 3.5 miles to the park. (State State becomes Mossyrock Road E and then Ajlune Road, which leads into the park.)

43 Taidnapam Park 🌲🌲🌲🌲

One of the newest and nicest campgrounds in western Washington, Taidnapam, southeast of Morton, was built in 1994 by Tacoma Power, which did some things right. It's a beaut of a location, with sites set in Doug fir and broadleaf maples on the Cowlitz River, at the head of Riffe Lake. The lake is open all year for fishing (see Mossyrock Park, above), and this park offers great access via a pedestrian and wheelchair-accessible fishing bridge across the Cowlitz. But there's plenty more to do here than wet a line. The 50-acre park is surrounded by the 14,000-acre Cowlitz Wildlife Area on the lake's north shore, home to nesting ospreys and bald eagles. Inside the park, family campers will appreciate the twin fish-cleaning stations, sandy swimming beach, boat launch, kid's playground, horseshoe pits, and other niceties. Campsites (your choice of paved pull-through or back-in) are set amidst Oregon grape, salal, and ferns, with nice tree cover, in one main loop. Also available are a 22-site group camp with a large kitchen shelter and 16 walk-in tent sites in a secluded, wooded area. The campground has an RV dump station and hot showers.

sites	68
🏕️ 🚐	52 full or partial hookups, RVs to 40 feet
open	All year, except December 20 to January 1
reservations	Recommended; 360/497-7707 or www.tacomapower.com
contact	Taidnapam Park, 360/497-7707

OK, now for the name. The moniker Taidnapam (pronounced tide-nuh-pom) honors the original campers here, the Upper Cowlitz tribe, a.k.a Taidnapam. Their history is highlighted at the park with a replica shovel-nose canoe and a kiosk detailing archaeological finds made here, with some artifacts dating back 4,600 years.

Getting there: From Interstate 5 south of Chehalis, take exit 68 (US 12) and drive about 37 miles east (about 5 miles east of Morton) to Kosmos Road. Turn right, then left onto gravel Road 100 (Champion Haul Road). Proceed about 4 miles to the park entrance, on the right.

44 Iron Creek 🌲🌲🌲🌲

Iron Creek is a popular and handy riverfront overnight spot for US 12 travelers or Mount St. Helens visitors. It's located right on the main access route for visitors bound for the more remote northeast side of the volcano (via Forest Roads 25 and 99), where popular hikes along Norway Ridge and an awesome view from Windy Ridge Viewpoint are found about 25 miles to the southwest. The Forest Service Woods Creek Information Center, on Forest Road 25 near the campground, is a good information source. The campground is in a pretty spot, set in a forest of tall

sites	98
🏕️🚐	No hookups, RVs to 42 feet
open	Mid-May to late September
reservations	Up to 240 days in advance; National Recreation Reservation Service, 877/444-6777 or www.reserveusa.com
contact	Gifford Pinchot National Forest, Cowlitz Valley Ranger District, Randle office, 360/497-1100

fir and hemlock at an elevation of 1,200 feet. Because it's one of only a few Cowlitz Valley Ranger District campgrounds accessible by primarily paved roads, this is a favorite RV camp for this area. Spaces are wide and easily maneuverable for trailers or motorhomes. Reservations are a good idea; 78 sites can be booked in advance. Also note that 17 sites here are double, family sites, able to accommodate two vehicles. The campground, set near the Cispus River, has pit toilets and piped water.

Getting there: From US 12 at Randle, follow Highway 131/Forest Road 25 about 10 miles south (following signs to Mount St. Helens National Volcanic Monument) to the campground, a short distance beyond the bridge over the Cispus River.

45 Tower Rock 🌲🌲🌲

Here's an alternative to the oft-full Iron Creek Campground (above) when you're making those summer Mount St. Helens vacation plans. However, RV owners probably will be more pleased with nearby North Fork (see below), which has

sites	22
🏕️🚐	No hookups, RVs to 22 feet
open	Mid-May to late September
reservations	Up to 240 days in advance; National Recreation Reservation Service, 877/444-6777 or www.reserveusa.com
contact	Gifford Pinchot National Forest, Cowlitz Valley Ranger District, Randle office, 360/497-1100

easier road access. Tower Rock, an older Forest Service camp, is set along the North Fork Cispus River, which is open for trout fishing in the summer. (If you're looking for better odds, visit the nearby private trout pond.) Campsites, in a mixed forest, are mostly flat, with ample space to pitch tents or spread out. Note that 15 of the sites can be reserved. The elevation is 1,100 feet. Mount St. Helens visitors bound for hikes around Norway Pass or mountain-watching at Windy Point View-point can stop for road and trail information at Woods Creek Information Center, on Forest Road 25 south of Randle.

Getting there: From US 12 at Randle, drive about a mile south on Highway 131 and veer left on Forest Road 23. Following signs to Tower Rock, proceed about 10 miles to the campground via Forest Roads 23 and 76.

The cold, clear waters of the North Fork Cispus River.

46 North Fork 🌲🌲🌲

Another favorite spot for eastside volcano visitors, North Fork is a pleasant camp along the North Fork Cispus River south of Randle. This is another good bet for RVers; campsites are large, road access is easy, and sites can be reserved well in advance, including the group camp with three sites. Campsites are set in a shady, forested area adjacent to the river. Several sites are double-wide, family sites, and some sites are pull-throughs. The elevation is 1,500 feet. Many good hiking trails and a few cycling trails are found in the area. Stop by the ranger district office in Randle for information. Note that this also is a good base camp for exploring the northeast side of Mount St. Helens, including the Norway Pass area and the Windy Ridge Viewpoint.

sites	33
🏕️🚐	No hookups, RVs to 32 feet
open	Mid-May to late September
reservations	Up to 240 days in advance; National Recreation Reservation Service, 877/444-6777 or www.reserveusa.com
contact	Gifford Pinchot National Forest, Cowlitz Valley Ranger District, Randle office, 360/497-1100

The Woods Creek Information Center, on Forest Road 25, south of Randle, is a good information source.

Getting there: From US 12 at Randle, follow Highway 131 a mile south, turn left (southeast) on Forest Road 23, and continue about 11 miles south to the campground.

47 Seaquest State Park 🌲🌲🌲

What in the world is going on here? Uninformed campers stumbling upon Seaquest State Park in the peak tourist season might be asking that, given the sell-out crowds at this otherwise unremarkable campground. What they won't know—and you will—is that this is the main spot for campers bound for Mount St. Helens up Highway 504 (Spirit Lake Highway), the only paved entrance road to the National Volcanic Monument. Seaquest is the only significant campground within a short drive of the volcano's spiffy new—and extremely popular—visitor facilities, which include Coldwater Ridge Visitors Center and Johnston Ridge Observatory. So expect large crowds here in the summertime, rain or shine, and get a reservation if you can. The campground is far from spectacular, with rather ordinary spaces spread through a flat, grassy area, and others (in the north, south, and middle loops) in the woods. It has coin-op showers, horseshoe pits, a baseball field, several Adirondack (three-sided sleeping) shelters, and an RV dump station. Across the road is the Mount St. Helens Interpretive Center, the original visitors center built after St. Helens erupted in 1980. An interpretive trail from the campground leads to a field where, weather permitting, Mount St. Helens comes into view. But the mountain isn't the only lure here. Across the highway is wide, flat Silver Lake, one of the state's most notable bass-, spiny ray-, and trout-fishing venues. (The closest boat ramp is 5 miles east on Highway 504).

sites	88
🏕️ 🚐	16 full hookups, 17 water/electrical hookups; RVs to 21 feet
open	All year
reservations	Up to 9 months in advance; 888/226-7688 or www.parks.wa.gov
contact	Washington State Parks, 360/902-8844; Seaquest State Park, 360/274-8633

Getting there: From Interstate 5 at Castle Rock, turn east on Highway 504 and proceed 6.5 miles to the park.

48 Lower Falls Recreation Area 🌲🌲🌲🌲

Lower Falls, high in the South Cascades along the Lewis River, is a hidden gem. It's close to the south side of Mount St. Helens, but because road access to the volcano itself is difficult from this side, the camp doesn't get a lot of use by St. Helens visitors. The place has its own contingent of fans, however, and little wonder. The campground, set in tall firs, is very near three scenic waterfalls on the Lewis River, as well as a wealth of good Gifford Pinchot National Forest hikes, such as the Lewis River Trail. (Beware abrupt cliff edges and seemingly safe, calm river water above the numerous falls in the area.) Campsites are very nicely spaced and fairly private. Some are pull-throughs. This, combined with the fact that the road here is paved except for the last half mile or so, makes this an increasingly popular RV destination. The campground has composting toilets and hand-pumped water. Two group sites for up to 20 campers each are available. The elevation is 1,300 feet.

sites	43
	No hookups, RVs to 60 feet
open	May through September
reservations	Up to 240 days in advance; National Recreation Reservation Service, 877/444-6777 or www.reserveusa.com
contact	Mount St. Helens National Volcanic Monument, 360/449-7800

Getting there: From Interstate 5 at Woodland, turn east on Highway 503 and proceed about 23 miles. Where Highway 503 turns south toward Amboy, continue straight (northeast) on what is now Highway 503 Spur (Lewis River Road). Drive about 7 miles, passing through Cougar, until the road becomes Forest Road 90. Continue an additional 21 miles northeast on Forest Road 90 to the campground, near milepost 29.

Other Mount St. Helens Campgrounds

They're a bit out of the way for most auto travelers visiting the volcano, but four campgrounds operated by a Portland utility company are located on the Swift Creek and Yale Reservoirs along Highway 503. They are **Cresap Bay** (73 sites), **Cougar** (60 sites), **Beaver Bay** (78 sites), and **Swift** (93 sites). Contact Pacificorp, 503/813-6666, for information. In the same general area is a free Department of Natural Resources camp, **Lake Merrill** (on Forest Road 8100, north of Highway 503 at Cougar; DNR Castle Rock office, 360/577-2025), with seven sites.

An alternate national forest campground is **Lewis River Horse Camp** (via Forest Roads 90/93 northeast of Cougar; Mount St. Helens National Volcanic Monument, 360/247-3900), with nine sites. Note: For Gifford Pinchot National Forest campgrounds south of North Fork Campground, see the Mount Adams section of this chapter.

Southern Gifford Pinchot National Forest

49 Beaver ▲▲▲▲

sites	21
	No hookups, RVs to 25 feet
open	Mid-April to late September
reservations	Up to 240 days in advance; National Recreation Reservation Service, 877/444-6777 or www.reserveusa.com
contact	Gifford Pinchot National Forest, Wind River Work Center, 509/427-3200

We've never seen one here. A beaver, that is. But we suspect more than a few have made their way past this site on the Wind River, the first Forest Service camp north of Stevenson and Carson. The campground has shady sites and a big, grassy day-use area for those (rare) sunny days. Beaver has pit toilets and piped water. Most of the sites offer easy RV parking. The elevation is 1,100 feet. Note to hikers: Falls Creek Trail and the little-visited Trapper Creek Wilderness are just to the north. Contact the Wind River Work Center in Carson for trail information.

Getting there: The campground is 12 miles north of Carson on Wind River Highway.

50 Panther Creek ▲▲▲

It's out of the way, it's lightly used, it's quiet. Three good reasons to drive up the scenic Wind River north of Carson (in the Columbia River Gorge) to check out Panther Creek Campground, a nice Forest Service site set in a very deep Douglas-

sites	33
	No hookups, RVs to 25 feet
open	Mid-May to mid-September
reservations	Up to 240 days in advance; National Recreation Reservation Service, 877/444-6777 or www.reserveusa.com
contact	Gifford Pinchot National Forest, Wind River Work Center, 509/427-3200

fir forest. The campground, at 1,000 feet, has creekside sites, hand-pumped water, and pit toilets. It also has paved sites and actually is quite well suited to self-contained RVs. Eight of the sites are double-wide, family sites, able to accommodate two vehicles. About two-thirds of the sites can be reserved in advance. A horse camp is located adjacent to the campground. The camp is close to a wide range of good hiking trails; the Pacific Crest Trail passes over the creek on a bridge nearby. Stop by the Wind River Work Center (formerly Wind River Ranger District) in Carson on the way here to check trail and road conditions.

Getting there: From Carson, drive 6 miles north on Wind River Highway to Forest Road 65. Turn right and proceed about 4 miles northeast on Forest Road 65 to the campground.

⑤ Paradise Creek 🌲🌲🌲

When you think about the wild inland areas of the Gifford Pinchot National Forest, you think of deep, old- and second-growth forest, clear streams, and a wide range of rocky, volcanic formations. All are in evidence in and around Paradise Creek, near the confluence of the creek and the scenic Wind River. The lightly used campground, which sits in heavy forest at 1,500 feet, has pit toilets and hand-pumped water. Thirty-one campsites can be reserved in advance; four are double, family sites, able to accommodate two vehicles. The camp offers good access to the Wind River, and a nearby trail leads to the top of scenic Lava Butte.

sites	*42*
🏕️ 🚐	*No hookups, RVs to 25 feet*
open	*Mid-May to mid-September*
reservations	*Up to 240 days in advance; National Recreation Reservation Service, 877/444-6777 or www.reserveusa.com*
contact	*Gifford Pinchot National Forest, Wind River Work Center, 509/427-3200*

Getting there: The campground is 20 miles north of Carson on Wind River Highway.

⑤ Moss Creek 🌲🌲🌲

Moss Creek is the first Gifford Pinchot National Forest camp encountered on the south-to-north journey up the Little White Salmon River, north of Highway 14 in the Columbia River Gorge. The campground, reached via paved roads, is a pleasant spot along the creek, with small, private campsites great for tents and OK for smaller RVs. This is a pretty area; bring the camera. The campground has pit toilets and piped water. Ten sites can be reserved in advance. Campground elevation is 1,400 feet.

sites	*17*
🏕️ 🚐	*No hookups, RVs to 32 feet*
open	*Mid-May to late September*
reservations	*Up to 240 days in advance; National Recreation Reservation Service, 877/444-6777 or www.reserveusa.com*
contact	*Gifford Pinchot National Forest, Wind River Work Center, 509/427-3200*

Note: The otherworldly Big Lava Bed, one of the state's most fascinating geologic features, is a short drive to the north on Forest Road 66. It really is big—12,500 acres of lava, varying in height from 2,000 to 3,350 feet. Trouble is, all lava looks pretty much the same, and it's easy to get lost in there. Bring a compass—and signal flares!

Getting there: From Cook on Highway 14 (near Drano Lake), turn north on County Road 1800 and drive about 8 miles north to the campground on Forest Road 18 (a.k.a Oklahoma Road).

⑤③ Oklahoma 🌲🌲

It's where the wind goes whipping down the plain. Actually, the flat spaces in and around this Oklahoma, high on the Little White Salmon River in the volcanically warped Gifford Pinchot National Forest, are more like meadows. But this far off the main highway, who's checking? The campground, at 1,700 feet, is a bit rough around the edges, with gravel roads (although it's paved all the way here) and campsites, pit toilets, and hand-pumped water. On the other hand, being this far away from the nearest bait 'n' video store has its advantages: It's quiet. But beware the killer mosquitoes in the summer. Fourteen sites can be reserved in advance. Check out the nearby Big Lava Bed (see Moss Creek, above).

sites	23
🏕️ 🚐	No hookups, RVs to 22 feet
open	Mid-May to mid-September
reservations	Up to 240 days in advance; National Recreation Reservation Service, 877/444-6777 or www.reserveusa.com
contact	Gifford Pinchot National Forest, Wind River Work Center, 509/427-3200

Getting there: From Cook on Highway 14 (near Drano Lake), turn north on County Road 1800 and drive about 14 miles north to the campground near the end of the pavement on Forest Road 18 (a.k.a Oklahoma Road).

⑤④ Peterson Prairie 🌲🌲🌲🌲

Ooh. Ooh. You've gotta see the stuff to be seen here. This is a truly grand place to come camping in the fall, when this area southwest of Mount Adams turns into the biggest wild huckleberry patch in the entire Northwest, and perhaps on the planet. Choice picking abounds if you time it right (usually late August through mid-September). Watch for black bears, and check with the Mount Adams Ranger District for berry-ripeness reports; the time varies from year to year. If the berry festivities don't hold your attention, mosey over to the nearby Ice Cave, a lava tube discovered by early settlers. The tube, accessible by a stairway, for many years served as the ice supply for pioneers in Hood River and The Dalles, both in the Columbia River Gorge. Worth a look. The campground is in a mixed evergreen forest (not too dark), with a range of pull-through sites for RVs and back-in sites

sites	30
	No hookups, RVs to 32 feet
open	May to late September
reservations	Up to 240 days in advance; National Recreation Reservation Service, 877/444-6777 or www.reserveusa.com
contact	Gifford Pinchot National Forest, Mount Adams Ranger District, 509/395-3400

with good privacy for tents. It has pit toilets and piped water. Sixteen sites can be reserved in advance. A group camp for up to 50 campers is available. The elevation is 2,800 feet.

Getting there: From Highway 14 west of White Salmon (66 miles east of Vancouver), turn north on Highway 141 and proceed about 25 miles to Forest Road 24 (5.5 miles beyond and southwest of the town of Trout Lake). Bear right and follow Forest Road 24 west 2.5 miles to the campground.

55 Goose Lake

Here's a nice spot to float your canoe, paddle your float tube, or set out on an air mattress in search of a few alpine-lake trout. Lots of campers do so in midsummer at Goose Lake, making this lakeshore fish camp a popular spot. That's in spite of

An old forest burn on the south side of Mount Adams.

somewhat primitive conditions, which include gravel roads; sketchy, hilly, ill-defined parking areas (most of the sites are walk-in, making them nice for tenters, but a pain for RV owners); pit toilets; and a lack of piped water. Other summer options include huckleberry picking and exploring the Big Lava Bed (see Moss Creek, above) and other local geologic features. The elevation is 3,200 feet. This campground melts out slowly in June, and you'll need to traverse about 5 miles of gravel roads to get here. Twenty-six of the sites can be reserved in advance.

sites 37

No hookups, RVs to 18 feet

open Mid-June to late September

reservations Up to 240 days in advance; National Recreation Reservation Service, 877/444-6777 or www.reserveusa.com

contact Gifford Pinchot National Forest, Mount Adams Ranger District, 509/395-3400

Getting there: From Highway 14 west of White Salmon (66 miles east of Vancouver), turn north on Highway 141 and proceed 25.5 miles to Forest Road 24 (about 5.5 miles beyond the town of Trout Lake). Follow Forest Road 24 about 2.5 miles west (near Peterson Prairie, see above) to Forest Road 60. Continue about 5 miles west to the campground on Forest Road 60. Note: This camp also can be accessed from Wind River valley to the west via Wind River Road, Forest Road 65 (Panther Creek Road) and Forest Road 60.

56 Cultus Creek 🌲🌲🌲🌲

Here's a perfect base camp for that long-considered, but never undertaken, backpacking expedition into the Indian Heaven Wilderness, one of the wildest portions of the very wild Gifford Pinchot National Forest. The somewhat rustic campground, which gets the most use during the fall huckleberry season, is pleasant all summer and receives only light use much of the time. The final 7 miles up here are on gravel road, and the campground roads are gravel. But the campsites are great, with flat, level spaces for tents and just the right amount of sun in a Douglas-fir and hemlock forest. Most sites are RV friendly, if you're willing to drive the beast all the way up here to 4,000 feet. The campground has

sites 51

No hookups, RVs to 32 feet

open June through September

reservations None

contact Gifford Pinchot National Forest, Mount Adams Ranger District, 509/395-3400

pit toilets and drinking water, but no garbage service. A Northwest Forest Pass parking permit is required in lieu of a camping fee. Local, um, "art" note: If he's still there, don't miss the campground's chainsaw-stump sculpture of "Smokey," the wooden forest worker. He looks a bit too much like the late Governor Dixy Lee Ray for our taste.

Getting there: From Highway 14 west of White Salmon (66 miles east of Vancouver), turn north on Highway 141 and proceed 25.5 miles to Forest Road 24 (5.5 miles beyond the town of Trout Lake). Follow Forest Road 24 (turning north at the junction near Peterson Prairie Campground) about 13.5 miles northwest to the campground.

57 Tillicum 🌲🌲

The Forest Service prospectus on this campground sounded dubious. "A few good camping spots," it said, "with numerous other poor ones." Let's just say the folks at Gifford Pinchot get high marks for truth in advertising. This isn't a great place to camp. It's not even a very good place to camp. But in a pinch, such as during the great human berry-picking waves down here in the fall, it might suffice. It also makes a decent base camp for backcountry hikes into the wilds of the Squaw Butte/Big Creek area north of the Indian Heaven Wilderness. The campground has pit toilets and is at 4,300 feet.

sites	32
🏕	
🚐	No hookups, RVs to 18 feet
open	Mid-June to late September
reservations	None
contact	Gifford Pinchot National Forest, Mount Adams Ranger District, 509/395-3400

Getting there: From Highway 14 west of White Salmon, turn north on Highway 141 and proceed 25.5 miles to Forest Road 24 (5.5 miles beyond the town of Trout Lake). Follow Forest Road 24 (turning north at the junction near Peterson Prairie Campground) about 20 miles northwest to the campground (about 6.5 miles north of Cultus Creek, above).

Other Southern Gifford Pinchot National Forest Campgrounds

On the far west side of Gifford Pinchot National Forest, a small, alternative camp with 18 sites is **Sunset Falls** (on Forest Road 42; Wind River Work Center, 509/427-3200). In the Trout Lake area (upper White Salmon River drainage), more primitive, alternative sites include **Trout Lake Creek** (on Forest Road 8810-011; 21 sites); **Smokey Creek** (on Forest Road 24), with 3 sites and no fee—the Forest Service describes it as "hardly a campground"; **Little Goose** (on Forest Road 24), with 28 sites, used primarily during fall berry season; **Saddle** (on Forest Road 2480 near Tillicum Campground, above), a poor campground with 12 free tent sites and bad road access; and **Atkisson Group Camp** with space for 50 (on Forest Road 24; reservations only, 877/444-6777 or www.reserveusa.com). Call the Mount Adams Ranger District (509/395-3400).

Mount Adams

58 Morrison Creek 🌲🌲🌲🌲

It's more a bivouac site than a campground, but Morrison Creek makes up for its lack of amenities with an awesome setting—the southern shoulder of 12,275-foot Mount Adams, second highest peak in Washington. It's a primitive site, with pit toilets but no piped water or anything else to speak of. Which is fine if you're here for what most Morrison Creek campers come for: A bit of rest before heading into the Mount Adams Wilderness for extended day hikes, backpack trips, or summit attempts. A grand day hike right from the campground is the Shorthorn Trail, a 5.6-mile round-trip to a scenic viewpoint on

sites	12
open	July through September
reservations	None
contact	Gifford Pinchot National Forest, Mount Adams Ranger District, 509/395-3400

the mountainside. Farther up the road from here is Cold Springs, an even less official hike-in climbers' campsite with one outhouse signaling its presence. Access to these campgrounds, at 4,600 feet and 5,700 feet, respectively, is on rough Forest Service roads. Leave that pretty Lincoln Navigator in the garage and take somebody else's beat-up four-by-four. Note: A Northwest Forest Pass parking permit is required here in lieu of a camping fee.

Getting there: From Highway 141 at Trout Lake, turn north on County Road 17. Following signs for Mount Adams Recreation Area, continue about 12 miles north on County Road 17 and Forest Roads 80 and 8040.

59 Blue Lake Creek 🌲🌲

sites	11
	No hookups, RVs to 22 feet
open	Mid-May to late September
reservations	Up to 240 days in advance; National Recreation Reservation Service, 877/444-6777 or www.reserveusa.com
contact	Gifford Pinchot National Forest, Cowlitz Valley Ranger District, Randle office, 360/497-1100

This small campground, one of the least used in the area, is a nice spot for tents, with flat, open spaces in a pleasant mixed forest. Roads are paved to the campground; those driving RVs can park here, but probably would prefer other local Forest Service camps, such as Iron Creek and North Fork, to the northwest (see the Mount St. Helens section of this chapter). Blue Lake Creek is set along a creek near the trailhead to Blue Lake (3.5 miles one way). Whether you like the place or flee in terror is up to chance; a number of ORV trails run nearby. If the blue-smoke belching machines are running, you won't want to stay long enough to get the bottoms of your shoes dirty. The campground has a swank pit toilet and hand-pumped water. The elevation is 1,900 feet.

Getting there: From US 12 at Randle, follow Highway 131 a mile south, turn left (southeast) on Forest Road 23, and proceed 16 miles to the campground.

⑥⓪ Adams Fork 🌲🌲🌲

Adams Fork is a very pretty campground on the upper Cispus River, below the northwestern flank of Mount Adams. Unfortunately, it can suffer from the same malady as nearby Blue Lake Creek (see above): ORV pollution, both the noise and air varieties. If that's not a problem for you, or if you're lucky enough to be here when they aren't, this is a pleasant spot in a nice stand of fir and hemlock. A nearby trail leads to Blue Lake. The campground has pit toilets and hand-pumped water. Seventeen campsites can be reserved in advance. The elevation is 2,600 feet.

sites	24
	No hookups, RVs to 22 feet
open	May through September
reservations	Up to 240 days in advance; National Recreation Reservation Service, 877/444-6777 or www.reserveusa.com
contact	Gifford Pinchot National Forest, Cowlitz Valley Ranger District, Randle office, 360/497-1100

Getting there: From US 12 at Randle, follow Highway 131 a mile south, turn left (southeast) on Forest Road 23, and proceed about 18 miles to Forest Road 21. Turn southeast (stay left) and continue about 5 miles to the campground, near the junction with Forest Road 56.

⑥① Horseshoe Lake 🌲🌲🌲🌲

Canoe lovers, this one's for you. Horseshoe Lake is a tiny, insignificant national forest camp on the northwestern flank of magnificent Mount Adams. But once you've been to this camp, it looms large in the memory of those who love to pitch a tent next to a serene alpine lakeshore, with the family canoe parked within range. Campsites are sort of ill-defined, but this dime-sized lake offers a billion-dollar view of Adams, and trout fishing can be good in season. Gas motors are prohibited on the lake. Even so, the serenity is spoiled from time to time by dirt bikes and other ORVs in this general

sites	10
	No hookups, RVs to 16 feet
open	Mid-June to late September
reservations	None
contact	Gifford Pinchot National Forest, Cowlitz Valley Ranger District, Randle office, 360/497-1100

vicinity. The campground has pit toilets, but no piped water. The elevation is 4,200 feet. A national forest road map will be a worthy investment to navigate the roads here, at least 12 miles of which will be gravel in various states of repair.

Getting there: From US 12 at Randle, follow Highway 131 a mile south, then turn left (southeast) on Forest Road 23. Continue 29 miles to a junction with Forest Road 2329. Turn left (northeast) and, proceeding around the north shore of Takhlakh Lake, drive 7 miles to Forest Road 078. Turn left and follow it about 1.5 miles to the campground.

62 Takhlakh Lake 🌲🌲🌲🌲

If you've only got enough energy to get up close to Mount Adams once in your life, expend it here. Takhlakh Lake, the stunning campground with the funny name (it's pronounced TOCK-lock), is the flagship camping area in the Gifford Pinchot National Forest. Sites are spread nicely through a slightly hilly, beautifully forested shore of the lake, where gas motors are prohibited and the view straight across to Mount Adams will melt your neoprene socks. This is a wonderful place to bring a canoe or kayak and spend a few days in awe of the mountain.

Takhlakh Lake and Mount Adams: Two jewels of the South Cascades.

Not that there isn't plenty to do nearby. The campground has a great beachfront day-use area, with picnic sites right along the shore. It also has a boat launch, and a 1.5-mile trail that runs around the lake, great for morning exercise. On the far side of the lake, that trail connects with another path that leads up to an impressive lava flow just off Forest Road 2329 (you can also drive here). Local roads make great mountain-bike paths, although they're very dusty in midsummer. Back at the lake, many people idle away the daytime hours fishing. Angling for trout can be productive, especially early in the season, just after the campground opens for the summer. If you get bored with all that, a host of hiking trails, from trailheads in the immediate vicinity, lead southeast onto Mount Adams itself.

sites	62
🏕️ 🚐	No hookups, RVs to 22 feet
open	Mid-June through September
reservations	Up to 240 days in advance; National Recreation Reservation Service, 877/444-6777 or www.reserveusa.com
contact	Gifford Pinchot National Forest, Cowlitz Valley Ranger District, Randle office, 360/497-1100

The campground has pit toilets, but no showers (this, plus notorious early-summer mosquitoes, keeps Takhlakh from a five-tree rating). The sites are paved, 12 are double-sized, family sites, and most are easily accessible by RVs. Thirty-seven of them can be reserved, and it's a good idea to get a reservation almost anytime you're planning to come here. Access note: The (long) drive down from Randle is mostly paved, with several miles of intermittent stretches of dusty gravel road. (It gets really narrow in a couple spots; use caution.) The campground elevation is 4,500 feet.

Getting there: From US 12 at Randle, follow Highway 131 a mile south, then turn left (southeast) on Forest Road 23. Continue 29 miles to a junction with Forest Road 2329. Turn left and drive about 1.5 miles to the campground.

Other Mount Adams–Area Campgrounds

Several other small, primitive Gifford Pinchot National Forest camps ring Mount Adams. These include **Chain of Lakes** (near the end of Forest Road 2329), with three dusty, scattered sites and a motorcycle trail nearby; **Cat Creek** (on Forest Road 21; 5 sites); **Twin Falls** (on Forest Road 90; 8 sites); **Killen Creek** (on Forest Road 2329 south of Horseshoe Lake Campground, above), essentially a wilderness trailhead with eight sites; nearby **Keene's Horse Camp** (dispersed camping for horse campers only); and **Olallie Lake** (on Forest Road 5601), a pretty, but very small, dusty, Adams-view campground with five sites. Call the Cowlitz Valley Ranger District (360/497-1100).

On the east side of the mountain, the Department of Natural Resources operates **Island Camp** (6 sites) and **Bird Creek** (8 sites), both primitive campgrounds with access through the Goldendale area. Call the DNR's Ellensburg office (509/925-8510).

Columbia River Gorge

⑥⑬ Beacon Rock State Park 🌲🌲🌲

Let's just say you don't need to follow many road signs to find Beacon Rock. The aptly named stone, a massive volcanic plug jutting from the soil along the banks of the lower Columbia River, is a wonder in itself: 850 feet high, with near vertical walls. It's believed to be the second largest monolith in the world, second only to that little rock called Gibraltar. A trail winds upward 1 mile—with 53 precarious switchbacks—to the top, where an unforgettable view awaits.

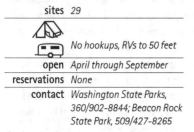

sites	29
	No hookups, RVs to 50 feet
open	April through September
reservations	None
contact	Washington State Parks, 360/902-8844; Beacon Rock State Park, 509/427-8265

The rock is so impressive, its summit trail so popular, that most of us ignore the large, diverse state park just across the road. Beacon Rock, the park, is in many ways nearly as impressive as Beacon Rock, the rock. The 4,650 acres contain a nice, albeit small, older campground that's really best suited for tents; a large group camp with Adirondack shelters for up to 200; a picnic area with five shelters; coinop showers; playground equipment; and other niceties. Above the park proper are many good hiking trails, including one up Hardy Creek to Rodney and Hardy Falls (about 2 miles round-trip) and beyond to the top of Hamilton Mountain. More than 13 miles of gravel fire roads run through the wooded upland area, providing a trail-riding bonanza for horse and mountain-bike riders. Below Beacon Rock is another strip of state park land with picnic facilities and a Columbia River boat launch.

Of course, all of this must wait until the entire camping party has made the obligatory march to the summit of the rock, which is believed to be a large andesite plug from a long-since-eroded volcano vent. (Keep a tight rein on the kids here; the handrails make this steep trail, which literally clings to the south face of the rock, fairly safe, but short people can slide underneath.)

Also take a moment to consider the fascinating history of Beacon Rock. It had legendary landmark status among natives who, before the Columbia was tamed by two dozen dams, knew it marked the last rapids on the river and the first tidal influence from the Pacific Ocean, 150 miles to the west. Lewis and Clark who camped nearby in 1805, are believed to have been the first white men to see the rock. They camped near its walls in the winter of 1805, and named it Beacon Rock in their journals. Years later, a man named Henry J. Biddle purchased the big rock and surrounding property. He built the impressive summit trail between 1916 and 1918. After his death, much wrangling occurred over the property. Oregon residents at one

The Beacon Rock Trail clings to the south face of the monolith.

point even attempted to make it an Oregon State Park to prevent commercial development. It ultimately was turned over to Washington State in 1935.

Today, the rock has a new constituency group keeping careful watch: rock climbers, who prefer the south face for its long, uninterrupted pitches. The face contains some 60 routes, many among the more technically challenging in the Northwest, with ratings up to 5.10. The rock is closed from February 1 to July 15 to allow peregrine falcons to nest on the cliffs. Note: Good day trips from here include the Bonneville Dam Fishway and Visitors Center (spring chinook pass through in April and May, other salmon species later), and the Carson National Fish Hatchery, near the Wind River Ranger Station north of Carson.

Getting there: Beacon Rock is 35 miles east of Vancouver on Highway 14.

64 Horsethief Lake State Park ▲▲▲▲

Have some spare time on your hands and want to take up a good cause? Petition Washington State Parks to change the name of Horsethief Lake State Park, one of the most historically significant—and misnamed—sites in the Northwest. The campground that lies on the shores of this 90-acre lake, a Columbia River backwater created by a railroad-crossing landfill, reportedly was named by 1950s surveyors, who said the nearby canyon looked like a hideout for horse thieves. Maybe so, but it also happens to be ground zero for a thriving native population that lived, traded, and fished near here for centuries. A park name reflecting and honoring that past seems more than appropriate. Historians note that this spot was a gathering and trading spot for coastal tribes and inland tribes. Lewis and Clark wrote that the land also was home to a permanent settlement of fishermen, who fished with spears and nets for salmon in the rapids of the now-flooded Celilo Falls area. The park site was also one of the largest native burial sites on the Columbia. Some graves remain in a small cemetery here, and rocks in its upland area contain some of the oldest known petroglyphs in the Northwest. Several are visible from a short trail that starts in the park. One of the more notable drawings, "She Who Watches," can be viewed on guided tours arranged with rangers by prescheduling at the number above.

sites	14
🏕	
🚐	8 partial hookups, RVs to 30 feet
open	April through October
reservations	None
contact	Washington State Parks, 360/902-8844; Horsethief Lake State Park, 509/767-1159

The campground here is unremarkable, with exposed, grassy campsites on the lake's west shore. The park has an RV dump station. Two boat launches get heavy use. The surrounding region is a great spring-wildflower-viewing venue, with plentiful bright balsam root. The lake (no gas motors allowed) is a popular trout- and bass-fishing venue. It also has become a practice area for up-and-coming windsurfers who aren't quite ready for the big waters of the adjacent Columbia River. Above the park, several trails lead up to 500-foot Horsethief Butte, where some rock-climbing pitches are available. Beware poison oak, rattlesnakes, and occasionally quite nasty Gorge winds.

Getting there: The park is near milepost 85 and the Dalles Dam on Highway 14, 17 miles east of White Salmon and 28 miles west of Goldendale.

⑥⑤ Brooks Memorial State Park 🌲🌲🌲🌲

We placed this lovely, forested state park in the Columbia Gorge section for two reasons: (1) It's truly a nice place to camp, especially for tenters; and (2) it's not really close to anything else. Brooks Memorial, 25 miles north of the Gorge on US 97, is in the unique type of dry pine forest that's typical of the beautiful Satus Pass area in the Simcoe Mountains, on the eastern slope of the South Cascades. The park, which has a large group camp (with cabins and teepees), substantial picnic shelters, and educational facilities, is most heavily used by organized groups. But it has a very pleasant campground in the portion of the park on the west side of US 97. It's equipped with flush toilets, piped water, and coin-op showers. The tent-designated campsites, scattered through two ponderosa pine–forested loops, are

sites	*45*
 🚐	*23 full hookups, RVs to 30 feet*
open	*All year; limited winter facilities*
reservations	*None*
contact	*Washington State Parks, 360/902-8844; Brooks Memorial State Park, 509/773-5382*

tidy and pleasant. Hookup sites are in a grassy area with paved parking strips. The park also offers hiking trails to local beaver dams on the Little Klickitat River, among other attractions. The entire place is beautiful in the spring, when wildflowers burst into blossom in local meadows. The high elevation (3,000 feet) makes this a popular cross-country skiing destination in the winter. Also note that the Goldendale Observatory, the largest telescope of its kind in the United States available for public use, is a short drive away, near Goldendale. (Call 509/773-3141 for schedules and details.) Historical note: The park was named for Nelson Brooks, a local citizen who helped establish and improve local roads.

Getting there: The park straddles US 97 13 miles north of Goldendale and 40 miles south of Toppenish, just south of Satus Pass summit.

The Columbia River Gorge is the only sea-level passage through the Cascade Mountains.

⑥⑥ Maryhill State Park 🌲🌲🌲🌲

Maryhill has long been one of our favorite state parks. Not so much for what it contains, which is nice enough, but for the spirit that comes along with this odd corner of the Evergreen State. Most of that, of course, is the legacy of local legend Sam Hill, son-in-law of railroad tycoon James Hill. The eccentric/inspired (take your pick) character of this man, who is entombed on the hillside above, lives on around Maryhill, named after Hill's wife, Mary. In the 1920s, he built a massive castlelike home on a bluff overlooking the river here, now known as Maryhill Museum. Hill, a Quaker and ardent pacifist, also built a near-scale concrete model

sites	70
	50 full hookups, RVs to 50 feet
open	All year
reservations	None
contact	Washington State Parks, 360/902-8844; Maryhill State Park, 509/773-5007

of Stonehenge on the hillside above this park, dedicating it to the victims of World War I. The state park that bears his family name is a pleasant spot on a broad, flat plain with 4,700 feet of frontage on the Columbia River. Camping spaces are mostly shaded and grassy, nice for tents. The beach area has breakwaters that cut the river current to provide swimming and windsurfing access. The park is also popular among fishermen, who launch here and pursue Columbia River salmon or sturgeon bigger than your car. The campground is nicely equipped, with picnic facilities with two kitchen shelters, flush toilets, piped water, an RV dump station, and coin-op showers. Reservations are a good idea in the summer.

Getting there: The park is 12 miles south of Goldendale on Highway 14, immediately east of the Sam Hill (US 97) Bridge over the Columbia River.

Other Columbia River Gorge Campgrounds

Visitors heading for the Columbia River Gorge can take advantage of two southwest Washington State Parks: **Paradise Point** near the East Fork Lewis River (15 miles north of Vancouver and 6 miles south of Woodland, take I-5 exit 16; 78 sites, no hookups); and **Battle Ground Lake** (northeast of Vancouver via Highway 503; 50 sites, no hookups). Call Washington State Parks (360/902-8844).

Central Washington

You get the sense that something really big happened here once. And by that we do not mean Dylan and The Dead at the Gorge. More than any other place in Washington, the central slice of the state—the heart of the Evergreen, as it were—looks, feels, and sometimes acts disturbed. It has good reason. This is the scene of the crime—the big spurt that made the rest of our state what it is today. We're referring, of course, to the Great Flood. Not the one Noah rode out; the one that came booming across the West after a massive glacial ice dam packed its bags in western Montana and fled for good to the Northwest Territories. In the process, much of what we now know as central and eastern Washington lived up to what at that time must have been its highest and best use—as a sink drain for the head and shoulders of North America.

Some truly Big Waters came ripping through central Washington in those days, 10,000 to 40,000 years ago, when massive floodwaters poured across the central state, creating waterfalls that would make Niagara look like the stream from a Super Soaker. It's all over with now, thank heavens. But the result is seen, enjoyed, boated in, and camped upon today by millions of sun-drenched outdoor lovers—without so much as a thought about how it all got here.

Which is fine. We're here to point you toward campsites, not spew out lectures for skipping Natural History 104. Now that you're properly schooled in the geologic forces that created the Grand Coulee, sandblasted the Channeled Scablands, and paved the way for the world's biggest, juiciest apple crop, feel free to roam the area at will and select a good place to park the Itasca Land Yacht.

There's a surprising amount from which to choose. Many western Washingtonians are amazed when they see figures that show central-state parks as some of the busiest in the Northwest. They're less surprised once they visit and see the obvious lures: The white mountains and deep blue inland sea of Lake Chelan. The calm, flat waters of the middle Columbia River. The awesome cliffs and watery reservoirs of the Grand Coulee.

See the pattern? It's the sun, stupid. And the water it warms. In these dry, wind-whipped lands surrounded by the comforting arms of the Columbia River, consistent warm, sunny weather combines with hundreds of square miles of cool, clear water to create an unbeatable recreation double team. Sun and water lovers—be they water-skiers, anglers, swimmers, Jet-ski cowboys, windsurfers, bird-watchers, or just misplaced beach bums—can't get enough of central Washington. That explains why many of its parks, particularly the state parks along the middle Columbia and in the Sun Lakes/Banks Lake area, are among the most consistently booked in Washington.

These parks draw hordes of repeat customers. If you don't believe it, visit North Bend on a Friday night and watch the long trail of boat trailers snake its way east, then come back the same way Sunday night. Luckily, most of these parks now are on the state reservation system, allowing you first-timers to make the trip over and see what all the commotion is about without worry.

We don't mean to suggest central Washington ever gets crowded, cramped, or even upset. This is a big, tough area—one quite used to large-scale commotion. And—nothing against all you folks in campers—but compared to the commotion that's gone on here before, you're little more than a gnat on the elephant's back. Dig in and hang on.

1. Wenatchee River County Park
2. Wenatchee Confluence State Park
3. Lincoln Rock State Park
4. Daroga State Park
5. Beebe Bridge Park
6. Entiat City Park
7. Alta Lake State Park
8. Bridgeport State Park
9. Lake Chelan State Park
10. Twenty-Five Mile Creek State Park
11. Lakeshore RV Park
12. Ginkgo-Wanapum State Park
13. Potholes State Park
14. Sun Lakes State Park
15. Coulee City Park
16. Steamboat Rock State Park
17. Spring Canyon
18. Keller Ferry
19. Fort Spokane
20. Hawk Creek
21. Yakima Sportsman State Park

Central Washington Map

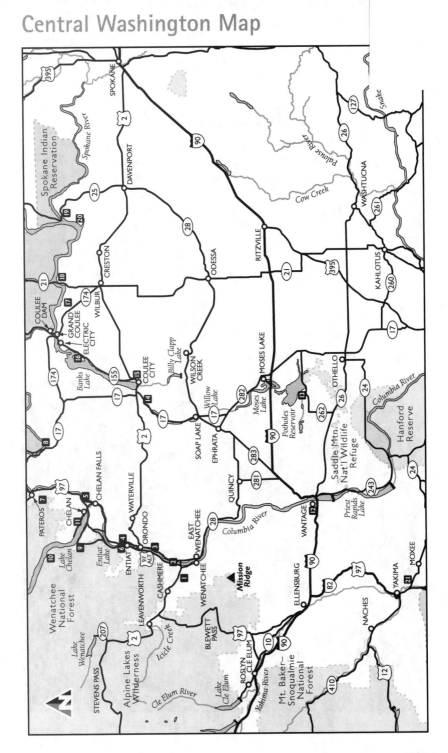

Middle Columbia

1 Wenatchee River County Park ▲▲⌅

Given its location—sandwiched between the rushing Wenatchee River and the roaring interstate—this campground doesn't exactly rate high on the serenity

sites	80
🏕️ 🚐	80 partial or full hookups, RVs to any length
open	April through October
reservations	509/667-7503
contact	Wenatchee River County Park, 509/667-7503

scale. But its convenience more than makes up for that, particularly if you're an RV-equipped camper on a long cross-state trek. The campsites are all close together in a flat, grassy, shaded area on a high bank above the river. The campground has flush toilets, showers, and other amenities. The park has some shade trees, a Wenatchee River put-in often used by rafters and kayakers, and some tent sites. Generally, though, it's best used as a convenient US 2 stopover for RVers.

Getting there: The campground is about 5 miles west of Wenatchee on US 2.

Kayaks lined up for Ridge To River, a spring Wenatchee River tradition.

❷ Wenatchee Confluence State Park

🌲🌲🌲🌲

First, some troubling news: Sadly, when this guide went to press, Wenatchee Confluence was one of a dozen Washington State Parks in danger of closing because of state budget problems. The park is on land leased from the Chelan County Public Utility District, which has agreed to help underwrite its operation temporarily. The same holds true for nearby Daroga and Lincoln Rock State Parks (see below). Call the contact number and check the park's operating status before departing.

For camping families who like to play, this is the Disneyland of the Washington State Parks system. The park, 200 acres of open, green space just north of the confluence of the powerful Wenatchee and Columbia Rivers, was for many centuries a gathering place of native peoples from both the east and west sides of the Cascades. The campground here today continues that tradition, offering visitors a wide choice of activities—land and waterborne—at a site fittingly located not far from the geographic center of Washington State. The campsites on this flat, sunny, riverside facility, built in the early 1990s, are tidy and beautifully manicured, although slightly antiseptic, since this is a new park and much of the vegetation is still only head high. Because of that, the park suffers from the same lack of shade as other new parks in this region. But cool breezes often emanate from the two rivers, and trees installed with the campsites will make this a more pleasant summer spot with the passage of each year. Besides, that very lack of rough natural vegetation makes this a completely wonderful place to pitch a tent, particularly for campers tired of fighting pine needles and mud. The sites are grassy, level, and clean. For RVers, full hookups, as well as pull-through sites, coin-op showers, and other niceties, make this a pleasant home away from home.

sites	59
🏕️ 🚐	51 full hookups, RVs to 65 feet
open	All year
reservations	Up to 9 months in advance; 888/226-7688 or www.parks.wa.gov
contact	Washington State Parks, 360/902-8844; Wenatchee Confluence State Park, 509/664-6373

The list of activities here makes this one of the best family campgrounds in the state. The park has playgrounds, basketball and tennis courts, dual boat-launch ramps, two picnic shelters, a Columbia River swimming area and bathhouse, and a delightful interpretive nature trail that winds through a riverside marsh home to many resident and migratory birds. An even greater lure is the Apple Capital Loop Trail, a new, paved recreation path that runs through this campground on its way around a 14-mile loop—a great day trip for campers. From the campground, the path crosses a bridge over the Wenatchee, then rolls through some lovely green city and utility-company waterfront parks near Wenatchee before

Cyclists head out from Wenatchee Confluence State Park, a grand spring escape.

crossing the Columbia on a railroad-bridge-turned-footbridge. On the east side, it follows the Columbia's shoreline north for 4 or 5 miles, then recrosses the river on a concrete highway bridge and returns to Wenatchee Confluence. Plans call for a northern extension of the trail to Rocky Reach Dam.

Getting there: Wenatchee Confluence is immediately north of the US 2/US 97A junction near Wenatchee. From US 2 eastbound, follow signs north on US 97A.

❸ Lincoln Rock State Park 🌲🌲🌲🌲

Lincoln Rock has long been one of our favorite state parks, mostly because of the amount of local character revealed by its namesake. History records that somewhere back around 1889, a local man, Billy Schaft, photographed a large rock outcrop across the river from this park and remarked how much it looked like a profile of Abraham Lincoln. Plenty of other local people who—let's face it, living in Wenatchee and all—had plenty of time to consider such things, agreed. Someone sent the picture to a photo contest in *Ladies Home Journal,* and it won first prize. Voila! Lincoln Rock went on the maps, and public gatherings soon followed. The park, on a broad, flat Columbia River shoulder across the river from the rock, now bears its name. If you look through the little fixed pipe near the Lincoln Rock upper restroom, you can see it. By George, it does look like Abe. Wake the kids.

The campground here is worthy of a visit on its own, however. It's the prototype for a series of Washington State Parks on the middle Columbia, all of which follow a wildly successful formula: sprawling grassy playfields, boat launches, a swimming area, and flat, open trailer and tent sites separated by young shade trees. All these parks are popular with boaters, who flock here in summer months to water-ski and soak up the sun. Lincoln Rock, on the Columbia's Entiat Lake behind Rocky Reach Dam, has all of these pleasures and more, including two boat launches, multiple moorage docks, tennis and basketball courts, coin-op showers, horseshoe pits, and an amphitheater. It's a very pleasant spot—too hot for some tastes in the summer, but just right for the lizard people among us. Just across the river is the popular Rocky Reach Dam visitors center, which you can only get to by driving back south to Wenatchee, crossing the river, and driving up US 97A.

sites	94
	32 full hookups, 35 water/electrical hookups, RVs to 65 feet
open	March to late October
reservations	Up to 9 months in advance; 888/226-7688 or www.parks.wa.gov
contact	Washington State Parks, 360/902-8844; Lincoln Rock State Park, 509/884-8702

Important note: See possible-closure notation in description of Wenatchee Confluence State Park, above.

Getting there: The campground is 7 miles north of East Wenatchee on US 2.

④ Daroga State Park ▲▲▲▲

KITE FLYING PROHIBITED. Now there's a welcome sign you don't see every day. About 30 seconds after arriving at Daroga State Park, however, you'll see why—a set of extremely high-voltage electric transmission lines runs right over the camping area at this diverse Columbia River park. Kite flying would be ill-advised, indeed. But you can get away with just about any other form of summertime fun here. Daroga, a relatively new, modern state park, actually is two parks in one. The RV camping area, which sits on a high bluff, is nicely equipped, with paved pull-through sites, modern picnic tables, and fire pits. Most of the sites have nice views of the Columbia—and the rather unique walk-in camping area below. Daroga, a former ranch site, has a lagoon separated from the main Columbia by a narrow earthen bar, which has been equipped with 17 walk-in campsites (the park provides wheelbarrow-type devices to help you move your

sites	45
	28 water/electrical hookups, RVs to 45 feet
open	Mid-March to mid-October
reservations	For group camping only; 509/664-6380
contact	Washington State Parks, 360/902-8844; Daroga State Park, 509/664-6380

gear). These are very nice spots, well worth the effort to get here. Note: This is a great place to set the kids up with a walk-in site and let Mom and Dad retreat to peaceful slumber in the RV! The entrance for the walk-in sites is a short distance south of the main park entrance on US 97. Daroga also offers boat launching and moorage, extensive picnic facilities, a gorgeous swimming area with a bathhouse, and a group camp for up to 100 campers. When the wind kicks up enough, the beach area here draws a few windsurfers. Local trivia: You just had to ask about the name. Here goes: Former property owner Grady Auvil developed a new strain of peach, which was named "Daroga" by local nurseryman Pete Van Well, Sr. The name contains the first two letters of the names of three Auvil brothers, Dave, Robert and Grady, who began working the ranch in 1928.

Important note: See possible-closure notation in description of Wenatchee Confluence State Park, above.

Getting there: The park is 18 miles north of Wenatchee on US 97.

⑤ Beebe Bridge Park 🌲🌲🌲

Chelan County Public Utility District used a lot of its own water to turn this former dusty riverbank shelf into a gleaming gem of a campground with ample shoreline frontage on the Columbia River. Beebe Bridge's campsites, most of which are pleasant pull-throughs with modern hookups, tables, and fire pits, are so clean and well-manicured, you almost feel the need to take off your shoes before stepping onto the grass. Smart design helps keep it that way: Every site has a level,

A flat, riverfront site at Beebe Bridge Park.

sandy tent pad to keep family campers from squishing the lawn. This is a clean, pretty spot, lacking, like most of its neighbors, summertime shade because the trees here are newly planted. Give it time, though, and Beebe Bridge's popularity is sure to grow. Amenities at the 56-acre park include picnic shelters, a swimming area, a two-lane boat launch, tennis courts, horseshoe pits, hot showers, boat moorage, a shoreline trail, and an RV dump station. It's a winner.

sites	46
	46 water/electrical hookups, RVs to any length
open	April through October
reservations	None
contact	Chelan County Public Utility District, 509/647-4208

Getting there: Beebe Bridge Park is about 34 miles north of Wenatchee and 4 miles east of Chelan on US 97, near the Beebe Bridge over the Columbia River.

❻ Entiat City Park ▲▲▲

Travelers who choose the US 97A route up the west side of the Columbia River have their choice of campgrounds: Entiat City Park or Entiat City Park. It's not all that bad a choice, actually. The riverfront park is close to downtown Entiat, but that's not exactly like being in downtown Pittsburgh. The 50-acre municipal park is quite nicely equipped, with hookup sites, a boat launch, pleasant picnic facilities, hot showers, playgrounds, and a swimming beach. It's a very popular RV stopover, so reservations are recommended.

sites	81
	31 water/electrical hookups, RVs to any length
open	April through September
reservations	Recommended; 800/736-8428
contact	City of Entiat Parks Department, 800/736-8428

Getting there: The park is in the town of Entiat on US 97A.

❼ Alta Lake State Park ▲▲▲▲

Here's the deal: We won't tell our small RV/tent-camping friends about Alta Lake. And you don't either. This well-hidden state park, tucked into a bowl behind two hulking, sheer ridges above the west shore of the Columbia River, is a favorite of fans of the dry, pine-forested, rocky terrain common to the east-slope Central Cascades. We have many fond memories of camping here in the brutally cold, crisp air of winter, tagging along while Dad went

sites	200
	32 electrical hookups, RVs to 45 feet
open	April through October
reservations	None
contact	Washington State Parks, 360/902-8844; Alta Lake State Park, 509/923-2473

Alta Lake State Park is one of Central Washington's better-kept secrets.

deer hunting in the Methow drainage. Campsites are split into two groups: two loops in the sweetly scented pine forest above the lake, and one near the still waters of the lake itself. The campground has coin-op showers, a swimming beach, a boat launch, a group camp for up to 88 people, and a trail that leads six-tenths of a mile to a viewpoint of the middle Columbia Valley (watch for snakes!). The lake is a popular trout-fishing venue; a private resort with a store and boat rentals is nearby. Local trivia: This former federal land was donated to the city of Pateros in 1928 by a Forest Service supervisor grateful for the services of a local man, who pulled the supervisor's car from the sand with a team of horses. When state auditors ruled the city couldn't own land outside its limits, the site was transferred to Washington State Parks in 1951. The lake was named for Alta Heinz, daughter of a man working a mining claim near here in 1900.

Getting there: From the US 97/Highway 153 junction near Pateros, drive about 2 miles northwest on Highway 153 to Alta Lake Road. Turn left and proceed about 2 miles to the campground, at the end of the road.

⑧ Bridgeport State Park 🌲🌲🌲

If you get a chance to pause and prop up your feet at Bridgeport, a state park just upstream from Chief Joseph Dam, say a word of thanks to the late Ralph Van Slyke, a retired U.S. Army Corps of Engineers employee who forged the beginnings of this park from the barren, rocky soil—using only common garden tools. With the help of some bigger equipment, the park has grown to a comfortable, shaded stopover, with campsites scattered beneath cottonwood trees, all in view of the massive hydro dam to the west. The park has coin-op showers, picnic facilities, and a boat launch and moorage docks. A pleasant, sandy swimming beach on the Columbia's Rufus Woods Lake will be popular with the kids. The 18-hole Lake Woods Golf Course is nearby. Several trails run through the park, and windsurfers use the beach on occasion. Be on guard for rattlesnakes.

sites	34
🏕️🚐	20 water/electrical hookups, RVs to 45 feet
open	April through October
reservations	None
contact	Washington State Parks, 360/902-8844; Bridgeport State Park, 509/686-7231

Getting there: From US 97 about 21 miles south of Okanogan and 70 miles north of Wenatchee, turn south on Highway 17 and proceed 8 miles to the park entrance.

Other Middle Columbia Campgrounds

For a more "out-there" camping experience nearly the opposite of the sprawling, grassy, lower-valley state parks, tent campers and hikers might want to take a hard left turn from US 97A south of Entiat and explore the long, narrow Entiat Valley, which connects the Columbia River Valley to the alluring alpine country in the Glacier Peak Wilderness. A string of picturesque Forest Service campgrounds, between 1,600 and 3,100 feet in elevation, awaits in the upper valley. Sites are primitive, but strategically located. The remote campgrounds are filled in summer months with small-stream anglers, horse or dirt bike riders, or hikers and backpackers headed into the wilderness; in the fall they're filled with hunters. Note that much of this valley was devastated by the massive Tyee Creek wildfire of 1994, one of the worst in modern history. The fire burned uncontrolled from midsummer to the first snows of October, stretching north nearly all the way to Lake Chelan. But vegetation and wildlife have been quick to spring back. The campgrounds, all accessed via Entiat River Road, are **Pine Flat** (10 miles up Entiat River Road; 7 sites, 30- to 50-person group camp); **Fox Creek** (27 miles; 16 sites); **Lake Creek** (28 miles; 18 sites); **Silver Falls** (32 miles; 31 sites, 30- to 50-person group camp); **North Fork** (33 miles; 9 sites); **Spruce Grove** (35 miles; 2 tent-only sites, closed at this writing due to dangerous trees); **Three Creek** (36 miles; 3 tent-only sites); and

Cottonwood (38 miles; 25 sites). All these campgrounds are open mid-May through October; all have pit toilets; and all except Pine Flat have piped water. Most are suitable for tents and small RVs. Call or visit the Wenatchee National Forest's Entiat Ranger District (2108 Entiat Wy, Entiat; 509/784-1511).

In the Wenatchee area, **Squilchuck State Park** (360/902-8844), near the Mission Ridge Ski Area, is a reservation-only group camp for up to 168 people. It reverts to a ski hill operated by Wenatchee Valley College on winter weekends. Follow Mission Street south from Wenatchee, then follow signs along Squilchuck Road.

Lake Chelan and Stehekin

⑨ Lake Chelan State Park ▲▲▲▲▲

If you close your eyes and concentrate, you can almost hear the grinding of the glaciers. OK, so maybe it's just the septic pump in that guy's 79-foot Winnebago next door. Never mind. Use your imagination, and conjure up the behemoth mass of ice it must have taken to carve the incredible gorge known as Lake Chelan. The glacier-carved trough, surrounded in some places by peaks approaching 9,000 feet, is among the deepest gorges in all of North America. And the lake, 55 miles long and never more than 2 miles wide, is a wonder of nature. Lake Chelan is 1,500 feet deep in places, a mark surpassed in America only by Lake Tahoe and Crater Lake. Get away from the water, and it only gets better. To the south rise the magnificent, glacier-draped mountains of the Glacier Peak Wilderness. To the west are the rugged peaks of North Cascades National Park. And due north is the impressive Sawtooth Range and other peaks in the Lake Chelan–Sawtooth Wilderness.

Many people choose to explore this wonderland via boat, either private pleasure craft or the commercial Lady of the Lake tour boats, which ferry visitors

Some sites at Lake Chelan State Park have their own docks.

to Stehekin and North Cascades National Park. But others come here just to admire, and partake of, the lake itself. That makes Lake Chelan State Park, a 127-acre waterfront getaway built with boaters, water-skiers, and Jet-ski riders in mind, one of the very busiest in the state park system. Little wonder. The park has the best of both worlds when it comes to camping: full hookup sites (in an older, private-resort setting; packed a bit too close together for our comfort) on one side of the park, and absolutely delightful, walk-in lakeshore tent sites on the other. The latter are the charmers here. Each has a flat tent pad, a table, a fireplace—and a view up the lake to die for. It's hard to imagine a more idyllic setting for campers with boats. Most sites are within a very short walk of modern moorage piers, making the park in high demand among water-skiers and anglers.

sites	144
	30 full hookups, RVs to 30 feet
open	Mid-March to early November; weekends/holidays in winter
reservations	Up to 9 months in advance; 888/226-7688 or www.parks.wa.gov
contact	Washington State Parks, 360/902-8844; Lake Chelan State Park, 509/687-3710

But there's plenty to do right in the park, which is equipped with a swimming beach, a bathhouse, coin-op showers, a picnic shelter, a playground, an RV dump station, and a boat launch. In the winter the park becomes a popular snow-play area, with cross-country skiers using it as a warming base for ski trips on local roads and trails. Get a reservation for this one. You'll need it. Local trivia: The name Chelan is at least some approximation of the Salish word for the tribe that once lived here. It is believed to translate to "lake" and/or "blue water."

Getting there: Southbound from Chelan: From US 97A about 3 miles south of Chelan, turn right on South Lakeshore Road and proceed 6 miles to the park entrance, on the right. Northbound from Wenatchee: On US 97A, about 9 miles north of Entiat, turn left onto Highway 971. Continue 7 miles to South Lakeshore Road. Turn right, then immediately left into the park.

⑩ Twenty-Five Mile Creek State Park 🌲🌲🌲🌲

You might think it looks more like an old resort than a state park. Give yourself a gold star. Twenty-Five Mile Creek is an old resort, converted to Washington State Parks use in 1975. Like Lake Chelan State Park just down the road, boating is the primary activity here; the park has a boat launch, ample moorage, a fuel dock, and other services. But the campground is a beauty, too, with nicely wooded, fairly private (and fairly small) sites near the lake and along Twenty-Five Mile Creek, where fishing for trout is popular. The park also has coin-op showers, a group camp for up to 40 people, an RV dump station, a pleasant picnic area, and even its own grocery store. Bring your mountain bike and ride down to Lake Chelan State Park, or

sites	71
[tent/RV icon]	23 full hookups, RVs to 45 feet
open	April through September
reservations	Up to 9 months in advance; 888/226-7688 or www.parks.wa.gov
contact	Washington State Parks, 360/902-8844; Twenty-Five Mile Creek State Park, 509/687-3710

up the hill and on to the wealth of backcountry roads in the Navarre Coulee, to the south.

Getting there: Southbound from Chelan: From US 97A about 3 miles south of Chelan, turn right on South Lakeshore Road and drive 15 miles to the park, on the right. Northbound from Wenatchee: On US 97A, about 9 miles north of Entiat, turn left onto Highway 971. Continue 7 miles to South Lakeshore Road. Turn left and proceed 9 miles to the park.

⑪ Lakeshore RV Park ▲▲▲▲

Everything that's good about Lake Chelan—fun in the summer sun, swimming, boating, tanning, paddling, and kid-sister-teasing—can be found at Lakeshore, the city of Chelan's pleasant camping and day-use park that becomes a bustling

sites	177
[tent/RV icon]	165 full hookups, RVs to 40 feet
open	All year
reservations	Recommended; 509/682-8023
contact	Lakeshore Park, 509/682-8023

activity zone in summer months. The campsites are pleasant, in partially shaded, grassy blocks near the lake. RV sites have full hookups with cable TV(!), and even many tent sites (the name is a bit of a misnomer) have electricity and water.

This is a big, modern park, with six main camping areas, a large marina, coin-op showers, an RV dump station, a covered picnic area, a boat launch, and other niceties. Prices are a bit steep in the peak season, rivaling private parks. But that does little to stem the flow of Lakeshore fans, many of whom book summer vacations here far, far in advance. Reservations for the summer are accepted beginning January 2 each year. Start dialing early.

Getting there: From downtown Chelan, follow signs to Highway 150 and Manson, proceeding about a half mile to the campground on the left.

Boat-in/Hike-in Lake Chelan National Recreation Area Campgrounds

Adventurers with hiking boots, boats, tents, and sleeping bags are in luck on Lake Chelan, whose waters lead to the greatest wealth of boat-in and hike-in campsites in Washington State. Many summertime visitors make use of both, ferrying by private watercraft to a shoreline campsite, then setting out on foot for hike-in sites in the same area. (One popular example: boating to Lucerne, riding the shuttle to Holden Village, then setting out on foot into the Glacier Peak Wilderness.) The starting points are a dozen small, primitive Forest Service campgrounds, all with floating docks or fixed moorage piers, that ring the lake. They are **Big Creek** (4 sites, 4-boat moorage); **Corral Creek** (2 sites, 6 boats); **Deer Point** (4 sites, 8 boats; at this writing, temporarily closed due to summer 2002 wildfire); **Domke Falls** (3 sites, 6 boats); **Graham Harbor** (5 sites, 10 boats); **Graham Harbor Creek** (4 sites, 6 boats); **Lucerne** (2 sites, 11 boats); **Mitchell Creek** (6 sites, 17 boats); **Moore Point** (4 sites, 3 boats); **Prince Creek** (6 sites, 3 boats); **Refrigerator Harbor** (4 sites, 4 boats); and **Safety Harbor** (2 sites, 6 boats).

The Forest Service also maintains a half-dozen primitive walk-in sites along the Chelan Lakeshore or Prince Creek Trails. They are **Cub Lake** (6.5 miles from Lake Chelan on Prince Creek Trail; 3 sites); **Boiling Lake** (10 miles from Lake Chelan on Prince Creek Trail; 3 sites); **Domke Lake** (2 miles from Lucerne via Trails 1230 and 1280; 8 sites); **Moore Point** (5.5 miles south of Stehekin on Chelan Lakeshore Trail; 4 sites); **Prince Creek** (18 miles south of Stehekin on Chelan Lakeshore Trail; 6 sites); and **Surprise Lake** (6 miles from Lake Chelan on Trail 1246; 3 sites). Another possible destination is **Holden Ballpark** (2 sites), near the Lutheran Camp/mining burg of Holden Village, reached by boating to Lucerne and riding the shuttle bus.

All the lakeshore campsites can be reached either by private watercraft or floatplane (call Chelan Airways, 509/682-5555). Or arrangements can be made for drop-offs by the Lady of the Lake (509/682-4584; www.ladyofthelake.com), with passenger boats that ferry visitors from Chelan to Stehekin in North Cascades National Park. The most popular drop-off camps are Prince Creek, where Chelan Lakeshore Trail walkers depart for an 18-mile walk north to Stehekin; and Lucerne, the drop point for hikers bound for Holden Village along Railroad Creek in the Glacier Peak Wilderness. Call the Wenatchee National Forest's Chelan Ranger District (509/682-2576) for more information.

Hike-in/Shuttle-in Stehekin-Area Campgrounds

In the Stehekin area, North Cascades National Park visitors, most of whom will have ferried up the 28-mile-long lake on boats operated by the Lady of the Lake company (509/682-4584; www.ladyofthelake.com), have their choice of walk-in sites, all reached by trail along the north end of Lake Chelan, or via the shuttle bus moving people up the Stehekin Valley Road (call the national park, 360/856-5700 ext. 340, for bus information; or visit the Lady of the Lake website). Campers will need to stop at Stehekin's Golden West Visitors Center for overnight permits. Choose from **Purple Point**, a short walk from the Stehekin landing; **Weaver Point,** a boat-in site; or **Harlequin, Rainbow Bridge, High Bridge, Tumwater, Dolly Varden, Shady, Bridge Creek, Flat Creek, Cottonwood,** or a half-dozen other walk-in sites. Consult with rangers, and remember that upper-valley campsites don't melt out until early July, and winter flooding often closes portions of Stehekin Valley Road. Call the park for updates, or visit the Lady of the Lake website for current conditions.

Other Lake Chelan–Area Campgrounds

A handful of primitive, tents-only, Forest Service campgrounds are scattered in the rugged hills above Lake Chelan's southern shore. All are on or near Forest Road 5900, reached by continuing beyond Twenty-Five Mile Creek State Park (see above) on South Lakeshore Drive. These campgrounds, most of which have pit toilets but no piped water or other services, are, in order, **Ramona Park** (8 sites; closed at this writing due to flood damage); **Windy Camp** (15 miles southwest of Ramona Park on Forest Road 8410; 2 sites); **Grouse Mountain** (8 miles west of Twenty-Five Mile Creek State Park on Forest Road 5900; 4 sites); **Junior Point** (14 miles west of Twenty-Five Mile Creek State Park on Forest Road 5900; 5 sites); **Antilon** (14 miles northwest of Chelan on Forest Road 5900; dispersed sites); **Handy Springs** (15 miles west of Twenty-Five Mile Creek State Park on Forest Road 5900; 1 site); and **South Navarre** (40 miles northwest of Chelan on Forest Road 5900; 4 sites at 6,475 feet). Campers who seek RV shelter before taking on the boat ride to Stehekin, and find Lake Chelan State Park or Lakeshore RV Park already booked, might consider **Lakeview Park** (on Highway 150; 509/687-3612; reservations suggested).

More often than not, the sun's shining on the Columbia River.

Columbia Basin and the Grand Coulee

⑫ Ginkgo-Wanapum State Park 🌲🌲🌲

It's hot, it's dry, it's occasionally gusty and dusty. For West Siders, it's the perfect introduction to the Columbia Basin. But hey, it's a short walk from the Columbia River and a short drive from the Gorge Amphitheater summer concert venue. And that's more than enough to keep this geologically fascinating state park packed with visitors in the summer, when it serves as one of very few regional campgrounds for music and sun lovers. The park has come into such demand, in fact, that it recently went on the state reservation system.

sites	50
🏕️	
🚐	50 full hookups, RVs to 60 feet
open	April through October; weekends only November through March
reservations	Up to 9 months in advance; 888/226-7688 or www.parks.wa.gov
contact	Washington State Parks, 360/902-8844; Ginkgo-Wanapum State Park, 509/856-2700

Reserving a site in advance is a good idea. The campground, on the west side of the Vantage Bridge over the Columbia, has a nice spread of picnic sites, a swim-

A typically busy summer weekend at Sun Lake State Park.

ming area and bathhouse, a boat launch, and partially shaded (thank heavens) campsites, all with full hookups to run the Winnie air conditioner. These sites work OK for tenters, but they're really designed for the RV crowd. Make time to visit the nearby Ginkgo Petrified Forest State Park, one of Washington's more fascinating geological oddities. It contains fossil remnants of an ancient forest, including the petrified remains of ancient ginkgo trees, now extinct. Several miles of trails lead through the petrified forest, discovered by highway workers in the 1930s. Watch for snakes! Note: Wanapum is one of only a handful of Washington State Parks that does not have an RV dump station.

Getting there: The campground is 30 miles east of Ellensburg on the Columbia River. Follow signs from Interstate 90 exit 136 at Vantage.

⑬ Potholes State Park ▲▲▲▲

Bring the binoculars, the oars, and a fly rod. Potholes State Park is the hub of waterborne activity in the Columbia Basin. The 640-acre splash of green amid the rather harsh surrounding desert won't be everyone's idea of a grand vacation getaway, but if fishing or canoeing are even medium-high on your list, the place deserves a visit. The water, naturally, is the star here. Most of it is seepage from the grandiose Columbia Basin Irrigation Project, which pumps millions of gallons of water from Banks Lake onto surrounding fields. When earthen O'Sullivan Dam was completed here in 1949, the water backed up and filled a series of low-lying glacial depressions: the Potholes. At about 29,000 acres when full in the spring, Potholes Reservoir is by far the largest body of water here. But literally hundreds of other small ponds and water canals are linked to it by the artificial water table, creating a serendipitous, navigable paradise for anglers and paddlers. The campground, on the southwest shore of the reservoir, is a mix of pleasant waterfront RV and rougher-cut tent sites (they're set in sand and sagebrush, exposed to the wind). The park also contains a mondo boat launch and day-use parking area, picnic facilities, an RV dump station, and a playground. This is a very popular springtime destination for Washington anglers and, increasingly, bird-watchers. Hundreds of species of birds migrating on the Pacific Flyway make stops here and at the nearby Columbia Wildlife Refuge.

sites	121
🏕 🚐	60 full hookups, RVs to 50 feet
open	All year
reservations	Up to 9 months in advance; 888/226-7688 or www.parks.wa.gov
contact	Washington State Parks, 360/902-8844; Potholes State Park, 509/765-7271

Getting there: From Interstate 90 at Moses Lake, take exit 179 and follow Highway 17 about 9 miles south to Highway 262 (O'Sullivan Dam Road). Turn right (west) and drive about 11 miles to the park.

⑭ Sun Lakes State Park 🌲🌲🌲

Close your eyes and imagine the flow. One of the most cataclysmic natural events ever to hit North America—the flooding of Missoula Lake, a glacier-dammed inland sea that covered huge portions of northwest Montana during the last ice age—created all of the many lakes within Sun Lakes State Park, as well as the amazing natural features all around it. These include the Grand Coulee, itself an ancient meander scar from one of the Columbia Basin's many incomprehensible ancient floods, as well as hundreds of other local lakes—wet and dry—that linger as flood scars in this area known as the Channeled Scablands. The upper Grand Coulee north of here is water-filled once more. It's now Banks Lake, a storage basin for irrigation water piped from the Columbia. But the lower Coulee remains in more of a natural (dry) state. And in between is Sun Lakes, a series of small lakes believed to have been former splash pools for Dry Falls, the awesome, 3.5-mile-wide, 400-foot-tall former waterfall north of here that dwarfed Niagara—

sites	180
🏕️ 🚐	18 full hookups, RVs to 50 feet
open	All year
reservations	Up to 9 months in advance; 888/226-7688 or www.parks.wa.gov
contact	Washington State Parks, 360/902-8844; Sun Lakes State Park, 509/632-5583; Sun Lakes State Park Resort, 509/632-5291

Dry Falls, lasting evidence of one of the greatest floods the earth has ever known.

and every other waterfall on Planet Earth—when water last flowed over it 10,000 to 15,000 years ago. A trip to the nearby Dry Falls Interpretive Center is a must.

That said, the campground here, wildly popular for generations of Washingtonians, leaves a bit to be desired. Many of the spaces are closely packed, with little privacy and dusty floors that can be downright dirty in summer months. Tent sites lack tent pads, RV sites lack fire pits. Some sites are grassy, and some are near the south shores of Park Lake. But the entire place is a bit busy for some campers' tastes (reservations are a must). The adjacent Sun Lakes State Park Resort lends a commercial, Palm Springsish air, adding rental cabins and trailers, a golf course, boat ramps and rentals, a store, laundry machines, a horse stable, and 110 full-hookup RV sites to the mix. If that's OK with you, the rest of this big 4,000-acre park will be, as well. The public portion of the park is similarly well outfitted, with a large group camp, picnic facilities, coin-op showers, an RV dump station, a boat launch, and more than 16 miles of hiking trails, one of which leads to nearby Lake Lenore Caves. The caves have produced some significant archaeological finds, such as pictographs still visible on the walls. Watch for snakes on trails here. Tenters: Be prepared for occasional strong winds.

Sun Lakes is a summer water-sport and angling hot spot. Lakes in this park, and the area in general, are among the very best in Washington for trophy trout. Park Lake, right at the park, and Blue Lake, just to the south, both are notable magnets on opening day of trout season (in late April; check state regulations), with good bank access and, often, easy limits. Other good fishing spots include Deep, Perch, Rainbow, and Dry Falls Lakes. The latter is a selective fishery, with bait and barbed hooks prohibited.

Getting there: From Interstate 90 at Moses Lake, follow Highway 17 about 38 miles north to the park, 17 miles north of Soap Lake and 6 miles south of Coulee City.

⑮ Coulee City Park ▲▲▲

This pleasant campground at Coulee City, on the south shore of Banks Lake, is a good alternative to the oft-booked Sun Lakes State Park (see above). It's not exactly scenic, but it is conveniently located near the lake and boat launches at the state park and elsewhere, making it very popular among anglers. Note that 100 sites here are designated tent sites, and the full-hookup RV sites are drive-throughs. The partially-shaded campground also has a playground, store, and showers.

sites	160
🏕	
🚐	32 full hookups, RVs to 35 feet
open	April to late October
reservations	None
contact	Coulee City Park, 509/632-5331

Getting there: The campground is in Coulee City, 2 miles east of the Dry Falls junction of Highway 17 and US 2.

⑯ Steamboat Rock State Park 🌲🌲🌲🌲

Steamboat Rock is Fun Central in the Grand Coulee. It's hard to imagine a better way to immerse oneself in the intriguing natural environs of the Columbia Basin than putting in some serious camping time at Steamboat Rock, named after the massive, prow-shaped basalt bluff jutting up from Banks Lake. The lake, an old Columbia River coulee, was turned in the 1940s into a massive reservoir for Columbia Basin irrigation water. This turned Steamboat Rock—formerly an island in the flooding Columbia—into a mighty peninsula and a grand outdoor playground was created. The state park, one of Washington's premier sunny-side vacation getaways, is a huge place—3,500 acres—with a very well-groomed, very well-attended campground. Steamboat was one of the first parks in the state to leap onto reservation status, and if you're seeking a campsite between Memorial Day and Labor Day, it's a good idea to get one. Most of the sites are clean, comfortable RV spaces, but you'll also find a dozen isolated, boat-in campsites at the north end of Steamboat Rock. Most sites are on flat, grassy land that's well suited to tents (be warned, however, about nasty winds and predatory late-night sprinklers).

sites	126
🏕️ 🚐	100 full hookups, RVs to 60 feet
open	All year; limited winter facilities
reservations	Up to 9 months in advance; 888/226-7688 or www.parks.wa.gov
contact	Washington State Parks, 360/902-8844; Steamboat Rock State Park, 509/633-1304

Most of the best things to do here are immediately obvious: For canoeists and water-skiers, the 27-mile-long, 4-mile-wide lake is paradise. Steamboat Rock is a water-sports recreation hub, with boat launches and moorage, a sandy-bottom swimming area, a water-ski float, bathhouses, and extensive waterfront picnic facilities. Also on the premises are a bathhouse, coin-op showers, an RV dump station, a group camp, and a nice playground. Anglers probably already know about this 30,000-acre reservoir's reputation as a hot spot for bass, walleye, perch, and other warm-water species.

If the weather's not baking hot, you can explore the park's 25 miles of paths on, around, and over Steamboat Rock. The access trail to the top is only about a mile, but gains 800 feet in elevation. Be sure to carry plenty of water, and to stay back from crumbly basalt cliffs. And do watch for rattlesnakes along the way. A more obscure attraction near here is across the highway from the park's northern rest area/boat launch (about 3.5 miles north of the main entrance): Northrup Canyon, the only natural forest in Grant County. The 3,120-acre area is filled with forested ravines between coulee walls, where bald eagles and other raptors sometimes are spotted. In the winter the park keeps hopping, with ice fishing and cross-country skiing drawing small but happy crowds.

Fishing in Banks Lake, near Steamboat Rock State Park.

Getting there: The park is on Highway 155, 11 miles south of Electric City, 16.5 miles north of Coulee City.

ⓗ Spring Canyon 🌲🌲🌲🌲

Spring Canyon, a national park site operated as part of the massive Lake Roosevelt National Recreation Area, is the closest public campground to the tourist-magnet of Grand Coulee Dam. That makes it the most popular of many campgrounds scattered along the shores of the 130-mile-long reservoir. Luckily, it's also among the largest and best-equipped. Campsites are spread through a series of loops in this dry, sagebrush-speckled area above the lake. The park also has a boat launch,

sites	87
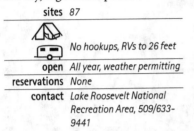	No hookups, RVs to 26 feet
open	All year, weather permitting
reservations	None
contact	Lake Roosevelt National Recreation Area, 509/633-9441

making it a favorite home base for anglers, water-skiers, and, in the winter, bald eagle–watchers. Roosevelt Lake is open all year for a variety of game-fish species (check the state fishing regulations book). The campground also has a very popular swimming area (even if you don't swim, you'll want to get in here on sweltering summer days), with a lifeguard on duty in the summer. The campground has piped water and an RV dump station, but no showers.

Getting there: From Grand Coulee, drive 3 miles east on Highway 174 to the campground, on the shores of Roosevelt Lake.

18 Keller Ferry ▲▲▲

If you close your eyes and use your imagination, you might think you were back on Puget Sound. Well, OK. Not really. But you almost have to take a ferry to get here. Keller Ferry, at the south side of the Roosevelt Lake ferry crossing on

sites	50
	No hookups, RVs to 16 feet
open	All year, weather permitting
reservations	None
contact	Lake Roosevelt National Recreation Area, 509/633-9441

Highway 21, is off the beaten path unless you're taking the ferry to somewhere else. But the Colville Confederated Tribes' boat ramp and moorage facility is nearby, and there's a playground here for kids. The lake is increasingly popular among walleye anglers. A lifeguard is on duty at the swimming area from July through Labor Day weekend.

Getting there: From US 2 near the town of Wilbur, turn north on Highway 21 and drive 14 miles to the campground, near Keller Ferry crossing.

19 Fort Spokane ▲▲▲▲

Lake Roosevelt National Recreation Area's second-largest campground (the largest is Spring Canyon, above) also has a fascinating history. There actually was—and is—a fort here, built in the late 1800s and occupied by the U.S. Army for about 20 years. The fort, strategically located near the confluence of the Spokane and Columbia Rivers, today is home to interesting historical exhibits describing the late 19th-century Indian wars. Fort Spokane has a noted swimming area

sites	67
🏕️ 🚐	No hookups, RVs to 25 feet
open	All year; limited winter facilities
reservations	None
contact	Lake Roosevelt National Recreation Area, 509/633-9441

(lifeguard included during summer months), a boat launch, and other goodies. The large park, with spaces in dry, sagebrushy loops is popular through the summer, thanks to its swimming area, boat launch, and central location on 130-mile-long Roosevelt Lake.

Getting there: From US 2 at the town of Davenport, turn north on Highway 25 and proceed about 22 miles to the campground.

20 Hawk Creek 🌲🌲🌲

This small, somewhat out-of-the-way Roosevelt Lake campground is a good alternate site if Spring Canyon and Fort Spokane (both above) are booked. A boat launch is nearby, and it is popular with anglers who troll around the mouth of

sites	25
🏕️ 🚐	No hookups, RVs to 16 feet
open	All year; limited winter facilities
reservations	None
contact	Lake Roosevelt National Recreation Area, 509/633-9441

Hawk Creek. Note that there is no drinking water here if the lake level drops below 1,265 feet.

Getting there: From US 2 at the town of Davenport, turn north on Highway 25 and proceed about 23 miles to Miles-Creston Road. Turn left and proceed about 10 miles to the campground.

Other Columbia Basin/Grand Coulee Campgrounds

In the Vantage area, most tent campers avoid RV-geared Ginkgo-Wanapum State Park, scooting instead over to the nearby **Vantage Riverstone Resort** (north of Vantage off I-90 exit 136; 509/856-2800; www.vantagewa.com)—formerly Vantage KOA—which offers more than 100 campsites (50 with full hookups) and the usual private-campground amenities. Gorge Amphitheater visitors also might consider another private campground, **Shady Tree RV Park** (at the Highway 281/Highway 283 junction 2 miles east of George; 509/785-2851), with 71 campsites (41 with full hookups).

In the Potholes area, a notable private development, **Mar Don Resort** (on O'Sullivan Dam Road/Highway 262 at the west end of O'Sullivan Dam; 509/346-2651; mardonresort.com), offers 300 sites with full hookups, a store, a motel, and extensive boating and fishing services.

To the north, in the thriving hub of Ephrata, **Oasis Park Resort** (on Highway 28; 509/754-5102 or 877/754-5102) is a quiet spot, complete with shaded picnic facilities, a swimming area, fishing ponds, and more than 100 campsites, 68 with utilities. It's a good possible stopover for travelers bound to or from Grand Coulee. In Soap Lake, **Smokiam Campground** (on East Beach; 509/246-1211), is a city facility with 52 sites (45 with utilities) that makes a decent RV stopover.

In the upper Grand Coulee, nearly three dozen small waterfront campgrounds, managed either by the National Park Service (because they lie within the Lake Roosevelt National Recreation Area) or the Colville Confederated or Spokane Tribes, literally ring Roosevelt Lake, the 130-mile-long reservoir behind Grand Coulee Dam. Four of these—Spring Canyon, Keller Ferry, Hawk Creek, and Fort Spokane—are profiled above. Contact the **Lake Roosevelt NRA** office in Coulee Dam (509/633-9441) for current information on others. All these campgrounds provide water access, most are open all year, and some have boat launches. Some of the campgrounds are so far up the lake that they land in a separate chapter of this guide (see Kettle Falls, Colville, and the Pend Oreille section, in the Northeast Washington chapter).

Yakima Valley

㉑ Yakima Sportsman State Park ▲▲▲

This just might be the best public campground in or around Yakima. Never mind that it's the only public campground in or around Yakima. It's not that bad a place to be, all things considered. And besides, you can't be too choosy in these parts, one of the least campsite-infested regions in all of Washington State (and yes, we're including the Palouse!). The park, which has good access to the Yakima River and it's increasingly impressive (and popular) Yakima River Greenway Trail, has convenient pull-through RV sites, a playground, kids' fishing ponds, and extensive (shady) picnic facilities. Two sites are wheelchair accessible. Some of the campsites are very near the Yakima, a pretty river with good fishing, even in

sites	65
🏕️ 🚐	37 full hookups, RVs to 60 feet
open	All year
reservations	Up to 9 months in advance; 888/226-7688 or www.parks.wa.gov
contact	Washington State Parks, 360/902-8844; Yakima Sportsman State Park, 509/575-2774

Central Washington: An enduring angler's vacation destination.

this semiurban setting. More than 140 species of birds have been recorded at this park, which gets heavy use during events at the Yakima fairgrounds or Sun Dome. Local trivia: The park owes its existence to members of the Yakima Sportsman's Association who, noting the lack of public parks in Yakima, purchased the land and began development here in the 1940s. The park was later turned over to Yakima County and, subsequently, Washington State Parks, in 1949.

Getting there: From Interstate 82 near Yakima, take exit 34 and follow signs about 2 miles mile east to the park, on Keys Road.

Other Yakima Valley Campgrounds

The riverside **Yakima KOA** (on Keys Road in Yakima, take I-82 exit 34; 509/248-5882 or 800/562-5773) is the other major campground in the area, with 50 tent sites and 90 RV sites with full hookups and the usual KOA amenities. Other private campgrounds include Yakima's **Circle H RV Ranch** (509/457-3683); **Trailer Inns RV Park** (509/452-9561); and **Yakama Nation RV Resort** (800/874-3087).

Far west of Yakima, in the Ahtanum Creek drainage, the Department of Natural Resources maintains four small, primitive campgrounds. Unless you're riding a dirt bike or really enjoy the exhaust from other people's, don't bother.

Northeast Washington

L et's dispense with the really important stuff right off the bat. If you ever want to be considered a serious or even capable Washington camper, do not—repeat, do not—walk into a Mountaineers meeting and tell the assembled masses you're taking the Trooper and tent over to "Penned Oriole" for the weekend. It's understandable. It's probably even happened. But just so you know, the river running through northeast Washington—that goofy thing spelled Pend Oreille—is pronounced POND-o-ray. The sooner you get that off your tongue without hurting yourself, the sooner people will stop asking to see your real driver's license—the California one—and the sooner you'll be out there in Washington's wildest corner, living happily with the ornery moose and largely indifferent bighorn rams.

This is the very problem with far-out places marked by far-out names, like northeast Washington. Nobody ever goes there, and if they do, they can't even explain where they've been once they get back. Anonymity is preserved. The cycle continues.

All of this, of course, works to your advantage. The fact is that, for whatever reason, northeast Washington, from year to year, stays right up there on Mr. Black's Top Ten Most Remote Areas list. This means, among other things, that you can go there without a reservation—yes, even on a Friday—and still snare a campsite at many of the region's fine campgrounds.

Once the shock from that wears off, take a look around. The northeast corner of Washington, a.k.a. "that big area up around Metaline Falls," hides in its second-growth pine trees a wide array of camping splendors. You can sip drinks festooned with umbrellas from a chaise lounge along sun-baked Franklin D. Roosevelt Lake, the giganto, 130-mile-long water way created by that little dam downstream at Grand Coulee. You can hike up a rocky peak east of Sullivan Lake and come face to face with your creator—assuming your creator is a Rocky Mountain bighorn sheep. Or you can drive far, far up badly maintained Forest Service roads into the heart of the Salmo-Priest Wilderness and shake hooves with a woodland caribou, a bona fide endangered species.

All around and in between, you can camp in relative solitude at a wide range of campgrounds, most operated by the federal government. It's a fine example of your tax dollars at work. Uncle Sam's long reach, which extends to the Columbia River (through the Lake Roosevelt National Recreation Area) and into the mountainous Okanogan Highlands, the Kettle Range, and the Selkirks (courtesy of the Okanogan and Colville National Forests), has strewn outhouses, fire pits, and picnic tables across this land. It's your land. My land. Our land. Go forth, multiply, and camp upon it.

1 American Legion Park
2 Conconully State Park
3 Sugarloaf
4 Cottonwood
5 Oriole
6 Kerr
7 Salmon Meadows
8 Crawfish Lake
9 Osoyoos Lake State Park
10 Bonaparte Lake
11 Beaver Lake
12 Beth Lake
13 Lost Lake
14 Tenmile
15 Ferry Lake
16 Swan Lake
17 Long Lake
18 Curlew Lake State Park
19 Sherman Pass Overlook
20 Canyon Creek
21 Kettle Falls
22 Kamloops
23 Marcus Island
24 Evans
25 North Gorge
26 Gifford
27 Pierre Lake
28 Little Twin Lakes
29 Lake Gillette/East Gillette
30 Lake Thomas
31 Big Meadow Lake
32 Edgewater
33 Sullivan Lake
34 Noisy Creek
35 Riverside State Park
36 Mount Spokane State Park
37 Pend Oreille County Park

Northeast Washington Map

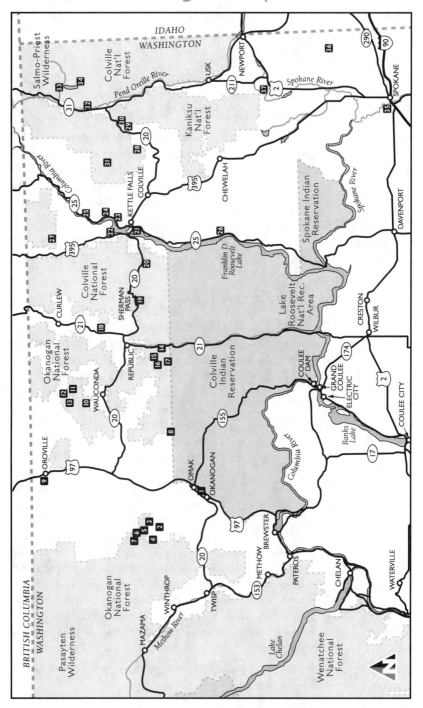

Okanogan Valley and Highlands

① American Legion Park 🌲🌲🌲

A small municipal park in Okanogan, American Legion is primarily an RV stopover along the Okanogan River. Sites are clustered in a gravel area with little shade or greenery. But it's close to the highway if you're just looking for a place to pull over for the night. The Okanogan Historical Museum is nearby.

sites	35
🚐	No hookups, RVs to any length
open	May to early October
reservations	None
contact	City of Okanogan, 509/422-3600

Getting there: The park is on Highway 215 in Okanogan.

② Conconully State Park 🌲🌲🌲🌲

Many private resorts and cabins ring Lake Conconully, an impoundment managed by the Federal Bureau of Reclamation. But public camping is found here, too, both on the lakeshore and the surrounding hillsides. Leading the way is Conconully State Park, an 80-acre site with 5,400 feet of shoreline on the reservoir.

sites	82
🏕️🚐	No hookups, RVs to 60 feet
open	April through October; weekends and holidays in winter
reservations	None
contact	Washington State Parks, 360/902-8844; Conconully State Park, 509/826-7408

The park, a very popular fishing spot, has broad lawns shaded by massive willow trees, making it a favorite summer lounging spot. Don't get too used to the location of the beach, however: Waterfront areas for swimming and boating are affected by broad fluctuations in lake levels as the water is drawn down. The camping area is divided between a main campground and a second, more primitive section closer to the lake. The campground has coin-op showers, a swimming beach, and a boat launch. Also within the property is a half-mile nature trail. Historical note: The name Conconully comes from Conconulp, an early English name for the area. That name was taken from the native Konekol'p, which meant "money hole"—a reference to the region's former status as a large producer of beaver pelts, which were traded to whites at an old trading post here.

Getting there: From US 97 at Omak, follow signs 22 miles northwest to the campground, on Conconully Road.

Lake Conconully, a reservoir with recreation benefits.

③ Sugarloaf 🌲🌲

You'll need to bring a big ol' stack of paper plates to make a sign trail long enough to enable your friends to find you at Sugarloaf, a tiny, lakefront campground north of Conconully. The national forest camp, elevation 2,400 feet, is primitive, with pit toilets and not much else. Strictly for the roughin' it campers among us. Although you'll find plenty of privacy here in late summer, when the lake level shrinks away from the shore. If you're looking for more creature comforts, try Conconully State Park (see above), or the other local Forest Service camps to the northwest, along Salmon Creek (see below).

sites	4
🏕️	
open	*Mid-May to mid-September*
reservations	*None*
contact	*Okanogan National Forest, Tonasket Ranger District, 509/486-2186*

Getting there: From Conconully, follow Sinlahekin Road (County Road 4015) northeast about 5 miles to the campground.

④ Cottonwood 🌲🌲🌲

If booming downtown Conconully comes across as just too much civilization for you, help is at hand along the sparkling water of Salmon Creek, northwest of town. Cottonwood, the first campground encountered along Forest Road 38, is

sites	4
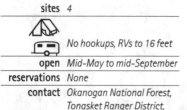	No hookups, RVs to 16 feet
open	Mid-May to mid-September
reservations	None
contact	Okanogan National Forest, Tonasket Ranger District, 509/486-2186

small but somewhat pretty, with four streamside sites set in a mixed forest. The campground has piped water and pit toilets, but no other amenities. It's open all year, with no garbage service or water in the winter. The elevation is 2,700 feet.

Getting there: From Conconully, follow Forest Road 38 2 miles northwest to the campground.

⑤ Oriole 🌲🌲🌲

If you visit during the dog days of summer, you just might find a wily old local stomping around in Salmon Creek near Oriole Campground, looking to land a rainbow on a dry fly. Whip out your gear and join him somewhere along the stream, then settle into your tent or small RV in this remote, quiet campground,

sites	10
	No hookups, RVs to 16 feet
open	Mid-May to mid-September
reservations	None
contact	Okanogan National Forest, Tonasket Ranger District, 509/486-2186

set amidst some lovely larch and fir trees. You'll find the Forest Service basics here: pit toilets, but few other amenities. But there's plenty of solace to go around. The elevation is 2,900 feet.

Getting there: From Conconully, follow Forest Road 38 and Forest Road 38-025 3 miles northwest to the campground.

⑥ Kerr 🌲🌲🌲

Kerr, the third of four campgrounds along Salmon Creek northwest of Conconully, is a quiet spot along the creek and a bit more primitive than other campgrounds on this road. It has pit toilets but no piped water or other services. The

sites	13
	No hookups, RVs to 16 feet
open	Mid-May to mid-September
reservations	None
contact	Okanogan National Forest, Tonasket Ranger District, 509/486-2186

campground has good fishing access to the creek—the main reason many people visit here, although the fishing is usually marginal. The elevation is 3,100 feet.

Getting there: From Conconully, follow Forest Road 38 4 miles northwest to the campground.

❼ Salmon Meadows 🌲🌲🌲

Ever have a hankering to pack up your entire work group and head way, way, way, way into the hills—away from even the most determined gearhead's cell-phone range—to talk about birds, fish, the unmitigated gall of the U.S. Forest Service to charge day-use hiking fees, and just life in general? Here's a good candidate for extreme solitude. Salmon Meadows, 8 miles beyond Conconully and 200 years beyond civilization, is high on Salmon Creek. The scenic campground has a group site with a community kitchen, around which all the campground citizens can gather to introduce legislation or just play cards. The campground has piped water and pit toilets, and it remains open in the winter with no water or garbage service. Note: Give your CEO the space next to the john. Let's just say that on our last visit, at least, it was not one of those newfangled, vented odorless jobs. The elevation here is 4,500 feet—bring a sweater in the off-season.

sites	7
open	Mid-May to mid-September
reservations	None
contact	Okanogan National Forest, Tonasket Ranger District, 509/486-2186

Getting there: From Conconully, follow Forest Road 38 about 8 miles northwest to the campground.

❽ Crawfish Lake 🌲🌲🌲

The Forest Service lists crawfish hunting as one activity at this scenic, lakefront campground, halfway to nowhere in the hills beyond the town of Riverside. We can't vouch for that, but we can vouch for summer days of fun in the canoe, kayak, or motorboat. That's what most campers make their way all the way out here to do, and it can get a bit noisy at times when the water-skiers and Jet-ski jockeys are doing their thing. Fishing can be productive in season. The campground is primitive, with no piped water or garbage service. You'll find pit toilets, lots of trees, and not much else here. The elevation is 4,500 feet. Local trivia: The far side of the lake actually is inside the northern border of the massive, seldom-trod Colville Indian Reservation.

sites	19
	No hookups, RVs to 31 feet
open	Mid-May to mid-September
reservations	None
contact	Okanogan National Forest, Tonasket Ranger District, 509/486-2186

Getting there: From US 97 at the town of Riverside (north of Omak and south of Tonasket), drive about 18 miles east on County Road 9320. After the road becomes Forest Road 30, continue 2 miles east to Forest Road 30-100, turn right, and proceed a half mile to the campground.

⑨ Osoyoos Lake State Park 🌲🌲

We have strong childhood memories of a particularly bad summer stopover here, during which: (1) It was so hot, the sun baked the ground in the campground to an asphaltlike surface, so replete with surface cracks and dust that we expected to see rhinos and giraffes gal-lumping through at any moment; (2) it was so crowded, we had to prey on departing families to snare a spot; and (3) the lifeguard yelled at us. Chances are, budget cuts have all but taken care of that life-guard. But we can't vouch for remedies for the other two problems. Osoyoos, the long-ago site of the Okanogan County Fair, is an unimpressive state park that gets plenty of use by virtue of its location—on a major interstate, close to the Canadian border. Swimming, fishing, water-skiing, and dumping ice on one's head to avoid wandering around in a heat-stroke stupor are the primary summer activities. The campground, on a 14-mile lake that stretches into British Columbia, has coin-op showers and an RV dump station. In the winter, RVs can park in the day-use parking lot.

sites	86
🏕️🚐	No hookups, RVs to 45 feet
open	Mid-March through October; weekends/holidays in winter
reservations	Up to 9 months in advance; 888/226-7688 or www.parks.wa.gov
contact	Washington State Parks, 360/902-8844; Osoyoos Lake State Park, 509/476-3321

Getting there: The park is 1 mile north of Oroville and 4 miles south of the Canadian border on US 97.

The day-use area at Osoyoos Lake State Park.

⑩ Bonaparte Lake 🌲🌲🌲🌲

Bonaparte Lake is the first, and most popular, of a handful of small Forest Service camps in the Five Lakes area, north of Highway 20 and east of Tonasket. It's a remote, quite pretty campground, set in the kind of picturesque, dry forest the Okanogan National Forest is known for. It's a good place for groups: 10 of the camping spaces are double sites, which can accommodate two cars or RVs. The campground also has a group site for up to 30 people. The campground, equipped with pit toilets and piped water, is popular with hunters in the fall.

sites	28
🏕️ 🚐	No hookups, RVs to 31 feet
open	Mid-May to mid-September
reservations	None
contact	Okanogan National Forest, Tonasket Ranger District, 509/486-2186

For much of the year, however, the primary draw is fishing. Brook and rainbow trout can be plentiful, and Bonaparte also holds some massive Mackinaw (lake) trout. A handful weighing over 20 pounds have been caught here. Boat rentals are available at nearby Bonaparte Lake Resort. The area also offers some good hiking trails, including the South Side Bonaparte Trail, an 11-mile round-trip hike to a stunning view atop 7,258-foot Bonaparte Peak, site of a pair of fire lookouts. A trail to the lookout begins in the campground, but you can shave several miles—and a lot of vertical—off the climb by driving to the upper trailhead at Lost Lake Campground (see below). The elevation at Bonaparte Lake is 3,600 feet.

Getting there: From Highway 20, about 20 miles east of Tonasket, turn north on County Road 4953 (Bonaparte Lake Road), which becomes Forest Road 32, and proceed about 6 miles to the campground, on the left.

⑪ Beaver Lake 🌲🌲🌲

It's small, quiet, and out of the way—and that makes it a perfect destination for what many campers come here for: solitude in the cracklin' dry forests of the Okanogan Highlands. Beaver Lake is a great place for hikers, thanks largely to the Beth Lake Trail, an easy, 3.8-mile loop that begins in the campground and follows a nearly flat course along both Beaver Lake and nearby Beth Lake (where there's another campground; see below). Other great local hikes include the 2-mile round-trip

sites	11
🏕️ 🚐	No hookups, RVs to 31 feet
open	Mid-May to mid-September
reservations	None
contact	Okanogan National Forest, Tonasket Ranger District, 509/486-2186

Pipsissewa Trail, and the Big Tree Botanical Loop, which begins on Forest Road 33 and weaves through an old-growth larch and pine forest. The campground, which has pit toilets and no piped water, is OK, but not remarkable. Two of the spaces are double sites that can accommodate two vehicles. The lake is stocked with trout in the spring. The elevation is 2,700 feet.

Getting there: From Highway 20, about 20 miles east of Tonasket, turn north on County Road 4953 (Bonaparte Lake Road), which becomes Forest Road 32. Proceed about 12 miles north to the campground.

⑫ Beth Lake 🌲🌲🌲

Another in the cluster of campgrounds in this Five Lakes region of the Okanogan National Forest, Beth Lake is a peaceful Forest Service camp on the north shore of a tiny alpine lake in the North Fork Beaver Creek drainage. It's a familiar Forest Service facility, with pit toilets, piped water, and a boat launch. Fishing in this and other nearby lakes can be productive. (See Beaver Lake and Bonaparte Lake campgrounds, above, for local hiking options.)

sites	15
🏕️ 🚐	No hookups, RVs to 31 feet
open	Mid-May to mid-September
reservations	None
contact	Okanogan National Forest, Tonasket Ranger District, 509/486-2186

Getting there: From Highway 20, about 20 miles east of Tonasket, turn north on County Road 4953 (Bonaparte Lake Road), which becomes Forest Road 32. Con-

Quiet, remote Tiffany Lake, northeast of Winthrop.

tinue about 12 miles north to Beaver Creek, and turn left (northwest) on County Road 9480. Proceed about a mile to the campground.

⑬ Lost Lake 🌲🌲🌲

Another campground high in the Okanogan's Five Lakes area, Lost Lake is a peaceful spot with good access to local hiking trails, most notably the South Side Bonaparte Trail, which climbs from Forest Road 100 north of here to spectacular views and fire lookouts atop 7,258-foot Bonaparte Peak. Fishing also is productive in this lake and the other four in the area. The campground has pit toilets, piped water, and a popular group-camp area.

sites	19
🏕️🚐	No hookups, RVs to 31 feet
open	Mid-May to mid-September
reservations	None
contact	Okanogan National Forest, Tonasket Ranger District, 509/486-2186

Getting there: From Highway 20, about 20 miles east of Tonasket, turn north on County Road 4953 (Bonaparte Lake Road). Continue north beyond Bonaparte and follow signs about 6 miles to the campground, on Forest Road 33-050.

⑭ Tenmile 🌲🌲🌲

Tenmile is one of four uncrowded, high-country campgrounds in the Sanpoil River drainage, which drains a giant slice of northeast Washington, and the Colville Indian Reservation, into the Columbia River. The campground, on the west side of the 1.1-million-acre Colville National Forest, is easy to reach from Republic, making it a good overnight stopover for Highway 20 travelers. It's also a good base for exploring the chain of local lakes in this area, each of which has its own Forest Service camp (see Ferry Lake, Beth Lake, and Long Lake, below). The campground has pit toilets, but no piped water.

sites	9
🏕️🚐	No hookups, RVs to 21 feet
open	Mid-May to mid-October
reservations	None
contact	Colville National Forest, Republic Ranger District, 509/775-3305

Getting there: From Highway 20 about 2 miles east of the town of Republic, turn south on Highway 21 and drive 10 miles to the campground.

⑮ Ferry Lake 🌲🌲🌲

Intrepid campers who make it this far into the heart of the sprawling lodgepole pine and clear-streamed lands south of Sherman Pass won't be displeased with

Ferry Lake, a scenic—if rough-around-the-edges—Forest Service campground in the Sanpoil River drainage. The small lake is a popular fishing spot, with a boat launch near the campground (gas motors are prohibited). The campground has some lakefront sites, which is a good thing, because there's no piped water here.

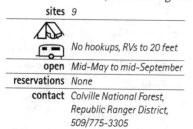

sites	9
	No hookups, RVs to 20 feet
open	Mid-May to mid-September
reservations	None
contact	Colville National Forest, Republic Ranger District, 509/775-3305

The campground has pit toilets and no other amenities. In general, this entire area is decent mountain-biking terrain. Three other local Forest Service camps in the area make nice day trips.

Getting there: From Highway 20 about 2 miles east of the town of Republic, turn south on Highway 21 and proceed about 7 miles to Forest Road 53 (Scatter Creek Road). Turn right (southwest) and drive 6 miles to Forest Road 5330. Turn right (north) and continue just over a mile to Forest Road 100. Turn right and proceed about a mile to the campground.

16 Swan Lake 🌲🌲🌲

Please, no ballet jokes. Swan Lake is the largest and most developed of four Colville National Forest camps in the Sanpoil River drainage south of Republic. It's also the only one in the area able to comfortably accommodate RVs longer

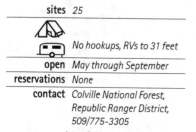

sites	25
	No hookups, RVs to 31 feet
open	May through September
reservations	None
contact	Colville National Forest, Republic Ranger District, 509/775-3305

than 21 feet. It's a pretty spot, with lakefront sites popular with anglers on the lake. A ban on gas motors keeps things peaceful here, and fishing can be good at times. A boat launch and mooring docks are nearby. The campground has pit toilets and, unlike others in the area, piped water. The elevation is 3,700 feet. If the campground is full, note the presence of Ferry Lake, Long Lake, and Tenmile, three similar, if smaller, Forest Service camps in the same area.

Getting there: From Highway 20 about 2 miles east of the town of Republic, turn south on Highway 21 and proceed about 7 miles to Forest Road 53 (Scatter Creek Road). Turn right (southwest) and drive 8 miles to the campground.

17 Long Lake 🌲🌲🌲🌲

Long Lake is one of the nicest of a cluster of four Forest Service camps in the Sanpoil River drainage south of Republic. It's a bit out there, but the camp has some great sites on scenic Long Lake, a noted cutthroat fishing spot. The campground has pit toilets and piped water. A trail around the lake is level and easy enough for

sites	12
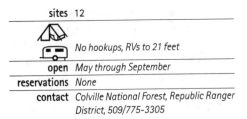	No hookups, RVs to 21 feet
open	May through September
reservations	None
contact	Colville National Forest, Republic Ranger District, 509/775-3305

the whole family, and a ban on gas motors at this fly-fishing-only lake keeps the shorelines quiet, even at the peak of fishing season.

Getting there: From Highway 20 about 2 miles east of the town of Republic, turn south on Highway 21 and proceed about 7 miles to Forest Road 53 (Scatter Creek Road). Turn right (southwest) and drive 8 miles to Forest Road 400. Turn south and proceed about 1.5 miles to the campground.

18 Curlew Lake State Park 🌲🌲🌲

There's gold in these hills. And some of it spreads to the shores of Curlew Lake, where one of Washington's more obscure—and more pleasant—state parks awaits on the east shore. The lake, long ago a center of local gold-panning activity, is a

Swimming and fishing are highlights at Curlew Lake State Park, near Republic.

recreation center these days. And the 123-acre park, a favorite fishing, swimming, and water-skiing spot in the dry, lodgepole pine forests north of the groovy mountain town of Republic, is a nice one, with campsites spread through a hilly area with green grass and shade trees along the lakeshore. This is one of the region's most notable rainbow trout fisheries, and the lake can be crowded with boats (both from

sites	84
	18 full hookups, 7 water/electrical hookups, RVs to 30 feet
open	April through October
reservations	None
contact	Washington State Parks, 360/902-8844; Curlew Lake State Park, 509/775-3592

the state park and from two private resorts on the lake) during peak fishing-season weeks in early summer. (The lake receives annual plants of trout, supplemented by fish raised here in net pens.) The park has coin-op showers, a swimming beach, a boat launch and mooring facilities, an RV dump station, and 10 picnic sites. Good mountain-bike trails are found in the area. The main camping area, to the right as you enter the campground, has particularly pleasant sites with grassy lawns and some shade trees. Some of the prime spots are walk-in tent spaces near the lake. The campground is located near what archaeologists believe was a Native American village; artifacts and some skeletons have been unearthed here. The campground is open summers only, but cross-country skiing and ice fishing are popular winter day-use activities. Note: If Curlew Lake seems a long way out there, get chummy with your favorite pilot. This 123-acre park has five primitive "fly-in" sites with tie-downs for planes landing at adjacent Merritt Field.

Getting there: From Highway 20, about 2.5 miles east of the town of Republic, turn north on Highway 21 and proceed about 7 miles to the campground.

19 Sherman Pass Overlook 🌲🌲🌲

They don't just hand out those National Scenic Byway plaques to every little road that applies. That's obvious after a trip across Highway 20, a.k.a. Sherman Pass National Scenic Byway. The road, which parallels the Canadian border between north-central and northeastern Washington, climbs to 5,575 feet—higher than any other mountain pass in Washington—to take visitors on a journey into some of the state's wildest natural areas, as well as some of its oldest and most colorful

sites	9
	No hookups, RVs to 21 feet
open	Mid-May to late September
reservations	None
contact	Colville National Forest, Three Rivers Ranger District, Kettle Falls office, 509/738-7700

history. Modern outdoor explorers will find a tiny-but-convenient roadside campground right near the summit of Sherman Pass. Sherman Pass Overlook offers tidy sites, pumped water, and pit toilets. It has no showers—a bummer,

A mirror image in a lake along Sherman Pass Scenic Byway.

given the wealth of great hiking opportunities in this area. A good example is the Kettle Crest Trail, which follows the top of the Kettle Range (a subgroup of the Rockies) 29 miles north and 29 miles south of the highway. Campsites are in a dark, wooded area just off the highway. The campground elevation is 5,300 feet—bring a sweater.

Getting there: The campground is on Highway 20 near Sherman Pass, about 20 miles west of Kettle Falls.

⑳ Canyon Creek 🌲🌲🌲🌲

Canyon Creek is a small but pretty campground just off the Sherman Pass National Scenic Byway (Highway 20). It's a popular fishing spot, thanks largely to the Canyon Creek Trail, an easy, 2-mile-round-trip path along the clear, rushing waters of Canyon Creek. Some campsites here are barrier free, as is the trail, which provides great angling access and makes a perfect short walk for camping families. The campground has pit toilets, but no piped water. The elevation is 2,200 feet.

sites	*12*
	No hookups, RVs to 30 feet
open	*late May to early September*
reservations	*None*
contact	*Colville National Forest, Three Rivers Ranger District, Kettle Falls office, 509/738-7700*

A frosty autumn morning near Sherman Pass.

Getting there: The campground is on Forest Road 136, just south of Highway 20, about 9 miles west of Kettle Falls.

Other Okanogan Valley/Highlands Campgrounds

In the southern Okanogan Valley, **Rock Creek** (on Loup Loup Canyon Rd; 6 sites), **Rock Lakes** (on Rocks Lake Road north of Rock Creek; 8 sites, no piped water), **Leader Lake** (on Leader Lake Road; 16 sites, no piped water), and **Sportsman's Camp** (on Sweat Creek Road; 6 sites, no piped water) all are small, primitive Department of Natural Resources camps north of Highway 20, east of Loup Loup Summit. Contact the DNR office in Colville (509/684-7474).

In the northern Okanogan River drainage, **Toats Coulee** (on Toats Coulee Road; 9 sites, no piped water), **Cold Springs** (on Cold Creek Road; 5 sites, no piped water), **North Fork Nine Mile** (near Toats Coulee; 11 sites), **Chopaka Lake** (off Toats Coulee Road; 16 sites), and **Palmer Lake** (8.5 miles north of Loomis; 6 sites, no piped water) all are small, primitive DNR camps in the Chopaka Mountain/Toats Coulee Creek/Palmer Lake area northwest of Tonasket. Contact the DNR office in Colville (509/684-7474). **Tiffany Springs** (1 mile from Tiffany Lake off Forest Road 39; 6 sites, no piped water) is a high (6,800-foot) remote Forest Service camp northeast of Winthrop. Far to the east, an equally remote camp high in the Sanpoil River drainage is **Lyman Lake** (on Forest Road 3785 southeast of Tonasket; 4 sites, no piped water). Contact the Okanogan National Forest's Tonasket Ranger District (509/486-2186).

On the east side of Sherman Pass, two small, primitive Colville National Forest sites are **Trout Lake** (on Trout Lake Road, north of Highway 20; 4 sites), and **Ellen Lake** (on County Road 412, south of Highway 20; 11 sites). Call the Three Rivers Ranger District, Kettle Falls office (509/738-7700).

Roosevelt Lake

㉑ Kettle Falls 🌲🌲🌲🌲

It's a long, long way from Kettle Falls to Grand Coulee. But you can paddle there from here, thanks to Grand Coulee Dam, which created the massive, 130-mile-long Franklin D. Roosevelt Lake. The damming of the Grand Coulee turned this lowland portion of northeastern Washington into a summer aquatic playground, and a series of campgrounds administered by the National Park Service rings the long, shimmering waterway. One of the most popular is Kettle Falls, a large, well-developed camp. Campsites are shaded and spread through three loops. Summer water sports—water-skiing, fishing, swimming, and boating—draw faithful legions to this camp's lakefront sites every summer. Kids, especially, love feeding the flocks

sites	77
🏕 🚐	No hookups, RVs to 26 feet
open	All year; limited winter facilities
reservations	None
contact	Lake Roosevelt National Recreation Area, 509/633-9441

Tent camping on 130-mile-long Franklin D. Roosevelt Lake.

of ducks and geese down at the marina (food is sold at the local store). Get there early if you're planning to spend a weekend. The campground has a boat launch and moorage. Note: The water level varies substantially on Roosevelt Lake throughout the year. Most Roosevelt Lake waterfront campgrounds, therefore, are left high and dry in the fall and winter, when the lake is drawn down.

Getting there: The campground is 2 miles west of Kettle Falls on US 395.

㉒ Kamloops 🌲🌲🌲🌲

Tenters, this one's for you. And only for you. Tent campers seeking respite from the RV- and boat-trailer-dominated world of camping on upper Roosevelt Lake will appreciate Kamloops, a smaller, peaceful waterfront camp on Kamloops Island. The campground has pit toilets but no piped water or showers. Nearby boat docks make this a decent place to launch a canoe. Squint really hard and try to imagine what the Columbia looked like here when it was still a real river. Note that there's no drinking water available if the lake level is drawn below 1,265 feet.

sites	17
open	All year
reservations	None
contact	Lake Roosevelt National Recreation Area, 509/633-9441

Getting there: Kamloops Campground is 7 miles west of Kettle Falls on US 395.

㉓ Marcus Island 🌲🌲🌲

Marcus Island is another popular waterfront camp on the north end of Franklin D. Roosevelt Lake. It's more remote and less crowded than Kettle Falls (see above), but still offers shore access as well as boat launching and moorage. The campground has pit toilets and a boat dock. Drinking water is available if the lake level is not drawn below 1,265 feet. Another Lake Roosevelt National Recreation Area camp, Evans (see below), is just north of here.

sites	27
	No hookups, RVs to 20 feet
open	All year
reservations	None
contact	Lake Roosevelt National Recreation Area, 509/633-9441

Getting there: Marcus Island is 4 miles north of Kettle Falls on Highway 25.

24 Evans 🌲🌲🌲

Evans is the largest and most developed Lake Roosevelt National Recreation Area campground north of Kettle Falls. It's easy to see why: The camp offers great lake access for anglers, water-skiers, swimmers, and other water lovers. The campground has a boat launch and moorage, an RV dump station, and a swimming area. Some of the sites are barrier free.

sites	43
🏕️ 🚐	No hookups, RVs to 26 feet
open	All year
reservations	None
contact	Lake Roosevelt National Recreation Area, 509/633-9441

Getting there: Evans is 8 miles north of Kettle Falls on Highway 25.

25 North Gorge 🌲🌲🌲

Another National Park Service camp on the northeast shores of Franklin D. Roosevelt Lake, North Gorge is small and a bit remote, but a suitable overnight spot that usually becomes more popular when all the waterfront camps closer to Kettle Falls are full. The campground has pit toilets and a boat launch. Drinking water is available unless the lake is substantially drawn down. A group site for 43 campers is available by reservation only (call the recreation area).

sites	12
🏕️ 🚐	No hookups, RVs to 26 feet
open	All year
reservations	None
contact	Lake Roosevelt National Recreation Area, 509/633-9441

Getting there: North Gorge is 20 miles north of Kettle Falls on Highway 25.

26 Gifford 🌲🌲🌲

Gifford, located about halfway up the eastern shore of Franklin D. Roosevelt Lake, the 130-mile-long impoundment behind Grand Coulee Dam, is one of the lake's largest waterfront campgrounds, and the major campground in this seldom-visited part of the state between the Columbia River and Chewelah. The campground is just far enough from civilization to make it a nice getaway for boaters, water-skiers, anglers, and canoeists who want to set up camp for a while and stay on the banks of the Columbia. It offers pit toilets, an RV dump station, boat docks, and moorage. Drinking water is available unless the reservoir level drops substantially.

sites	42
🏕️ 🚐	No hookups, RVs to 20 feet
open	All year
reservations	None
contact	Lake Roosevelt National Recreation Area, 509/633-9441

A time-honored time-passer for lakeshore campers.

Getting there: The campground is on Highway 25, 60 miles north of the US 2 junction.

Other Roosevelt Lake Campgrounds

Many smaller and/or more remote campsites, administered by the Lake Roosevelt National Recreation Area, ring the northern shores of Roosevelt Lake. These include westside camps such as **Kettle River** (13 sites), **Barnaby Island** (4 sites), and **Cloverleaf** (9 sites), and eastside camps such as **Haag Cove** (16 sites), **Bradbury Beach** (4 sites), and **Hunters** (39 sites). Contact the Lake Roosevelt NRA (509/633-9441).

Kettle Falls, Colville, and the Pend Oreille

㉗ Pierre Lake ▲▲▲

It's not quite in Canada. But you can almost see it from here. Pierre Lake, a small camp on a small (105-acre) lake in the northern Colville National Forest, is known primarily to anglers, who use the boat launch here to pursue trout. But it's a pretty spot, with the added attraction of a nice day hike: The Pierre Lake Trail (easy, 1.6 miles round-trip), begins in the campground and leads through a forested area on the lake's west shore. It's a good family walk, with the added advantage of bank-fishing access to the entire lake. The campground has nine picnic sites and pit toilets, but no piped water or garbage service. The elevation is 2,100 feet.

sites	15
🏕️🚐	No hookups, RVs to 24 feet
open	Mid-April to mid-October
reservations	None
contact	Colville National Forest, Three Rivers Ranger District, Kettle Falls office, 509/738-7700

Getting there: Pierre Lake is 20 miles north of Kettle Falls via US 395 and County Road 4013.

㉘ Little Twin Lakes ▲▲

Leave the Winnebago at home. It wouldn't fit if you could get it here, and the thing is, you can't. Access roads to this remote camp on a tiny lake in the Colville National Forest are rough, especially up high. When it's in bad shape, in fact, it's probably not even a good idea for passenger cars. The campground, used largely by anglers, has pit toilets and a boat launch, but no piped water, showers, or anything else. It's pretty rough around the edges, even for those who really, really want to get away from it all.

sites	20
🏕️🚐	No hookups, RVs to 16 feet
open	Mid-May through October
reservations	None
contact	Colville National Forest, Three Rivers Ranger District, Colville office, 509/684-7010

Getting there: From Colville, follow Highway 20 about 12.5 miles east to County Road 4915. Turn north and proceed 1.5 miles to Forest Road 4939. Turn north and drive just over 4 miles to the campground.

The Pend Oreille River, constantly pointing the way to Canada.

29 Lake Gillette/East Gillette 🌲🌲🌲

Here's a pretty spot: pretty noisy. Which is too bad, because Lake Gillette and East Gillette, two camps right across the road from one another in the chain of seven Little Pend Oreille Lakes (see also Lakes Thomas and Leo, below), are in a beautiful setting. Unfortunately, they're also popular with ORV riders, even one of whom can destroy solitude for hundreds of people for many square miles. Still, if you can get here at a time when they're all at a convention in Yakima or something, this is a nice spot. Lake Gillette Campground has 14 sites, East Gillette has 30. Five of the sites are multifamily sites with room for two or more vehicles. Both campgrounds have pit toilets and access to a boat launch and moorage. An interpretive trail runs through the area, and trout-fishing in the lake is a major activity in season. The elevation is 3,200 feet. Note: RVers seeking hookups and other modern amenities might prefer the private Beaver Lodge Resort (509/684-5657), just to the north on the shore of Lake Gillette. Tent campers seeking quieter climes likely will prefer Lake Thomas (below).

sites	44
🏕️ 🚐	No hookups, RVs to 31 feet
open	Mid-May to late September
reservations	None
contact	Colville National Forest, Three Rivers Ranger District, Colville office, 509/684-7010

Getting there: From Colville, follow Highway 20 about 20 miles east, turn right on Lake Gillette Road, and follow signs about a half mile north to the campground.

30 Lake Thomas 🌲🌲🌲

Here's the quieter alternative to Lake Gillette/East Gillette (above) for campers seeking solitude in the chain of seven Little Pend Oreille Lakes. The tents-only campground, on the shores of scenic Lake Thomas, is easy to reach from Highway 20. Bring the mountain bikes, the fishing rod, and the camera and stay for a while, exploring each of the lakes in the Little Pend Oreille drainage. It's pretty country. The campground has pit toilets and drinking water. The elevation is 3,200 feet.

sites	44
🏕️ 🚐	No hookups, RVs to 31 feet
open	Mid-May to late September
reservations	None
contact	Colville National Forest, Three Rivers Ranger District, Colville office, 509/684-7010

Getting there: From Colville, follow Highway 20 about 20 miles east, turn right on Lake Gillette Road, and follow signs about a mile north to the campground.

③ Big Meadow Lake 🌲🌲🌲🌲

This remote campground doesn't earn high marks because of its creature comforts. But it does get extra credit for its comfort to creatures. The camp is primitive, with pit toilets and no piped water, showers, or other amenities. And the road up here can establish all new levels of hell in the springtime, when the ground is soft. But the campground is in a gorgeous, waterfront location on 70-acre Big Meadow Lake. And campground builders have taken full advantage of the large amount of wildlife in the area. The camp has an interpretive trail and a wildlife viewing platform from which deer, beaver, osprey, and—loosen your lens caps—moose(!) are sometimes spotted. This is only one of several grand wildlife observation posts in this remote corner of the state. See Sullivan Lake and Noisy Creek (below) for other places to spot moose, mountain goats, and bighorn sheep. The elevation is 3,400 feet.

sites	16
🏕️ 🚐	No hookups, RVs to 32 feet
open	May through November
reservations	None
contact	Colville National Forest, Three Rivers Ranger District, Colville office, 509/684-7010

Getting there: From Highway 20, 1.1 miles east of Colville, turn northeast on Aladdin-Northport Road and continue about 20 miles to (rough and rocky) Meadow Creek Road. Turn right (east) and drive about 6 miles to the campground.

③ Edgewater 🌲🌲🌲

Look on the bright side: If not for Box Canyon Dam, a couple miles downstream from here, they would have had to call Edgewater something like High Above the Water. As it is, the small Forest Service campground makes proper use of this reservoir on the Pend Oreille River, which drains north to meet the upper Columbia River in British Columbia. The campground, a popular fishing base camp, has pit toilets and no garbage service. The elevation is 2,200 feet.

sites	23
🏕️ 🚐	No hookups, RVs to 20 feet
open	Late May to early September
reservations	None
contact	Colville National Forest, Sullivan Lake Ranger District, 509/446-7500

Getting there: Edgewater is 2 miles northeast of the town of Ione via Highway 31 and County Roads 9345 and 3669.

33 Sullivan Lake

Everything you need to know about what first brought people to the harsh northeast corner of Washington—and what keeps them coming back—can be found within a short distance of East and West Sullivan, adjacent campgrounds on the north shore of Sullivan Lake. In other words, if you're just passing through the area and only have a day or two to spare, spend them here. The campgrounds themselves are nice, with sites well spaced between pleasant, shady pine and fir trees. Amenities include piped water, pit toilets (unusually clean!), an RV dump station, and great access to the 3-mile-long lake, which is a very popular water-skiing, swimming, and fishing (rainbows and brown trout) venue in the summer. But you'd be remiss if you wasted all your time in these campgrounds east of Metaline Falls.

sites	*44*
	No hookups, RVs to 50 feet
open	*Late May through August*
reservations	*Up to 240 days in advance; National Recreation Reservation Service, 877/444-6777 or www.reserveusa.com*
contact	*Colville National Forest, Sullivan Lake Ranger District, 509/446-7500*

Much of the best of the northeast—manmade and wild—is within a short distance of your tent or trailer door. Three miles to the east, you'll encounter the western border of the 40,000-acre Salmo-Priest Wilderness, a vast, unspoiled area filled with 6,500-foot rocky peaks. The wilderness contains the last old-growth forest in eastern Washington, and a wealth of rare animals, including woodland caribou, mountain goats, Rocky Mountain bighorn sheep, and the occasional moose. Not all this wildlife stays up in the hills, out of sight, either. Local bighorn sheep, in particular, often are viewed from trails around and to the top of 6,325-foot Hall Mountain (strenuous, 5 miles round-trip), which looms above the eastern shore of the lake. Wildlife managers sometimes place salt licks near the summit, to supplement the sheep's diets.

Other local attractions include a wide range of beautiful, unpeopled trails in the Salmo-Priest Wilderness, as well as the short, fascinating (barrier-free) Millpond Interpretive Trail at nearby Millpond Campground, just up Sullivan Lake Road. Signs along the trail explain the creation of the lake and its connecting waterway: Sullivan Lake was raised 40 feet by a dam built in 1910 to supply water to Metaline Falls. The way it got there was fairly unique—via a massive wooden flume, wide enough to drive a car through. A boardwalk atop the flume, which was considered an engineering marvel in its day, provides a path between the lake and Metaline Falls. The elevation of the two campgrounds is 2,600 feet. Note: East Sullivan is by far the larger campground, with 38 sites in three loops, while West Sullivan has 6 sites. An airstrip between the East and West Sullivan Lake Campgrounds allows pilots to "fly-in camp" here.

Swimmers take a dip in Sullivan Lake, near Metaline Falls.

Getting there: From the powerhouse in Metaline Falls, follow Highway 31 about 1.5 miles north, turn east on Sullivan Lake Road (County Road 9345) and proceed about 6.5 miles to the campground.

㉞ Noisy Creek 🌲🌲🌲🌲

Noisy Creek is a smaller, somewhat less crowded version of the East and West Sullivan Lake Campgrounds, and it shares the wide variety of great activities in this area (see Sullivan Lake, above). The campground has vault toilets, piped water, and a boat launch. Reservations are a good idea; about 60 percent of the sites can be reserved in advance. Note that Sullivan Lake shrinks away from the camping area when the reservoir is drawn down.

RVers can find plenty of quiet spots in Northeast Washington.

sites	19
	No hookups, RVs to 45 feet
open	Late May through September
reservations	Up to 240 days in advance; National Recreation Reservation Service, 877/444-6777 or www.reserveusa.com
contact	Colville National Forest, Sullivan Lake Ranger District, 509/446-7500

Getting there: From the powerhouse in Metaline Falls, follow Highway 31 about 1.5 miles north, turn east on Sullivan Lake Road (County Road 9345) and proceed about 9.5 miles to the campground, on the south end of Sullivan Lake. Alternatively, turn right (east) on Sullivan Lake Road from Highway 31 near Ione and proceed about 8 miles northeast.

Other Kettle Falls/Colville/Pend Oreille Campgrounds

In the Colville National Forest, an alternative to the popular camps on Sullivan Lake is **Millpond** (5 miles northeast of Metaline Falls; Sullivan Lake Ranger District, 509/446-7500), with 10 sites. An alternative to camps at Lakes Thomas and Gillette in the Little Pend Oreille Lakes chain is **Lake Leo** (Colville Ranger District, 509/684-7010), with 8 sites and popular with cross-country skiers in winter. Farther south in the Newport Ranger District (509/447-7300) are **Panhandle** (13 sites), **Brown's Lake** (18 sites), **South Skookum Lake** (25 sites), and **Pioneer Park** (17 sites).

A handful of primitive Department of Natural Resources camps allows campers to really rough it in this region. They are **Sheep Creek** (on Sheep Creek Road, just off Highway 25 near the Canadian border; 8 sites); **Upper Sheep Creek** (1.2 miles up the road, near Sheep Creek Falls; 2 sites, no piped water); **Douglas Falls Grange Park** (on Douglas Falls Road north of Colville; 18 sites); **Williams Lake,** (on Williams Lake Road north of Kettle Falls; 8 sites); **Rocky Lake** (off Highway 395 south of Colville, near the Little Pend Oreille Wildlife Area; 7 unimpressive sites—and lots of dirt bikes); **Flodelle Creek** (off Highway 20 northeast of Colville; 8 sites and lots of dirt bikes); **Starvation Lake** (east of Colville off Highway 20; 8 small sites and canoe/fishing access, no piped water); **Sherry Creek** (24.2 miles east of Colville off Highway 20; 3 sites, no piped water); and **Skookum Creek** (on the Pend Oreille River near Usk; 10 sites, with access to a Native American painting interpretive site). Most of these campgrounds are free. For details, call the DNR office in Colville; (509/684-7474).

Spokane

㉟ Riverside State Park 🌲🌲🌲🌲

It's not often that the very best place to camp, explore, and relax in a given place is close to the urban core of the same area. But such is the case in Spokane, where sprawling Riverside State Park takes care of an amazingly wide range of city recreational needs. The 10,000-acre park is scattered in separate parcels along 9 miles of the Spokane River. The camping area lies in a broad meander curve, in a park section called the Bowl and Pitcher, named for unique rock formations along the river. Even without hookups, recently renovated campsites are comfortable, with niceties such as coin-op showers. Note that winning a site here in summer might be more difficult than it once was: Riverside no longer accepts reservations.

sites	101
🏕️🚐	No hookups, RVs to 45 feet
open	All year
reservations	None
contact	Washington State Parks, 360/902-8844; Riverside State Park, 509/456-3964

Spokane Falls: A highlight of the 37-mile Centennial Trail.

The campground, however, is only one of a dozen good reasons to visit. Inside Riverside's 7,600 acres are 36 miles of hiking and equestrian trails, a large group camp, multiple picnic areas, fascinating rock formations, Native American petroglyphs, white-water rapids on the Spokane and Little Spokane Rivers (novice paddlers should keep to the latter), an ORV park, a scenic river gorge, and Spokane House Interpretive Center. The latter, which has been open sporadically of late because of budget problems, is on the site of Spokane House, explorer David Thompson's 1810 fur-trading outpost.

If none of that is enough to goad you from your lawn chair, you can seriously recreate from here by hoofing or pedaling up the Centennial Trail, the 37-mile paved multisport path between Riverside State Park and Coeur d'Alene, Idaho, that follows the Spokane River. By Washington standards, the trail isn't wildly scenic. But the trail does pass local attractions like Riverfront Park, raging Spokane Falls, Gonzaga University, and Mission Park, and the Walk in the Wild Zoo, and it's a walk with plenty of historical flavor. Native American petroglyphs are visible from the trail near Long Lake, and the trail itself follows a route pounded out over the centuries by native peoples—and after that, white fur traders. The entire length is open to strolling and cycling, with some portions also open to horseback riding. For details and trail events, contact Friends of the Centennial Trail (509/624-7188; www.spokanecentennialtrail.org).

Getting there: From Interstate 90 near Spokane, take exit 280, Maple Street North. Cross the Maple Street Bridge and proceed about a mile to Maxwell Street. Turn left (west) and drive about 2 miles (it becomes Pettit Street), passing Downriver Golf Course, to the park entrance.

㊱ Mount Spokane State Park 🌲🌲🌲

Mount Spokane's main claim to fame is that it is the closest ski mountain to downtown Spokane. As such, it doesn't get much attention as a summertime getaway. But this is a nice day-trip destination out of Spokane that can turn into a pleasant overnighter, or a longer stay for equestrians making use of horse trails that ring this 5,800-foot mountaintop. The small campground is unremarkable. But the park has an extensive, 86-mile trail system, and the view from the Vista House restaurant at the summit is memorable.

sites	14
🏕	
🚐	No hookups, RVs to 30 feet
open	June through September
reservations	None
contact	Washington State Parks, 360/902-8844; Mount Spokane State Park, 509/238-4258

Getting there: Mount Spokane State Park is 30 miles northwest of Spokane via Division Street (US 2) and Highway 206.

㊲ Pend Oreille County Park 🌲🌲🌲

It's nothing to write home about, but 440-acre Pend Oreille County Park will do in a pinch for eastern Washington travelers. These are mostly tent sites, although two are described as RV sites. The campground has flush toilets and hot showers—

sites	34
open	Memorial Day through Labor Day
reservations	509/447-4821
contact	Pend Oreille County Department of Public Works, 509/447-4821

a rarity for a campground geared for the tent crowd. There's not much to do in the local area, so most people use this camp as a one-night stopover.

Getting there: From Interstate 90 near Spokane, turn north on US 2 and drive about 31 miles to the campground, on the west side of the highway.

Other Spokane-Area Campgrounds

Three Department of Natural Resources campgrounds offer primitive alternatives. They are **Long Lake** (on Long Lake Dam Road north of Reardon; 12 sites); **Dragoon Creek** (on Dragoon Creek Rd north of Spokane; 22 sites); and **A. J. Pat Kehn** (on Bruce Road east of Chattaroy; 4 sites, no piped water). For details, call the DNR office in Colville (509/684-7474).

Private campgrounds within Spokane city limits include **KOA Spokane** (509/924-4722) and **Trailer Inns RV Park** (509/535-1811). Also, a number of private resorts are located west of town in the Medical Lake region. They include **West Medical Lake Resort** (509/299-3921); **Picnic Pines on Silver Lake** (509/299-6902); **Mallard Bay Resort** (509/299-3830); and **Rainbow Cove** (509/299-3717). A private resort west of town is **Yogi Bear's Camp Resort** (800/494-7275).

Medical Lake: A good place to spend the dog days of summer.

Southeast Washington

Let's be honest. The closest most of us West Siders want to get to summer in southeast Washington is that bag of Walla Walla Sweets we brought home from QFC. Just thinking about the place makes the brain start squinting from the sun. Southeast—isn't that where Washtucna is? Not much out there except sand, sun, and the campus of Washington State University. And we all know what the combination of those three poisons can do to an otherwise sound mind.

That may be a bit harsh. But, well, so's the climate. That's why camping in the southeast corner of the state—where peas and lentils are often the most vibrant living creatures for miles—requires a bit of an attitude adjustment. Don't call it a campout. Consider it an expedition. Would Lawrence of Arabia have had a chance if he'd told his troops they were going for a restful weekend over at Aquaba? Precisely. To quote everybody's junior-high football coach: You've gotta want it.

And even in lowly southeast Washington, he or she who wants it shall find it indeed. In the most forlorn corner of this splendid state, a few nuggets of pure gold emerge from the billions of tons of rough ore. Camping can be good in the southeast corner, if you know where to look, when to go, and how to keep the rattlesnakes out of your boots once you've arrived. Not surprisingly, most of these oases in the great desert of the southeast are found along the banks of the life-giving rivers that cross the region, particularly the Snake. From the sun-and-water riverfront playgrounds of the Tri-Cities to the solemn, historic gravesites at Chief Timothy State Park near Clarkston, the Snake can be a savage but beautiful land to visit.

Speaking of Chief Timothy, one major caveat for campers: At this writing, four of the best sun-and-fun getaways in this region, Crow Butte, Central Ferry, Lyons Ferry, and Chief Timothy State Parks, were closed because of lease cancellations by the cash-strapped Washington State Parks system. (See the Crow Butte description for details.) Budget cuts also claimed another of this region's prime campgrounds, Fort Walla

Walla—a highly rated campground in the first edition of this guide. A troubling trend, indeed. Their future as state parks is strongly in doubt, but they might live on as campgrounds managed by another agency.

In any case: You can still find places to get lost in the region. A lot of wide-open space lies north and south of the Snake River. Southeast Washington is marked by a few notable getaways where time has stood still since long before white people arrived. There's something reassuring about that. Last time we stood in the Blue Mountains of the Wenaha-Tucannon Wilderness east of Walla Walla, things looked a lot like they must have 1,000 years ago. Here's hoping they'll look just the same when you get there next summer—and 1,000 years after you leave.

① Columbia Park
② Hood Park
③ Charbonneau Park
④ Fishhook Park
⑤ Crow Butte State Park
⑥ Central Ferry State Park
⑦ Lyons Ferry State Park
⑧ Palouse Falls State Park
⑨ Chief Timothy State Park
⑩ Lewis and Clark Trail State Park
⑪ Fields Spring State Park

Southeast Washington Map

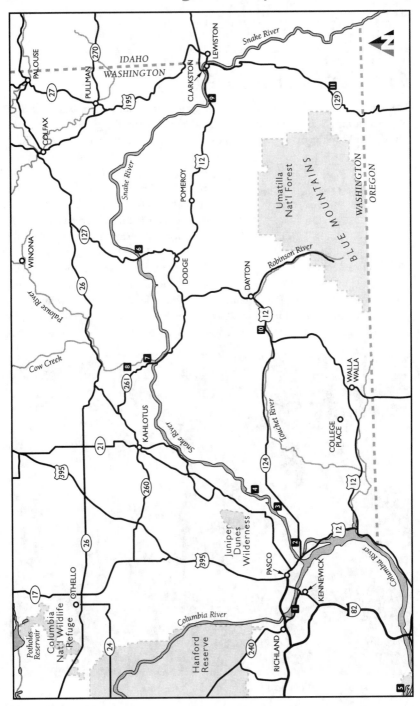

Tri-Cities Area

❶ Columbia Park 🌲🌲🌲

Everybody must get wet. The Tri-Cities, situated nicely in the oven-baked climate of southeastern Washington, fortunately also are situated nicely in a rich water world, thanks to the many dams on the Columbia and Snake Rivers. Lake Wallula,

sites	*100*
🏕️🚐	*18 water/electrical hookups, RVs to any length*
open	*All year*
reservations	*Recommended; 509/585-4529*
contact	*Columbia Park, 509/585-4529*

the 64-mile-long Columbia impoundment behind McNary Dam near Umatilla, Oregon, makes for a broad, smooth boating track. So does Lake Sacajawea, the Snake River backup created by the Ice Harbor Dam, 9 miles east of Pasco. That's why you'll find—no joke—three actual yacht clubs in town, and it's not difficult to find boating supplies and services. Major public launches are found at all the local public waterfront parks—most of which also welcome campers. Columbia Park is a good example. This 605-acre park, not exactly wild, is in a grassy area in downtown Ken-

A coyote stops by the Columbia River for a drink after work.

newick. In addition to the obligatory boat facilities (including nine lanes of boat launching!), the adjacent campground offers flush toilets, piped water, coin-op showers, hiking and biking trails, and tennis courts. The park, operated by the city of Kennewick, also has an RV dump station and a day-use area with shaded picnic shelters, a swimming beach, a snack bar, and a playground. A municipal marina is adjacent to the park. Invest heavily in SPF 1.5 million sunscreen if you plan to stay here in August.

Getting there: The campground is well-signed off Columbia Drive in Kennewick.

❷ Hood Park ▲▲▲

Hood Park is the most centrally located of a number of Army Corps of Engineers campgrounds on Tri-Cities impoundments (see Charbonneau and Fishhook Parks, below). The 99-acre park provides good river access, basketball courts, horseshoe pits, flush toilets, piped water, showers, and an RV dump station. Like most parks in this area, it also has a boat launch and moorage facilities. More than two dozen of the sites here are paved pull-throughs with utilities—great for RVs. And the biggest bonus in this sun-baked camp: mature shade trees and grass in most sites. The campground is popular with swimmers, anglers, water-skiers, and sunbathers. Sacajawea State Park, a popular day-use area at the confluence of the Snake and Columbia Rivers, is nearby. An overflow area at Hood Park has an additional 90 sites. It's a good base camp for exploring Tri-Cities-area wineries and other sights.

sites	69
	69 electrical hookups, RVs to any length
open	April through September
reservations	Up to 240 days in advance; National Recreation Reservation Service, 877/444-6777 or www.reserveusa.com
contact	U.S. Army Corps of Engineers, 509/547-7781

Getting there: From Pasco, drive about 5 miles southeast on US 12 to Highway 124. Turn east and follow signs to the campground.

❸ Charbonneau Park ▲▲▲

Next time you're in the Tri-Cities area, stop by here to see what the lingering controversy about dams on the Columbia and Snake Rivers is all about. Charbonneau Park, an Army Corps of Engineers site, is very near one of them: Ice Harbor Dam. It's one of a series of dams built on the Snake between the Tri-Cities and Lewiston, Idaho, from the late 1960s through the 1970s. The dams and locks—Ice Harbor, Lower Monumental, Little Goose, and Lower Granite—are used mostly for barge navigation. They accomplished the seemingly impossible, turning Lewiston into a

sites	54
	18 full hookups, 36 electrical hookups; RVs to any length
open	April through October; all year for day use
reservations	Up to 240 days in advance; National Recreation Reservation Service, 877/444-6777 or www.reserveusa.com
contact	U.S. Army Corps of Engineers, 509/547-7781

seaport, of sorts. They also helped snuff out what was left of the struggling Snake River salmon runs, which long have been listed as endangered. Not a good tradeoff, perhaps, but one that reaped many recreational benefits for this area. Charbonneau Park, on 31-mile-long Lake Sacajawea, is but one example. Eighteen of the sites are drive-throughs favored by big-RV drivers. The park also has showers, boat launching and moorage, and a nice playground. The primary activities are fishing, boating, water-skiing, and touring the dam, which is open daily April through October.

Getting there: From Pasco, drive about 5 miles southeast on US 12 to Highway 124. Turn northeast on Highway 124 and proceed 8 miles to Sun Harbor Road. Turn north follow signs about 2 miles to the park.

④ Fishhook Park ▲▲▲

Like its big brother, Charbonneau, Fishhook Park is an Army Corps of Engineers site off Highway 124 northeast of Pasco, with good access to the Snake River's Lake Sacajawea, behind Ice Harbor Dam. The campground is in a wooded

sites	61
	41 water/electrical hookups, RVs to any length
open	April through September
reservations	Up to 240 days in advance; National Recreation Reservation Service, 877/444-6777 or www.reserveusa.com
contact	U.S. Army Corps of Engineers, 509/547-7781

area that provides some shade; many of the utility sites are pull-throughs. Nonhookup sites are walk-in tent spaces. Facilities include flush toilets, showers,a playground, a swimming area, a boat launch and moorage, and an RV dump station.

Getting there: From Pasco, drive about 5 miles southeast on US 12 to Highway 124, turn northeast and proceed 18 miles to Fishhook Road. Turn left and continue about 4 miles to the park.

⑤ Crow Butte State Park ▲▲▲▲

First: The bad news. When this guide went to press, Crow Butte, along with sister parks Lyons Ferry, Chief Timothy, and Central Ferry—all on land owned by the U.S. Army Corps of Engineers and leased to Washington State Parks—were in danger of

sites	51
	50 full hookups, RVs to 60 feet
open	All year; limited winter facilities
reservations	Up to 9 months in advance; 888/226-7688 or www.parks.wa.gov
contact	Washington State Parks, 360/902-8844; Crow Butte State Park, 509/875-2644

permanently closing. Reason: State Parks, facing the latest in a seemingly endless series of budget cuts, was forced to cancel or renegotiate leases for about a dozen state parks on lands leased from the federal government or public utilities. Some of these agencies offered to pay part of the operating costs and keep the parks open. But the Corps said it had no money to do so, and therefore: all four parks closed in October 2002. Crow Butte, because it is on Columbia River property adjacent to a federally operated dam pool, could be claimed permanently by the Department of the Interior for treaty fishing. Plenty of efforts were underway to prevent that, and perhaps keep the areas open as state parks, or parks managed by another entity. But be advised: You'll need to call the contact number and check on these parks' status before heading this way. Last word on the subject: If you live in Washington, it never hurts to contact your state representative and let them know many people consider parks a priority at budget time.

Second: The good news. If it remains open, Crow Butte is more than worth the drive south from the Tri-Cities. One of Washington's most unique parks, it sits on an island in the middle of a portion of the Columbia River called Lake Umatilla (created by the John Day Dam). The 1,300-acre property is situated on what once was a high river bluff. The campsites are in a grassy area with some shade. Fortunately, windbreaks have been constructed to cut stiff breezes that buffet this large, flat knoll. The park also has a spiffy boat launch and moorage in a protected basin, a 60-person group camp, and a swimming area. Short hiking trails lead to the top of 670-foot Crow Butte, which offers views of Mount Hood. Watch for rattlesnakes!

Getting there: From Highway 14, about 13 miles west of Paterson, cross the bridge southwest to the island.

Other Tri-Cities-Area Campgrounds

The state's **McNary Habitat Management Area** (southeast of Pasco, follow signs from US 12; 509/456-4082), next to the McNary National Wildlife Refuge, has a Fish and Wildlife campground with 24 primitive sites and no piped water. It's open all year and it's free, but it's not your best choice unless you're a very enthusiastic birder. The keeper of local waterways, the U.S. Army Corps of Engineers, allows camping at nondesignated sites near many of its public day-use areas and boat launches on Lakes Wallula and Sacajawea (try to whip out those names with a mouth full of peanut butter). Some riverfront parks with "primitive" (read: parking-lot style, or sandbar tent sites) camping include **Madame Dorion** and **Sand**

Deer keeping cool on the shoreline of the Columbia River's Hanford Reach.

Station on Lake Wallula; and **Big Flat, Lake Emma, Matthews, Walker,** and **Windust,** all on Lake Sacajawea. Contact the Corps' Ice Harbor Project office in Pasco (509/547-7781; or visit www.nww.usace.army.mil, click "recreation"). Also, note that the Corps' Portland, Oregon, branch operates another campground, **Plymouth Park** (541/298-7650; reservations, 877/444-6777 or www.reserveusa.com), with 32 sites and 16 partial hookups. It's all the way at the edge of the map—on Lake Umatilla, near the Interstate 82/US 395 bridge below McNary Dam.

The Palouse
and Snake River

⑥ Central Ferry State Park ▲▲▲▲

(Important note on park closure: See the Crow Butte State Park description, p. 268.) Sun worshippers, unite. You'll see lots of boat trailers and swim fins at Central Ferry State Park, which fronts on the Snake River and draws many boaters and water-sport fans. This is the most developed full-service RV campground in this corner of the state. Spaces here often are reserved well in advance. The park was built specifically to take advantage of Lake Bryan, the large waterway created by Little Goose Dam on the Snake River. Two basins were dug to protect moored boats from nasty winds that occasionally whip through the river gorge—often taking haphazardly staked tents with them. (Stake those babies down!) The campground sites are in six loops located in a flat, grassy area. Loops two through five are closest to the water. The campground has flush toilets, coin-op showers, an RV dump station, three horseshoe pits, a boat launch and moorage, water-ski launch ramps, a marine sewer pumpout station, a nonpatrolled swimming beach and bathhouse, a group camp, and sheltered picnic sites near the river. The eight tent sites are primitive, walk-in spaces.

sites	68
🏕️ 🚐	60 full hookups, RVs to 45 feet
open	Mid-March to mid-November
reservations	Up to 9 months in advance; 888/226-7688 or www.parks.wa.gov
contact	Washington State Parks, 360/902-8844; Central Ferry State Park, 509/549-3551

Getting there: Central Ferry is on Highway 127, 17 miles south of aptly named Dusty and 34 miles southwest of beautiful downtown Colfax.

⑦ Lyons Ferry State Park ▲▲▲▲

(Important note on possible closure: See Crow Butte State Park description, p. 268.) It's as rich in history as it is hot and dry. And out here, that's saying something. Lyons Ferry, which sits on a point at the confluence of the Palouse and Snake Rivers, is much like Central Ferry (see above), a state park farther upstream (east) on the Snake. As at Central Ferry, the boat that crossed the river here for 108 years—very often with skipper Dan Lyons at the rudder—long ago was replaced by a bridge. Unlike Central Ferry, however, the Lyons Ferry, which operated on river current alone, is still here, tied up onshore, where it serves as a fishing pier and historical display. The

sites	*52*

	No hookups, RVs to 45 feet
open	*April through September*
reservations	*None*
contact	*Washington State Parks, 360/902-8844; Lyons Ferry State Park, 509/646-3252*

park lies on either side of the north end of the Lyons Ferry Bridge on Highway 261. On the west side is a plain, poorly landscaped campground. Not exactly a garden spot, but it'll do for an overnight, particularly if you're in an RV. The campground has an RV dump station and coin-op showers. At the north end of the day-use area, a trail leads about a mile up a bluff to a canyon overlook, where you'll find historical information about Marmes Rock Shelter, an ancient Palouse Indian burial cave below here, now flooded by the lake waters. Before the flooding, archaeologists discovered human remains carbon-dated to 10,000 years ago.

Getting there: Lyons Ferry is at the confluence of the Palouse and Snake Rivers, 8 miles northwest of Starbuck on Highway 261.

Someone's always telling you where to go in Washington State Parks.

⑧ Palouse Falls State Park 🌲🌲

Absolutely do not, under any circumstances, drive all the way here from Bellingham just to camp. The campground at Palouse Falls State Park, which is upstream from Lyons Ferry State Park (see above), isn't much. The primitive camp, which has pit toilets and an RV dump station but no other amenities, is often used as a day-use area by the many nature lovers who come to see the real attraction: Palouse Falls itself. The 200-foot waterfall is one of Washington's most spectacular natural sights, plunging from the top of a half circle of wall-like columnar basalt into a deep pool. The falls are at their peak in the spring (usually late March), when the Palouse River is at high flow. The prolific spray at the bottom often forms a rainbow, making this a photographer's dream. The falls are believed to have been formed by the same prehistoric floods that carved other eastern Washington features, such as the Grand Coulee. Our suggestion: If it's still open, camp at Lyons Ferry State Park, and make this a day trip.

sites	10
	No hookups, RVs to 40 feet
open	Mid-March to late September
reservations	None
contact	Washington State Parks, 360/902-8844; Palouse Falls State Park, 509/646-3252

Getting there: The park is 16 miles northwest of Starbuck via Highway 261 and Palouse Falls Road.

⑨ Chief Timothy State Park 🌲🌲🌲

(Important note on possible closure: See Crow Butte State Park description, p.268.) Hmm. I think we've seen this theme before. A state park situated on a Snake River impoundment, popular with boaters and anglers (see Lyons Ferry and Central Ferry, above). Chief Timothy State Park, near Clarkston, is another water-world. It sits on an island in Lower Granite Lake, a Snake River dam creation. The proximity of the island to the shore creates a nicely protected waterway—an ideal swimming and water-play area made even better by a broad, flat, sandy beach. The day-use area has eight shaded picnic sites, playground equipment, a bathhouse, four boat-launch ramps, and moorage. The campsites are split into three camping loops. A historical display tells of Timothy, a Nez Perce chief, and

sites	68
	25 full hookups, 8 water/electrical hookups; RVs to 60 feet
open	All year; limited winter facilities
reservations	Up to 9 months in advance; 888/226-7688 or www.parks.wa.gov
contact	Washington State Parks, 360/902-8844; Chief Timothy State Park, 509/758-9580

Palouse Falls is a great day trip from Lyons Ferry State Park.

describes Alpowai, an old Nez Perce village located here long before the old pioneer town of Silcott was built on the same site. Unfortunately, like many other Snake River historical sites, most of it now lies beneath the lake waters.

Getting there: Chief Timothy State Park is 8 miles west of Clarkston, just off US 12.

Other Palouse/Snake River Campgrounds

In the Clarkston area, alternate camping is available at **Wawawai County Park** (509/397-6238; 9 sites) on Lower Granite Lake, about 25 miles west of Clarkston, and across the river at **Boyer Park and Marina** (509/397-3791). Around Pullman, the city's **Pullman RV Park** (Riverview Road and South Street; 509/334-4555; 24 full-hookup sites) has decent RV spots in the summer. **Kamiak Butte County Park** (11 miles north on Highway 27; 509/397-6238) has 9 sites.

Walla Walla and Blue Mountains

⑩ Lewis and Clark Trail State Park 🌲🌲🌲🌲

They came, they saw, they stepped in the ocean—and came back. The latter part is how Lewis and Clark touched this part of Washington—on their return trip east in 1806. Lewis and Clark Trail State Park (not to be confused with Lewis and Clark State Park in western Washington) is a small place set in a very pleasant forest of big, straight ponderosa pines with a tinder-dry grassy floor. The park, which fronts on the Touchet River (good rainbow and brown trout fishing), is an oasis in this flat, dry area—no doubt one reason the Lewis and Clark Expedition chose it as a picnic spot of sorts. The park is split by US 12; day-use areas, playfields, and picnic grounds are on the south side, camping on the north. The two riverside loops contain nice, tidy campsites, as well as a 50-person group camp. In the winter, 17 primitive sites in the day-use area remain open for camping, and the park provides ample cross-country skiing and snowshoeing trails. Other facilities include flush toilets, piped water, coin-op showers, an RV dump station, and two group sites for up to 100 campers each. The park also has several hiking trails, including a three-quarter-mile designated bird-watching trail and a mile-long interpretive trail. Interpretive programs about the Lewis and Clark Expedition are presented Saturday evenings in the summer. This is a popular camp for hunters in the fall.

sites	41
🏕️ 🚐	No hookups, RVs to 28 feet
open	April to mid-September; day use and limited facilities in winter
reservations	None
contact	Washington State Parks, 360/902-8844; Lewis and Clark Trail State Park, 509/337-6457

Getting there: The park is on US 12, 4.5 miles west of Dayton, 25 miles northeast of Walla Walla.

⑪ Fields Spring State Park 🌲🌲🌲🌲

Wouldn't you know it: One of the nicest state parks in Washington, particularly for tenters, is located about as far away from most of the state's population as you can get without being in Idaho. Fields Spring is well worth the long trip for West Side campers frustrated by big crowds. This park—located 29 miles south of Clarkston, just north of the Grande Ronde River Canyon, and east of just about everything—lies in a thicket of trees marking the transition from flat plains to the

sites	20
⛺🚐	No hookups, RVs to 30 feet
open	All year; limited winter facilities
reservations	None
contact	Washington State Parks, 360/902-8844; Fields Spring State Park, 509/256-3332

high, dry forests of the Blue Mountains. The park, spread across 4,500-foot Puffer Butte above the Grande Ronde, is a lovely spot, rich with wildflower blooms on mountain slopes in the spring, and with wildlife year-round. Don't miss the hiking trail to the grand view atop Puffer Butte, where (legend has it) the first homesteaders would trek every morning and watch for Indians coming up the canyon. The campground is quite pleasant, especially for tenters. It's equipped with flush toilets, piped water, coin-op showers, and an RV dump station. It's also a good spot for RVs, although the 30-foot sites are too short for the larger land yachts. The 800-acre park also has extensive play-fields, a six-person teepee camp, 7 miles of mountain-bike trails, a picnic area with a covered shelter, electricity, and a woodstove, and other day-use facilities. It's a popular winter hangout too, with lighted sledding and tubing runs near the park's twin Environmental Learning Centers, and numerous marked cross-country ski routes on local fire roads.

Getting there: The park is 29 miles south of Clarkston on Highway 129.

Other Walla Walla/Blue Mountains Campgrounds

For a remote campout—and we're talking really remote here—consider one of five small Umatilla National Forest campgrounds in or near the Blue Mountains, in the Wenaha-Tucannon Wilderness. Most of them make excellent jump-off points for wilderness backpacking or fishing treks and are used most heavily in the fall, when elk and deer hunters flock to the wilderness area. All these campgrounds are free, and none have piped water. Bring a filter, or pack in your own water. They are **Tucannon** (20 miles south of Pomeroy on Forest Road 47; 6 sites, good access to the Tucannon River); **Alder Thicket** (20 miles south of Pomeroy on Forest Road 40; 6 small sites at 5,100 feet); **Big Springs** (23 miles south of Pomeroy on Forest Road 42; 6 small sites at 5,100 feet); **Teal Spring** (26 miles south of Pomeroy on Forest Road 40; 8 small sites at 5,600 feet); **Godman** (on Forest Road 46; 8 sites, horse-hitching rails and other facilities); and **Wickiup** (34 miles southeast of Pomeroy via Forest Roads 40 and 44; 9 sites). For forest maps and other information, contact the Umatilla National Forest's Pomeroy Ranger District (509/843-1891).

Ratings Index

Campground Index

A

Adams Fork, 195
A. J. Pat Kehn, 262
Alder Creek Horse Camp, 128
Alder Lake Park, 178
Alder Thicket, 276
Aldrich Lake, 38
Alpine Meadows, 128
Alta Lake State Park, 211
Altaire, 48
American Forks, 168
American Legion Park, 234
Antilon, 219
Aqua Barn Ranch, 23
Atkinson Flats, 128
Atkisson Group Camp, 193

B

Baker Lake Resort, 98
Ballard, 108
Barnaby Island, 251
Battle Ground Lake, 202
Bay View State Park, 14
Bayview Group Camps, 98
Beach 77-79, 37
Beach 83, 37
Beach 85, 37
Beacon Road State Park, 198
Beaver, 188
Beaver Bay, 187
Beaver Creek, 88
Beaver Lake, 239
Beaver Plant Lake, 88
Beckler River, 122
Bedal, 84
Beebe Bridge Park, 210
Belfair State Park, 35
Berthusen Park, 18
Beth Lake, 240
Beverly, 146
Big Beaver, 105
Big Creek, 74
Big Creek, 169
Big Creek, 218
Big Flat, 270
Big Meadow Lake, 255

Big Springs, 276
Birch Bay State Park, 17
Bird Creek, 197
Black Pine Lake, 116
Blackpine Creek Horse Camp, 133
Blake Island State Park, 35
Blue Lake Creek , 194
Blue Sky RV Park, 24
Boardman Creek, 82
Boat-in North Sound/Islands Campgrounds, 19
Boat-in/Hike-in Lake Chelan National Recreation Area Campground, 217-218
Bogachiel State Park, 55
Boiling Lake, 218
Bonaparte Lake, 239
Boulder Creek, 53
Boulder Creek, 95
Boundary Bay, 105
Boyer Park and Marina, 274
Bradbury Beach, 251
Bridge Creek, 130
Bridge Creek, 218
Bridgeport State Park, 213
Brooks Memorial State Park, 200
Brown Creek, 76
Brown's Lake, 258
Buck Creek, 86
Buck Lake, 113
Buck Meadows, 148
Bumping Crossing, 164
Burlington KOA, 18
Buster Brown, 105

C

Camano Island State Park, 4
Camp Spillman, 38
Campbell Tree Grove, 61
Canyon Creek, 245
Cascade Island, 104
Cascadia Marine Trail, 37
Cat Creek, 197
Cat Island, 105
Cedar Springs, 163
Central Ferry State Park, 271
Chain of Lakes, 197
Charbonneau Park, 267
Chatter Creek, 132
Chief Timothy State Park, 273

Chiwawa Horse Camp, 128
Chopaka Lake, 247
Circle H RV Ranch, 230
Clark's Skagit River Resort, 105
Cle Elum River, 140
Clear Creek, 84
Clear Lake North, 174
Clear Lake South, 175
Cloverleaf, 251
Coal Creek Bar, 88
Coho, 76
Coho Resort, 53
Cold Springs, 247
Collins, 71
Colonial Creek, 103
Columbia Park, 266
Conconully State Park, 234
Coppermine Bottom, 61
Corral Creek, 218
Corral Pass, 160
Cottonwood, 61
Cottonwood, 168
Cottonwood, 214
Cottonwood, 218
Cottonwood, 235
Cougar, 187
Cougar Flat, 164
Cougar Island, 105
Cougar Rock, 154
Coulee City Park, 223
Crawfish Lake, 237
Cresap Bay, 187
Crow Butte State Park, 268
Crow Creek, 166
Crystal Springs, 137
Cub Lake, 218
Cultus Creek, 192
Curlew Lake State Park, 243

D

Daroga State Park, 209
Dash Point State Park, 22
Deception Pass State Park, 8
Deep Creek, 128
Deer Creek, 128
Deer Park, 46
Deer Point, 218
Denny Creek, 136
Devils Junction, 105
Doe Bay Village Resort, 19
Dog Lake, 173